THE REFERENCE SHELF   VOLUME 35 NUMBER 5

THE NEW STATES: ALASKA AND HAWAII

EDITED BY WILLIAM P. LINEBERRY

Associate Editor, Foreign Policy Association

38546

THE H. W. WILSON COMPANY
NEW YORK   1963

THE REFERENCE SHELF

The books in this series reprint articles, excerpts from books, and addresses on current issues, social trends, and other aspects of American life, and occasional surveys of foreign countries. There are six separately bound numbers in each volume, all of which are generally published in the same calendar year. One number is a collection of recent speeches on a variety of subjects; each of the remaining numbers is devoted to a single subject and gives background information and discussion from varying points of view, followed by a comprehensive bibliography.

Subscribers to the current volume receive the books as issued. The subscription rate is $12 ($15 foreign) for a volume of six numbers. The price of single numbers is $3 each.

PRINTED IN THE UNITED STATES OF AMERICA

PREFACE

Surely no two states in the American Union of fifty are as alike — and yet as different — as the new states, Alaska and Hawaii.

Consider the striking similarities: Both states are the latest to join the Union, having come to each other's aid in the long and agonizing quest for entry. Both are the only noncontiguous states, Alaska being separated from the mainland forty-eight by another nation (Canada), Hawaii by a vast expanse of ocean (the Pacific). Both states (even if for vastly different reasons) are considered tourist paradises and are heavily dependent upon tourism for their livelihood. Both play a key role in the nation's defense— Alaska bulking within sight of the Soviet Union across the Bering Strait, Hawaii anchored in the Pacific as a forward staging area for America's Far Eastern defenses. Both states have advanced political systems, with up-to-date constitutions that are models of progressive good government. And in spirit, both are character-ized by the same open-hearted friendliness, the same congenial attitude of tolerance and brotherhood, from which the other states might well take example.

Despite these and other similarities, however, the two states are dramatically the opposite of each other in many ways. Alaska is the largest and least densely populated. Hawaii is one of the smallest and most densely populated. Alaska's rugged, frozen wildernesses contrast sharply with Hawaii's balmy, sun-drenched tropicality. The one has an electrifying frontier history of men battling nature and the elements for gold and for land. The other embodies the romantic tale of a lush island kingdom wrapped in charm and innocence.

Together, the new states make a fascinating study in same-ness, contrast and paradox. Having entered the Union less than a decade ago, how are Alaska and Hawaii faring under their new status? What advances have come with statehood? What prob-lems? And what are their prospects for the future, now that the initial excitement of a new and coveted standing has simmered down?

The first section of this book attempts to recapture the historic moments when Alaska and Hawaii won statehood. How was it achieved, what did it mean, and where did the new states stand upon entering the Union? The next section is devoted to contemporary life and society in the new states, with special attention going to the "native" problem in Alaska and interracial relations in Hawaii. The third and fourth sections explore the political and economic meaning of statehood, respectively. New responsibilities have brought new burdens and new opportunities. How are Alaska and Hawaii dealing with these emerging conditions? The fifth and final section deals with defense, a matter of crucial concern to both states.

The compiler wishes to thank the authors and publishers who have courteously granted permission for the reprinting of their materials in this book. I would also like to thank the staffs of Senators Ernest Gruening and E. L. Bartlett of Alaska and Senator Hiram L. Fong of Hawaii for their cooperation and assistance. I am especially indebted to Katherine Woodroofe, whose able assistance in preparing the manuscript proved invaluable and made light an otherwise difficult task.

WILLIAM P. LINEBERRY

September 1963

CONTENTS

1. ALASKA AND HAWAII ENTER THE UNION

EDITOR'S INTRODUCTION

Both states have a word for it. In Alaska it's *cheechako*. In Hawaii it's *malihini*. They mean the same—*newcomer*—a word that fittingly describes the condition of the latest states to join the American Union, Alaska and Hawaii. Like newcomers everywhere, the new states are not without their problems, as succeeding sections of this book will indicate. But first, for perspective, a flashback to those happy and hectic days attending statehood is in order.

Alaska and Hawaii were admitted to the Union in 1958 and 1959, respectively. Congressional approval climaxed decades of petitioning, maneuvering, and beseeching by territorial delegates determined to add new stars to the flag. In the final moments, it was only through the mutual bolstering of each other's cause that statehood, somewhat rapidly and surprisingly, became a reality. How and why did Alaska and Hawaii win admission to the Union? And what did admission mean for the "other forty-eight"?

The first four articles in this section discuss Alaska's history and its admission in 1958, the last four Hawaii's history and its admission in 1959. Following a brief historical survey, an Alaskan publisher describes his state's continuing endeavor to enter the Union, detailing the strategy that brought final victory. In the third article an active participant in the Alaskan statehood drive explains the advantages—political and economic—which statehood was expected to bring. The next article presents a fact-and-figure breakdown of the status of the forty-ninth state, its population resources and relation to the Federal Government, in the year of admission.

After an introductory historical sketch, "Hawaii's Struggle for Statehood" gives a detailed and lively account of Hawaii's efforts to enter the Union. The next article presents a resident's view of what statehood means to Hawaii in terms of self-rule, the transi-

tion from territorial status, and the economic and social impact
on both Hawaii and the United States as a whole. In the final
article, the noted novelist James A. Michener provides a glowing
description of the fiftieth state, its people and culture, in the year
of admission.

ALASKA'S RUGGED PAST [1]

Some historical and geographical experts believe that Asia and
North America were connected by a land bridge long before the
period of recorded history. Wandering native tribes from the
continent of Asia came across this bridge to North America.
While some of those dark-skinned people settled in Alaska, others
went south to what is now Canada and the United States. This
theory also explains the apparent similarities between the Alaskan
natives and other North American Indian tribes.

As early as 1579, a Russian Cossack named Yermak, in search
of furs, had conquered Siberia for the Czars. By 1650, a permanent Russian settlement had been established at Anadyrsk, on
the Bering Sea, within about four hundred miles of Alaska's
nearest point. Russia was interested in further exploration to the
east, but could not continue it because she became involved in a
series of wars with China.

Russian Exploration and Settlement

Almost a century passed before the Russians ventured in the
direction of Alaska again. In 1724, Peter the Great, a powerful
and ambitious Czar, ordered Captain Vitus Bering, a Dane who
had been in the Czar's service since childhood, to explore the
land east of Siberia and see whether Asia and America were
joined. Bering outfitted an expedition at Okhotsk, a village on
the Siberian mainland across the Sea of Okhotsk from Kamchatka, a large peninsula of southeastern Siberia. In 1728 he
sailed into the sea now named for him and sighted the St. Lawrence Islands and the Diomedes. But winter was approaching
rapidly, and he returned to Russia without seeing the mainland
of Alaska.

[1] From *A Pocket Guide to Alaska*, pamphlet prepared by the Office of Armed Forces
Information and Education. (DOD Pam 2-9) Department of Defense. Washington 25,
D.C. '56. p 6-15.

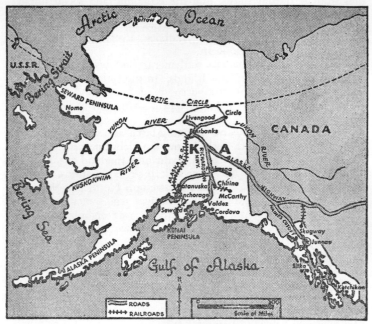

ALASKA

From *Senior Scholastic.* 56:10. My. 17, '50. Reprinted by permission from *Senior Scholastic.* ©1950 by Scholastic Magazines, Inc.

Bering organized another expedition in 1740, and with two ships again set sail for Alaska. Chirikof, in command of one of the ships, sailed along the southeastern coast and lost a landing party to hostile natives near Sitka. In the meantime, Bering skirted the south-central coast and made a landing near Mount St. Elias. On the way back his ship stranded on Bering Island where he and half of his men died from hardship and scurvy. The remnants of the expedition, after enduring more hardships, finally returned to Kamchatka and made their way back to Russia.

Stimulated by the explorers' tales of fabulous wealth in the newly discovered land, Russian fur traders and trappers began to enter the area. These exploiters gradually depleted the country of furs and almost exterminated the sea otter. They enslaved the Aleuts and made war on the Indians. Everything went out of Alaska, and nothing came in.

By 1800 a few Russian settlements had been established at Kodiak and on the Pribilof Islands. In the following years others sprang up along the mainland coasts of Alaska and Canada. At one time the Russians actually had a settlement at what is now Ross, California!

Russian activity in and around Alaska aroused the interest of other nations eager to cash in on the rich fur trade. Between 1774 and 1780, explorers from Spain and England made surveys along the Alaskan coast. It was Bering's explorations, however, that gave Russia her claim to northwestern North America.

Wholesale killing of Alaska's natives was somewhat reduced when the Russian-American Company was organized in 1799. The company's charter, granted by the Czar, required it to promote discovery and commerce and to spread the Russian Orthodox faith, a branch of the Christian religion. One of the early directors of this company was Alexander Baranof, whose word was law and who ruled accordingly. Under his direction, Sitka, the Russian capital of Alaska, became a highly cosmopolitan town and an extremely active business and trading center. It was Baranof and Russian missionary priests who founded the churches with their bulb-like steeples . . . principally in the Aleutians, at Kodiak, and at Sitka. . . .

"Seward's Folly"

As early as 1855 the Russian Czar tried to sell Alaska to the United States. He feared Great Britain might take it anyway, because Russia was losing the Crimean War to Britain. Russia had other troubles, too. Her attention was being turned more and more toward Europe because of Prussia's growing military strength. For these reasons Russia believed that Alaska was a definite liability.

Soon after the American Civil War ended, the Czar sent Baron de Stoeckl, an able diplomat, to Washington. The Czar's instructions were simple: Get rid of Alaska—sell it if possible, give it away if necessary.

After a considerable period and many conferences, the United States Secretary of State, William H. Seward, and the Baron finally signed a treaty on 30 March 1867, on behalf of their respective countries, for the United States to purchase Alaska for $7.2 million.

Seward was severely criticized for agreeing to purchase Alaska. Many persons called the region "Seward's Folly" or "Seward's Icebox," because it was generally believed that the land was absolutely worthless. But, after much controversy, the United States Senate finally approved the treaty, and on 18 October 1867, the Great Land became American property. The Russian flag was lowered and Old Glory was hoisted.

Still smarting at spending the sum of 2 cents an acre for what was thought to be an ice heap, Congress paid practically no attention to the new district (which became a territory in 1912) for about seventeen years. During this period there was no civil government in Alaska, but it was governed at various times from Washington by the Army, the Navy, and the Treasury Department. Little exploration was done and little use was made of its natural resources.

But were Seward alive today, few critical voices would be heard. From almost any standpoint the decision to buy Alaska has proved to be wise. Exports of fish, gold, and furs alone have repaid its purchase price many times over; and the land is rich in untapped resources. The production of gold, incidentally, has amounted to about $660 million.

Gold!

Who hasn't heard of gold strikes in Alaska? Klondike, Nome, Fairbanks, and others! The first strike was made in the Klondike in 1898. (Actually, the Klondike region is in Canada, but its most accessible route, before the airplane, was through southeastern Alaska via Skagway and the treacherous Chilkoot Pass.) Before the Klondike strike subsided, a fresh gold rush began at Nome. Within a few months eighteen thousand people jammed the short, desolate Nome beach in a feverish scramble. Again in 1902, the magic word of "gold" came from the interior, and the "sourdoughs" (oldtimers) rushed to Fairbanks.

During this period hard-boiled adventurers, miners, confidence men, gamblers, and opportunists came to Alaska by the thousands. Lights blazed in hotel lobbies until dawn. Bars and gambling houses never closed their doors, and beneath their chandeliers pistols barked and knives flashed. Our early West was tame compared to this period in Alaska's history!

Fantastic prices accompanied the early gold strikes. Cheap whisky was dispensed across bars at $10 a shot. A few eggs were available at a dollar each. Turkey dinners cost $175 apiece. Traders, who set up shop right after the first stampeders arrived, reaped high profits selling grub, clothing, and equipment. No wonder pennies went out of fashion during this period—everything was on the "gold standard"! (As a matter of fact, in the interior of Alaska, until recently, a quarter was the smallest coin in general circulation.)

Much has been written about the fabulous gold strikes. Adventure stories and poetry—favorites of many Americans—tell about the men who made fortunes, those who went broke, and those who died in the stampedes. Rex Beach, Robert Service, and Jack London are some of the better-known writers who "panned" the literary gold. To this day Hollywood is mining that rich lode.

Although there haven't been any big gold strikes in recent years, interest in mining still runs high. Today a few "sourdough" prospectors roam the hills, but modern mining is scientific. Engineering know-how has replaced hit-or-miss methods; necessary capital for mining operations now comes from cautious investors rather than from get-rich-quick "wildcatters."

ALASKA'S STRUGGLE FOR STATEHOOD [2]

The idea, or dream, of statehood for Alaska dates back to the time of its purchase by the United States from Russia in 1867.

Senator Charles Sumner of Massachusetts, in a learned speech supporting ratification of the treaty of purchase, dedicated Alaska to future statehood. Two years after the purchase, Secretary of State William H. Seward, whose vision and courage brought

[2] Article by Robert B. Atwood, editor and publisher of the Anchorage (Alaska) *Daily Times*, chairman of the Alaska Statehood Committee, 1949-1959. *State Government*. 31:202-8. Autumn '58. Reprinted by permission.

about the purchase, said in a speech at Sitka that Alaska would some day be one of the great states of the Union. . . . The enthusiasm of those two men, however, was not shared by the rest of Washington officialdom. Alaska was generally deemed of little value and was ignored.

Congress was the ultimate authority on everything pertaining to the new American territory, and the prevailing sentiment in that body was a disparaging one. The members' attitude was that the nation was "stuck" with the useless northland area, and "we'll run it with the least expense possible."

As a result of this attitude, the courageous Americans who went to Alaska found that they lived in a state of anarchy. There were no laws, no government in any form. People in Alaska could not own property. They could not marry. Upon death they could not be sure that the beneficiaries they named would get so much as their prospector's pick.

The first political activity of Alaskans was to seek some form of government. Nothing as refined as statehood was within the realm of possibility. They sent delegations to Washington requesting "any form of civil government." Seventeen years after the purchase, in 1884, Congress passed the first basic law and it proved to be totally inadequate.

Alaskans continued sending representatives to Congress requesting more adequate government. In 1906, just thirty-nine years after the purchase, Congress created the post of Delegate to Congress so that Alaskans could quit sending delegations at their own expense. The delegate, a voteless member of Congress, was to be their "voice."

In 1912, Congress enacted an Organic Act to replace the old law of 1884. It created a territorial legislature with powers so limited that it crippled its effectiveness.

First Moves for Statehood

Statehood became of real interest to Alaskans in 1915 after they realized that they would never be able to do much with their homeland without it.

The first forty-eight years of American ownership had brought more frustrations than anything else. What little government there was had been rendered ineffectively, by men not elected or responsible to the people they governed.

First sentiment for statehood crystallized at Valdez, a city which was then a thriving political center in western Alaska. O. P. Hubbard, a territorial senator from Valdez, introduced a bill in the legislature memorializing Congress to grant statehood. . . .

Delegate James Wickersham introduced the first statehood bill in Congress on March 30, 1916. In his diary he noted that he selected that date because it was the forty-ninth anniversary of the signing of the treaty of purchase. The bill was referred to a committee and died.)

Tax Issue

Delegate Wickersham had his hands full in a battle which involved protecting the powers of the little government Alaska had.

The territorial legislature had levied a small tax on the salmon fisheries in Alaska. The packers, most of whom lived in the Pacific Northwest and the East, had turned to the courts and to Congress for protection from such a surprising turn of events. The packers had operated without any taxes up to then.

In Congress, the Bureau of Fisheries, the Secretary of Commerce and President Wilson favored legislation that would exempt the fisheries from territorial taxation. Delegate Wickersham succeeded in having the bill defeated only by convincing the Congressmen that the multimillion-dollar industry was exploiting the resources of Alaska at the expense of the American taxpayers living in the states.

The fish interests took their complaints to court and argued that the territorial legislature had no authority to tax either the fishing or mining industries. The courts, however, upheld the taxing powers of the territory.

This was the first pitched battle between the fish interests and Alaskans. It is of historical interest because it continued many years after this incident. The fish packers had opposed every effort of Alaskans to establish a government. They opposed the Organic Act of 1884, the delegate's seat in 1906 and the legislature in 1912. Indeed, it was the fish opposition that delayed the realization of those small steps toward self-government. . . .

The tax problem proved an absorbing one for Alaskans, but the nation was fascinated by the statehood proposal in Delegate

Wickersham's bill. Many newspapers gave it support.

Opponents, however, came up with the arguments that were to be heard for the next forty-two years. They contended that Alaska was not ready, could not afford it, had insufficient resources and the population was too sparse and migratory. . . .

The first sixty-six years of American ownership had witnessed the gigantic efforts and the small successes of Alaskans in getting the first semblance of government, and the first collisions with the fish packers.

The first successes sharpened the awareness of Alaskans to the need for the traditional American form of self-government. The collisions with the packers served to identify their main enemy and drew battle lines that endured down to the final roll call on statehood in the United States Senate in 1958.

Changes in the Thirties

(Changes came to Alaska under President Franklin D. Roosevelt in 1933 just as they did for the rest of the nation.

He appointed Harold L. Ickes as Secretary of the Interior, a man who seemed to appreciate the czar-like powers over Alaskan affairs and enjoyed using them.

Ickes jolted Alaskans out of the apathetic attitude that prevailed. He compelled them to widen their concern beyond their small business ventures and community problems.

He proposed colonization schemes involving the introduction of large foreign populations into Alaska. He proposed making the Rat Islands in the Aleutian chain a penal colony. He forbade the issuance of patents to homesteaders because he disapproved of the separation of any more land from the public domain. In this action he proved himself more powerful than the United States Congress. His rule superseded and replaced the land laws enacted by Congress.)

Statehood Movement Revived

Alaskans were . . . alarmed when he proposed a tax of 8 per cent on the gross production of gold mines. They were convinced it would force many mines to be abandoned. The tax proposal brought Alaskans together in a new movement for statehood as a means of eliminating the rule of Ickes.

In 1939, the Anchorage Pioneer Lodge by resolution asked the territorial legislature to name a committee to study statehood. The organization condemned Ickes as making "Alaska's venture in home rule a bitter and regrettable jest."

The sentiments of the pioneers found ready acceptance by Alaska's governor, Dr. Ernest Gruening. Gruening had been appointed by the President over the objection of the Secretary of the Interior.

The outbreak of World War II brought an upheaval in Alaska. The military "discovered" the strategic value of the territory. Roads, docks, airports and housing were built in crash programs. Military leaders pleaded with Congress to enact measures assisting community growth because "we can't defend a wilderness."

The wartime prosperity gave the territory an economic lift that revived the lagging statehood movement.

On April 2, 1943, Congress for the first time since 1916 received the statehood bill. It was introduced by Senator William Langer (Republican) of North Dakota on behalf of himself and Senator Pat McCarran (Democrat) [of] Nevada. This was the start of a bipartisan effort that was to meet with success fifteen years later.

Alaska's Delegate to Congress, Anthony J. Dimond, followed with a similar bill, introduced December 3, 1943. Both the Senate and House bills were referred to a committee and died, but the spark they kindled would not die.

The new generation of Alaskans undertook studies of the duties, responsibilities and privileges that would come with statehood. When the Seventy-ninth Congress convened in 1944 new statehood bills were introduced. Alaskans were optimistic because both political parties had included statehood for Alaska and Hawaii in their platforms. The war precluded progress, however. Four Federal departments—War, Navy, Justice and Interior—recommended against action for the duration.

Postwar Action

It was in 1945, after the war had ended, that the statehood movement got under way in earnest. Thousands of veterans came to Alaska to find homes. Sentiment in favor of statehood grew with the population. Opponents became scarce, and those who were identified as opposed declined to appear publicly with their arguments. Senators Langer and McCarran reintroduced their bills. Representative Ervin [Democrat] of North Carolina put one in the House. The Alaska delegate always had one pending.

In August 1945, Secretary Ickes surprised Alaskans by going on record in favor. The territorial legislature memorialized Congress for favorable action and also provided for a referendum vote at which all Alaskans could express themselves.

Advocates of statehood formed the Alaska Statehood Association for the purpose of sponsoring research and informational work which could be the base for an intelligent vote in the referendum. . . .

The referendum resulted in a vote of 9,630 for, and 6,822 against, statehood. This proved to be a great impetus for the statehood movement.

In 1947 the first Congressional hearings were held. Alaskans flew to Washington to testify, following which the committee, with Representative Fred L. Crawford [Republican] of Michigan as chairman, came to Alaska and heard 150 more Alaskans. The committee reported favorably on the bill.

The bill, however, died in the Rules Committee. The members did not allow it to go to the floor for debate. But death of the bill did not kill statehood. The 1949 territorial legislature created the Alaska Statehood Committee and appropriated $80,000 for it to use in promoting statehood legislation, making studies of transitional problems and compiling information to aid delegates to a constitutional convention.

Stepping up the Pace

Creation of the committee took the initiative out of the hands of volunteers who, up to that point, had been carrying full responsibility. Statehood became a part of the official territorial program.

After the committee was created, an organized effort toward statehood was initiated. As a result, many national organizations such as lodges, civic groups, labor unions and others adopted resolutions in behalf of Alaska statehood. A national committee of prominent Americans for statehood was organized.

The House committee held hearings again and reported the bill favorably in 1949. The movement gained more and more prestige and power.

In 1950 a Gallup poll showed the public 81 per cent for, 8 per cent against, and 11 per cent no opinion. The House voted 186 to 146 to pass it, and another big victory for Alaska statehood was noted.

The bill then moved to the Senate, and Alaskans chartered an airplane to take fifty-five witnesses to Washington. They were dismayed, upon arrival, to find certain members of the committee hostile. W. C. Arnold, managing director of the Alaska Salmon Industry, Inc., had made a private presentation of the packers' arguments at a luncheon the day before. He had given the senators copies of his testimony, with charts and graphs, nicely bound in a leatherette cover.

Undaunted, the Alaskans presented their testimony over a period of one week. They also listened to Arnold give his testimony formally, reading from the document he had already presented to the senators privately.

The senators held the matter under advisement for almost two months after the hearings and then reported favorably. The Alaskans had done what they had been told was impossible. The merits of statehood had outweighed the elaborate opposition presented by Arnold.

During the two months' waiting period, the committee invented a new land formula for the proposed state of Alaska. Instead of granting lands from the public domain by chance of surveyed numbers, they provided for Alaska to select the land in large blocks regardless of survey. This was the origin of the generous land provisions that made the Alaska statehood bill unique.

Despite the favorable report and enthusiastic support by Chairman O'Mahoney of the Senate committee, the bill was not allowed to come to the floor of the Senate. It died with the Eighty-first Congress without further action.

New bills went into the Eighty-second Congress immediately after it convened. The leadership decided that inasmuch as the House had acted favorably before, the first action should now come from the Senate.

The Senate committee held executive sessions and approved the bill without delay. The bill carried the names of nineteen senators as authors. When it went to the floor for action, however, a Republican-Southern Democratic coalition prevented enactment. They recommitted it to the committee with a margin of one vote, 45 to 44.

This action came at the end of eleven days of debate over a period of four weeks. The outcome was a setback, but the closeness of the vote added to the prestige of the legislation. It was obvious then that the bill would pass if it could be brought to a vote again. But it required five more years to bring about that vote.

Another Fresh Start

Alaskans started all over again with new legislation when the Eighty-third Congress convened in 1958. They were braced by the platforms of both political parties, an impressive legislative history and growing sentiments in favor. They were surrounded by strength, but their forces had one great weakness. Certain key men in the Interior Department were cool toward statehood or were known opponents.

Despite this gap, statehood was a lively issue. Representative John P. Saylor (Republican) of Pennsylvania proved an effective new leader for statehood. He pressed for action on Alaska while the Administration at that time sought action only on Hawaii.

Further maneuvers appeared. The Democrats feared that Hawaii would be approved and Alaska left wanting statehood, so they combined the two bills.

It was during these maneuvers that Senator Hugh Butler (Republican) of Nebraska, as Chairman of the Senate Interior Committee, went to Alaska with the committee to hold more hearings. In previous sessions of Congress Senator Butler opposed statehood. In Alaska he indicated that he wished to hear testimony of "little people" who could not afford to go to Washington for hearings.

Senator Butler and his committee held hearings in Ketchikan, Juneau, Fairbanks and Anchorage. While emphasizing that he had an open mind on the statehood question, he prefaced most of the sessions with statements that pointed to the possibility that statehood would mean higher taxes and other undesirable burdens.

The "little people" testified in force. Out of 140 who appeared there were only 10 against statehood.

Senator Butler was impressed with the dedication of Alaskans to statehood. In Anchorage he found that the citizens had organized a "Little Man's Club" and had signs in store windows, on automobiles and buildings saying, "I'm a Little Man Who Wants Statehood." Wherever Senator Butler looked he saw the message. He and his committee reported the bill favorably.

This action brought a new device into the legislative picture. It was a suggestion that Alaska be made a commonwealth, like Puerto Rico, instead of a state. Senator Monroney [Democrat of Oklahoma] was the author of the idea. The suggestion was denounced immediately by Delegate Bartlett of Alaska and Delegate Farrington of Hawaii. It received virtually no public support.

The commonwealth proposal was defeated 60 to 24 in the Senate. The combined statehood bill was passed 57 to 28 and went to the House, where it died without further action.

Operation Statehood

While the bill was pigeonholed in the House, the "Little Man's Club" in Anchorage was reorganized into "Operation Statehood" for the purpose of continuing work in behalf of statehood.

The new organization literally flew into action in May 1954, when opponents of statehood proposed partitioning Alaska. . . . Alaskans refused to be divided. The Delegate to Congress and the Chairman of the Alaska Statehood Committee denounced the plan. "Operation Statehood" chartered a plane and flew Alaskans to Washington to oppose it. The partition plan died while some of the officials favoring it were still trying to find a likely place for a boundary.

The Eighty-fourth Congress had eight statehood bills in the two houses. They won committee approvals readily but they made little headway. The only chamber action was in the House, where a combined Hawaii-Alaska bill was recommitted to committee. After this unfavorable action the Senate decided not to waste any time on the subject.

Constitution and Tennessee Plan

Alaskans were not inclined to allow statehood to languish in Congress. They turned to the home front to build their case. In the winter of 1955-56 they held a constitutional convention on their own motion, without waiting for authorization from Congress.

Besides submitting the constitution for ratification, the convention also put before the voters a proposal that Alaska adopt the so-called "Tennessee Plan" for seeking statehood. This was its name for a program under which the territory would act like a state by electing two senators and a representative and send them to Washington to request Congress that they be seated. This approach had been successful when statehood was sought by Tennessee, Michigan, Oregon, California, Minnesota, Kansas and Ohio.

The constitution was ratified by a vote better than two to one. The Tennessee Plan also carried, and three men were elected as provisional senators and representative.

Eleven statehood bills went before the Eighty-fifth Congress. They were approved by the committees promptly and were in line for floor action. The House Rules Committee once more stopped them. For ten months it failed to act.

House Action, 1958

Representative Clair Engle (Democrat) of California, Chairman of the House Interior Committee, then invoked an old rule under which statehood legislation is privileged. He got a bill to the floor without action by the Rules Committee.

During debate the opponents found they could not stop enactment, but they could amend the bill. They provided for a referendum vote on three propositions before Alaska could become a state. These propositions required that Alaskans indicate that they (1) want immediate statehood, (2) accept the boundaries of the territory as the boundaries of the state, and (3) accept conditions as to transfer of public lands to the state and power of the President to withdraw certain military lands in emergency.

The bill was also amended to have the Federal Government retain control over the fisheries until the Secretary of the Interior certifies that the new state is ready and able to assume management responsibilities. This reduced the opposition of fish packers.

The House passed the measure May 28, 1958, by vote of 208 to 166.

Victory in the Senate

In the Senate the road to success was found sprinkled with hurdles, many of them formidable. Party concerns appeared. Republicans held that Democrats were pressing Alaska statehood and had no intention of acting on Hawaii. This made some Republicans reluctant to help enact the Alaska measure.

Additionally, some Republicans expressed fear that there were "no Republicans" in Alaska. The three in the "Tennessee Plan" delegation were Democrats, as was the Delegate to Congress.

The situation was complicated further by the fact that the Senate bill was, in the minds of its sponsors, better than the House bill. They preferred to act on their own measure. If they did, however, it was certain that no bill would result, as the two chambers would never agree in conference. The Rules Committee would bottle it up again.

Statehood supporters undertook a three-pronged challenge. It was that of (1) convincing the senators to forgo action on their own bill and consider the bill that had passed the House, (2) persuade the senators to accept the House bill without amendment so that no conference with the House would be necessary, and (3) allay the fears of Republicans that their party was non-existent in Alaska.

The friends of statehood were persuasive enough to accomplish all three phases of that program, largely because Secretary of the Interior Fred A. Seaton proved a devoted supporter and leader. The Secretary won strong support from all Administration quarters, and inspired the Republican side of the Senate to favor enactment of the bill.

During six days of debate on the floor of the Senate, certain of the southern senators sought by various means to upset the legislation. But repeated attempts to amend it were voted down.

Five Alaska Republicans went to Washington to bolster the Democratic delegation. They called on every Republican, and in the final tally Republican senators for statehood outnumbered the Democrats.

The final vote came on the evening of June 30. The vote was 64 to 20, a landslide for statehood. The bill was signed by the President on July 7.

Victory in Alaska

Alaskans went to the polls August 26. They approved the three referendum propositions by five to one, and ran up the biggest vote in the history of Alaska.

Even during the final days before the referendum, Alaskans found themselves pitted against fish packers still opposing statehood. The Alaska Statehood Committee sponsored another informational program for the voters, to put down rumors that were circulated in the hope of stirring up enough votes to defeat at least one proposition.

Secretary Seaton accepted an invitation of the Alaska Statehood Committee to come to Alaska for the purpose of explaining that Federal functions and agencies would continue to operate after statehood, that Indians would not be confined to reservations, and that they would not lose their lands and fishing rights.

The final chapter was written by the Alaskans when they gave the five-to-one decision in favor of statehood. It was only natural that they should, because they had been working for it for forty-two years.

WHAT STATEHOOD MEANS TO ALASKA [3]

On August 26, 1958, more than 48,800 Alaskan voters recorded at the polls their overwhelming endorsement of statehood for Alaska. The ratio of "yes" to "no" votes over the entire territory was five to one, but even this figure does not indicate the strength of the popular support for statehood. An emphasizing underline may be added to the quoted ratio by noting that 20,000 more persons voted on the statehood question than had

[3] From "The Meaning of Statehood to Alaska," by Thomas B. Stewart, attorney, executive officer of the Alaska Statehood Committee and secretary of the Alaska Constitutional Convention. *State Government.* 31:215-19. Autumn '58. Reprinted by permission.

ever before voted in Alaska, the largest previous vote cast having been 28,903 ballots at the general election in 1956. And an indication that the people of Alaska came to the polls especially to record their desire for statehood is revealed by the fact that nearly 3,000 more persons voted on the proposition as to whether statehood be granted than voted for United States senators, the contest drawing the next greatest number of votes.

Self-Government the Key

This fact of the tremendous popular majority for statehood, in a proportion not anticipated by even the most optimistic supporters, points up the central and basic meaning of statehood to Alaska and for Alaskans: the achievement of full self-government, in its unique American form. This vote itself was a vigorous exercise of self-determination in government by the people of Alaska.

Some few spokesmen for statehood in the pre-election campaign dwelt expressly on the fundamental proposition that the question before the voters was whether to accept the full responsibility of self-government or to continue in territorial, colonial status without the rights of self-determination held by full-fledged American citizens, i.e., those residing "in the states proper" (in the territorial idiom).

The debate on statehood just prior to this election focused principally on economic problems and on the general tax burden, and not so significantly on the more idealistic question of obtaining democratic rights. But the response of the voters to the challenge of the statehood question, on the other hand, implied a widespread and perhaps deeply emotional feeling amongst Alaskans for the central idea: statehood means the right of self-government for the people of Alaska.

Beyond this dominant proposition, the meaning of statehood principally assumes the character of possibilities. Having the right of self-determination, Alaskans now have the possibility of realizing many advantages and benefits not heretofore within their reach, as a practical matter. Whether the possibilities will become realities is to be determined largely by the wisdom and care with which the people of Alaska, and their leaders, exercise the newly gained rights of self-government.

Earlier Restrictions

There are some significant meanings of statehood of more certainty, however, and these include the immediate removal of positive restrictions on the powers of the territorial government imposed by the Organic Act of 1912, by the act of Congress which created the territory in its present form, and by other Federal laws.

These restrictions are too numerous to list in detail, but they include such things as a prohibition against the territory or municipal corporations assuming any bonded indebtedness. This barrier has been modified during the years prior to statehood in various ways, but it still has operated to prevent adequate capital improvements and a sound program of public financing. A most drastic prohibition has been that of preventing the territory from entering the field of regulation of its fish and wildlife resources— a restriction which has given rise to some of the most bitter, local feelings with regard to Federal administration in Alaska. This particular restriction on the governmental power has been temporarily retained in Public Law 85-508, Eighty-fifth Congress, the act providing for admission of the state of Alaska into the Union.

Perhaps the most significant restriction has been that preventing the election of the governor by the people of Alaska. The consequence of having a federally appointed governor, not responsible to the will of the electorate of the territory, has been a long history of bitter conflict in past decades between the legislature and the governor. In some instances, the governor has simply not given regard to the popular will—in circumstances in which an elected governor would need to do so, at the almost certain price of loss of office should he not respond. This situation has given rise to a distrust of the chief executive by the legislature which has produced much bad legislation in the territory in terms of decentralization in the executive organization and consequent lack of coordination in executive programs.

Strong Executive Becomes Possible

The removal of the restrictions of Federal law on Alaskan governmental power suggests the area in which there are perhaps the greatest possibilities for advantages to Alaska from statehood.

This is the matter of organization of the executive branch of the Alaskan government.

The general outline of its organization is already provided in the constitution for the state of Alaska, adopted by its framers on February 6, 1956, and ratified by the people of Alaska in an election held on April 24, 1956. The constitution has been accepted, ratified, and confirmed by Congress as being republican in form and in conformity with the Constitution of the United States and the principles of the Declaration of Independence. It provides for a strong executive, with powers to appoint the major department heads who will serve at his pleasure. It provides for a limited number of major departments of the executive branch, and otherwise expresses a policy of simplicity and clear lines of authority and responsibility. . . .

Thus a most important meaning of statehood to Alaska is the possibility of creating a workable and responsible executive branch. The constitution already adopted not only will permit this but encourages it. . .

Legislative Apportionment

Statehood means for Alaska an opportunity to make the legislative branch continuously representative of the population and its distribution to a degree seldom achieved by any state. The territorial legislature in recent years has been particularly unrepresentative, in the sense that most of its members came primarily from a few of the largest communities, although numerous smaller communities had sufficient population to warrant representation in the legislature on a proportionate basis. While it recently became theoretically possible for the legislature to redistrict for purposes of legislative elections, this was not done.

A sure consequence of statehood is an immediate redistricting along logical lines, providing for maximum representation of people and a constitutional scheme for reapportionment carefully designed to insure its operation despite legislative inertia on reapportionment.

It is noteworthy that the constitutional convention which determined upon the scheme of apportionment adopted by the people was itself composed of delegates whose election was based upon a special districting for the purposes of the election to the convention. This scheme of districting for the convention, which unquestionably produced a group of delegates far more widely representative than had ever assembled in the territorial legislature, was an instance of self-government. It indicates the quality of governmental action that arises from the promise of statehood.

A Better Court System

Statehood means that for the first time there will be a court system designed and operated by the people of Alaska rather than for them by absent powers. Perhaps one of the most significant facets of this change is that the judges will be selected by Alaskans—and, as provided by the state constitution, under the pattern of the American Bar Association plan for the selection of judges.

There is another and equally significant facet of Alaska's finally having its own judicial system. Heretofore, appeal from decisions of the district courts in Alaska has been through the Federal system to the Court of Appeals for the Ninth Circuit at San Francisco, and thence to the United States Supreme Court. This process of appeal has been prohibitively expensive for litigants. Consequently it has meant many decisions by the district courts without appellate review. There has also been little opportunity to review the validity of Alaskan laws and to interpret their meaning, which was needed to put flesh on the statutory skeletons. Statehood offers an opportunity to give the judicial system its proper place in the scheme of government.

Power at the Federal Level

A vitally important part of the meaning of statehood to Alaska is the opportunity to exercise political power at the Federal level. The history of Alaska as a territory is filled with frustrations of the elected delegates to Congress who have sat in the House of Representatives without the right to vote. This has meant almost no representation at all on critical issues where the practical processes of legislation required political power to accomplish governmental action for the constituency.

The lack of power in the voteless delegate to Congress evidenced itself in many ways. Often the Alaskan delegate's opportunity to be heard before a committee, for example, was lost in the press of time when voting members of Congress were given priority in hearing. The delegate from Alaska, of course, sat only in the lower house, and his opportunity to obtain action by the Senate was severely restricted since he had no privilege in that body.

Under statehood Alaska will have two senators and a representative in Congress. In an area as undeveloped as Alaska, and with so much of its surface in the category of Federal land, there are unlimited opportunities for enhancing development by Federal action. It is only with statehood that Alaska is in a position properly and adequately to urge necessary Federal action. The obtaining of a voice in Congress is a key feature of statehood that can affect Alaska's growth and development.

Transport and Natural Resources

Two of the most critical problems facing Alaska today are the development of an adequate transportation and communication system and the control and development of natural resources. Statehood holds the opportunity to reach sound answers in these fields.

Alaska today is economically a high-cost region, toward which venture capital for development therefore is not readily attracted. At the root of the problem of high costs is Alaska's remoteness from the manufacturing centers of the United States and the high cost of transporting goods from them. Under territorial status Alaska has suffered certain discriminations which have tended to restrict competition in transportation and otherwise to produce extremely high freight rates.

Statehood means that some of these restrictions will automatically be removed, and the possibility will exist for new competition, especially in ocean freight.

Under statehood Alaska will become eligible for Federal assistance in road building in a manner that heretofore has been denied it. By careful planning of the development of road and air facilities the new state has an opportunity to make available for economic use and development resources presently not used because of the difficulties of transportation.

Perhaps the greatest opportunity offered by statehood is that of planning for and, with accepted conservation standards, encouraging the use of Alaska's natural resources. At present the largest single industry is the taking and canning of fish, especially the various species of the Pacific salmon. A potentially large industry, just now awakening, is in the timber products field, including lumber and pulp. Mining remains one of the most important industries, although its future is uncertain in the face of existing depressed prices on the national and international levels. The prospect of extensive oil reserves is promising. There are known sites in Alaska for development of tremendous quantities of inexpensive hydroelectric power, and this offers great challenge for possible industrial development—the potential being available in many cases in the near vicinity of deep-water and ice-free ports that may accommodate ocean shipping. Not the least of the new state's economic advantages is its magnificent scenic beauty; the possibilities for development of tourism present an immediate opportunity. Finally, Alaska's vast land area is one of its major resources. Making land available for use and occupation to settlers offers a prime opportunity for governmental action looking toward the healthy, economic growth of the state. . . .

Alaska and the World

The strategic position of Alaska, located as it is athwart the growing polar transportation routes by air and sea, places it in a particularly sensitive international status. The significance of statehood reaches out, militarily and otherwise, into international affairs, with possibly wide consequences for the international position of the United States.

Alaska's statehood has every possibility of contributing to the best defensive system for the United States. With statehood there will now be added, for the Federal determinations on such matters as military appropriations, the voices of Alaska's two senators and its congressman. It is important to America to have a strong Alaska as its northernmost bastion. And Alaska is much more likely to be strong when occupied by people with roots in the land, supported by good transportation facilities, with a well-developed industry and agriculture, and a sense of being full participants in the destiny of all the United States.

Not the least of the consequences of statehood for the international position of the United States is the tangible evidence it provides that America practices the democracy it preaches. The granting of statehood is an obvious demonstration of America's belief in self-determination, self-government, and the superiority of democratic processes. The situation of the entire free world argues for an extension of the principle of union; in joining Alaska to the forty-eight states, America asserts a leadership in the development and spread of that principle. As a demonstration of faith in democracy the significance of Alaska's admission cannot be missed by the nations of the world. That it has had this value is evidenced by the weak attempt of the Russian government to minimize its importance, labeling it an effort by the United States to extend a military threat toward Russia. It is very clear that no such motives lay behind the decision of Congress to extend statehood. On the contrary, the passage of the bill was the culmination of long, hard efforts by Alaska and its many friends in Congress, the national Government and private life to achieve full rights of self-government for the people of Alaska.

The meaning of statehood for Alaska will become fully known only when its people have exercised these new rights of self-determination.

BACKGROUND ON THE FORTY-NINTH STATE [4]

Alaska is about one fifth the size of the continental United States. The distance from Ketchikan in southeastern Alaska to the westernmost Aleutian Island is greater than from New York to San Francisco. The distance from Ketchikan to Point Barrow is about the same as from Seattle to the Mexican border. Yet this large area—586,000 square miles—is thinly settled although its young population is growing rapidly.

For July 1957 the Bureau of the Census estimated the civilian population of Alaska at 165,000, an increase of 56,000 (52.0 per cent) over the 1950 figure of 108,000. Nevada's gain in civilian population for the 1950-1957 period was 63.8 per cent. In the period between the 1940 and 1950 censuses, Alaska's gain of 77.4

[4] From "The 49th State." *Social Legislation Information Service Bulletin*. 82:540-7. N. 25, '58. Reprinted by permission.

per cent in total population was larger than any state's. California was nearest with 53.3 per cent for this period.

While Alaska's population increased 77 per cent between 1940 and 1950, the population of the continental United States increased 14 per cent. The population of Alaska is still growing much faster than any state except Nevada. About two thirds of this growth is accounted for by natural increase—excess of births over deaths—and about one third to net immigration. About one quarter of the population is nonwhite.

Much of the population increase has taken place around Anchorage, the largest city in the state, whose total population is now 32,000. Fairbanks, the second city in size, has approximately 16,000 people. Juneau, the state capital, and Ketchikan in the southeast both have less than 10,000 inhabitants. About three people live in the country to every city dweller in Alaska. The "stateside" ratio is roughly two urban dwellers to one rural resident. Alaska has a population density of about 1 person per 4 square miles, as compared with 57 persons per square mile in the continental United States. Nevada, with two persons per square mile, has heretofore held the record for population sparseness.

The birth rate in Alaska (number of births per 1,000 population per year) stands at 35, ten points higher than the United States average and a rate close to those of several Latin American countries. The high Alaskan birth rate reflects the youthfulness of the population and the high proportion of married women. The median age of the Alaskan population is only 26, five years below that of the United States. In 1950, 42 per cent of Alaska's population was in the prime reproductive ages of 20 to 40, as compared with only 32 per cent in the United States as a whole.

The forty-ninth state of the Union has by far the largest proportion of males of any state and the highest proportion of married women. There are 16 males to every 10 females in Alaska. Nearly three fourths of all women there are married. In the continental United States, women slightly exceed men in numbers, and only two thirds of the women are married.

The extremely youthful age structure of the population also accounts for Alaska's phenomenally low death rate of 5.8. This is almost four points below the 9.6 death rate of the continental

United States. But if birth and death rates were adjusted for the age differences, the marked differences in birth and death rates between Alaska and the continental United States would be greatly reduced. . . .

Tuberculosis is probably the most serious health problem among the 34,000 Eskimos, Indians and Aleuts who are known as "Alaska natives." In 1957 the known case rate was 1649.7 per 100,000 in the native population. The number of cases among the Indian population in the United States in the same year was 426.9 and 51.4 cases among the general population. Although mortality from tuberculosis remains high among Alaska natives, it has dropped from a rate of 630 per 100,000 population in 1951 to 89.2 in 1956.

Programs: Special Federal Aid

The Federal Government now owns 99.5 per cent of the land in Alaska. The land north of the Yukon River and west of its porcupine tributary—plus much of the Alaska Peninsula in the southwest—will remain subject to exclusive Federal jurisdiction whenever the President deems this necessary for national defense. This "withdrawal area" is about half of Alaska, containing 15,000 Indians, Aleuts and Eskimos and 5,000 employees of the Defense Department.

Under the Alaska Statehood Act, over the next twenty-five years, the new state may select up to 103,350,000 acres of land, of which 400,000 acres may be within the withdrawal area. Alaska may sell or lease its land "dowry," except that land within the withdrawal area may be used only for recreational purposes and community expansion and may not be sold. Although the Federal Government will retain some 70 per cent of the land in Alaska, the new state is receiving more land than has been granted any other state joining the Union. . . .

The Government is turning over to the new state the Federal building in Juneau, as well as the Governor's Mansion. Of great benefit also will be continuance, for at least several years, of special Federal aid for welfare, health and education in Alaska:

Until 1900 all Alaskan public schools were operated by the Federal Government. Since then the territorial public school system, which accounts for about half the territorial budget, has grown to total 125 schools, of four types:

28 schools in organized districts supported by local funds and directed by local school boards. Elementary enrollment, 20,000 (about 20 per cent native); secondary enrollment, 4,700 (about 18 per cent native).

68 schools outside incorporated districts are supported and operated by Alaska's Department of Education. Elementary enrollment, 3,100 (about 48 per cent native); secondary enrollment, 250 (about 35 per cent native).

21 former Federal schools now operated by Alaska's Department of Education, although the Federal Government still owns and finances them. Enrollment is about 650, entirely elementary and virtually all native.

8 schools on military bases, operated by Alaska's Department of Education but supported by Federal funds.

There are also some 20 or 25 private and denominational schools in Alaska, most of which are elementary. Their enrollment totals 1,600 (about half native).

The Department of the Interior operates 86 schools in Alaska. Two on the Pribilof Islands of St. George and St. Paul are the responsibility of the Fish and Wildlife Service of the Department, while the others are managed by its Bureau of Indian Affairs. Most have only one or two teachers; three fourths have enrollments between 15 and 55. In southeast Alaska the Bureau maintains two boarding schools: Wrangell Institute, an elementary school with an enrollment of 250; and Mount Edgecumbe, a secondary school with an enrollment of 740. Only native children may attend. . . .

The Bureau of Indian Affairs of the Interior Department provides general assistance to Alaskan natives who are not eligible for categorical public assistance under the Social Security Act. The BIA also provides child welfare services to native children who are not eligible for Territorial services and social casework services for families with serious problems. . . . [In 1958] BIA allocated $960,000 for its Alaskan welfare program.

The Federal Government provides health and medical services for Alaska natives on essentially the same basis that these services are rendered to Indians who live on reservations within

the continental United States. Until July 1955, health services
for Alaska natives were provided by the Bureau of Indian Affairs
of the Department of the Interior, but since then the Indian
health program has been the responsibility of the Public Health
Service of the Department of Health, Education and Welfare.
In general, all services to the natives are designed to reach natives
who live in unincorporated villages and rural areas. Those living in larger towns depend for services upon the same territorial
agencies that serve the entire population.

The eight PHS hospitals in Alaska have a combined total of
more than 1,000 beds, of which about 650 are for tuberculosis
patients. However, there are not enough beds to meet the needs
of the unusually high number of tuberculosis patients and some
general patients in remote communities. To serve these people,
the Public Health Service contracts with community hospitals
and sanatoria for about 25 general beds and for more than 100
beds for tuberculosis patients, as well as for about 300 beds in
three sanatoria in the state of Washington. Native tuberculosis
patients are transported by air to the hospitals in Washington.

For a number of years the Bureau of Indian Affairs had contracted with the Alaska Department of Health for public health
nursing services to the native population. This contractual arrangement has been continued and expanded since the transfer
of the program to the PHS. The current contract provides for
public health nursing services, medical care, tuberculosis control
and sanitation and health education services to the Alaska native
population. Under this contract, native sanitarian aides are being
trained and employed in the Alaska native health programs.

The PHS program also includes itinerant nursing services to
natives in 113 remote villages. The Service operates a nationally
accredited practical nurse training school at Mount Edgecumbe,
in which about forty Alaska native girls are in training annually.
Graduates of this school are employed in the hospitals and other
Alaskan health facilities of the PHS.

Three Federal grant programs in the health field apply only
to Alaska. The former territory has been appropriated $638,000
annually to supplement territorial, local and other funds received by the Alaskan Department of Health. . . . [In 1957 and
again in 1958], Congress also made a special $1 million grant
to help the territory meet the cost of treatment and care of the

mentally ill. In July 1956, Congress provided for the progressive transfer—over a decade ending June 30, 1967—of responsibility for the mentally ill in Alaska from the Federal Government to the territory. Appropriation of $6.5 million was then authorized for construction of suitable facilities in Alaska, where none now exist, patients being hospitalized in Oregon. . . .

The Public Health Service program currently [1958] includes $527,000 for direct operations in Alaska. The territory has been aided through loan of personnel, procurement of supplies and provision of other services necessary for control of venereal diseases, tuberculosis and sanitation and other general health problems. At Anchorage, the PHS also operates its Arctic Health Research Center, which studies environmental sanitation, epidemiology, entomology, animal-borne diseases transmissible to man, biochemistry, nutrition and physiology.

Grants: Special Treatment for Alaska

In . . . [many] programs of Federal aid to the states, no distinction is made between the former Territory of Alaska and the states. . . .

In other Federal grant programs, however, Alaska is presently accorded treatment differing from that received by the forty eight states. For the most part, the current laws give Alaska less favorable treatment. The Library Services Act sets the Federal share of Alaska's rural libraries at two thirds of the annual costs, although in the states the Federal share varies from two thirds to one third, depending upon state per capita income.

On the other hand, the section of the Smith-Hughes Vocational Education Act providing grants for teacher training does not include Alaska. Under the National Defense Education Act of 1958, financial assistance to Alaska for instruction in science, mathematics and modern foreign languages will be determined by the Commissioner of Education, as is also true of the Act's provisions for guidance, counseling and testing. Special provisions of other laws affecting Alaska are:

The 1958 amendments to the Social Security Act . . . specified for Alaska the Federal share of four matching grant programs in which the former territory participates. Starting with the 1960 fiscal year—which begins July 1, 1959—the Federal share of state child welfare programs will depend on state per capita income, varying from one third to two thirds of the total. The Federal share in Alaska, though, was fixed at half the cost of the program.

In the public assistance programs of Old-Age Assistance, Aid to Dependent Children and Aid to the Blind, the Federal grants are in two parts. The Federal share is $15 of the first $18 paid monthly to adult recipients and $14 of the first $17 received monthly by dependent children. With respect to this portion of the OAA, ADC and AB grants, Alaska is treated as other states.

The Federal share of additional payments made under these programs depends upon state per capita income and varies from 50 to 65 per cent. The Federal share of the cost of Alaska's OAA, AB and ADC programs is fixed at 50 per cent, without regard to per capita income in the forty-ninth state.

Alaska is treated like the states under most public health programs. Exceptions are the Federal grants for water pollution control and construction of (Hill-Burton) medical facilities. In these two programs, the Federal share of project costs depends upon state per capita income and may vary from one third to two thirds of the total. In Alaska the Federal contribution does not depend on per capita income and is fixed at half the cost of projects.

Alaska is also treated differently in one portion of the Federal-state vocational rehabilitation program—the grant-in-aid for support of services. Under the law, available funds are allotted among the states on the basis of a formula involving per capita income, with allotments ranging from one third to three fourths. The allotment percentage for Alaska is fixed by law at three fourths. The matching provisions of this law call for the Federal contribution to vary from 50 to 70 per cent, depending upon state per capita income. In Alaska the Federal share is fixed by law at 60 per cent.

The only distinction made between Alaska and the states under the Housing and Home Finance Agency's authority to provide defense housing and community services and facilities is with respect to maximum cost per family dwelling unit. At the discretion of the HHFA, the cost in Alaska may be 50 per cent higher than the maximum allowed in the forty eight states. Similarly, in the low rent public housing program, Alaska is permitted $500 additional over the maximum cost of $2,000 per room in the continental United States. Congress authorized establishment of the Alaska Housing Authority, which may borrow up to $20 million from HHFA. Up to $1 million of this sum may be used to make character loans to individuals and co-operatives. . . .

Under a law passed in 1949, donations of surplus Federal property may be made to the states only for purposes of education, public health, civil defense or for research in these fields, and all such donations are subject to certain restrictions and controls by the donor agencies. In 1954 this law was amended, however, to authorize donation of surplus movable Federal property to the territorial government of Alaska without regard to other requirements of the law, providing only that the territorial governor indicates, before the end of 1959, that the property is needed.

Prospects: Continued Federal Generosity?

. . . [The] Department of the Interior, with the concurrence of the Attorney General, has circulated a legal opinion to encourage uniform interpretation of the Alaska Statehood Act by the various Federal departments and agencies.

The legal memorandum recalls that Section 8(d) of the Act, provides that "All of the laws of the United States shall have the same force and effect within said state (Alaska) as elsewhere within the United States." The memorandum then categorizes "the laws of the United States" as follows:

1. Those generally applicable but not applying to Alaska,
2. Those equally applicable to the United States and Alaska and
3. Those which accord territories or possessions, including Alaska, more or less favorable treatment than the several states.

In the opinion of the Interior Department's attorneys, laws of the first two types continue or will be extended to apply to the new state of Alaska. With respect to the third category of laws, they believe it would be "clearly inconsistent with statehood to apply to Alaska provisions expressly applicable only to territories and possessions." This reasoning would seem to dictate the end of the special provisions regarding Alaska that have been described above.

However, the Interior Department's legal memorandum regards as an exception to the third category laws "which prescribe distinctive treatment for Alaska attributable to some factor other than the territorial status of Alaska. . . . The distinction may have been made, for example, because of area, population, climate, terrain, or any of a number of other factors. We think it entirely compatible with statehood that those distinctions be preserved until such time as the Congress manifests an intention to the contrary.

HAWAII'S EXOTIC PAST [5]

[One of the mysteries of the Pacific is] where . . . the native Hawaiian . . . [came] from, and how . . . [he got] to Hawaii. This much is obvious: the ancient Polynesian was a daring and venturesome navigator. He had to be, when you consider the distances he traveled over uncharted seas, in small craft, to get to Hawaii.

Many theories have been advanced through the years to account for the arrival of these intrepid voyagers to the Islands. Most authorities agree that they first came to Hawaii about one thousand years ago. Their origin is obscure but it is generally believed that they were Polynesians who came up from Tahiti, two thousand miles away.

The Polynesians are said to be the descendants of a tribe of Caucasian people who left their homeland in India. They roamed through Malaya to the island groups of the Pacific. Along the route they intermarried with Malayans and people of the Orient. From the people of the southwestern Pacific islands they acquired their darker complexion, so that by the time they reached Tahiti, now considered the ancient homeland of the Polynesian, they were a light brown people.

During the thirteenth and fourteenth centuries, new groups of Tahitian Polynesians rediscovered Hawaii. They came in large double canoes, laden with families, food, plants, and animals, and they settled down. The era of long voyages ended. Hawaii remained isolated from the world for . . . several centuries.

    [5] From *A Pocket Guide to Hawaii*, pamphlet prepared by the Office of Armed Forces Information and Education. (DOD Pam 2-1) Department of Defense. Washington 25, D.C. '55. p 15-27.

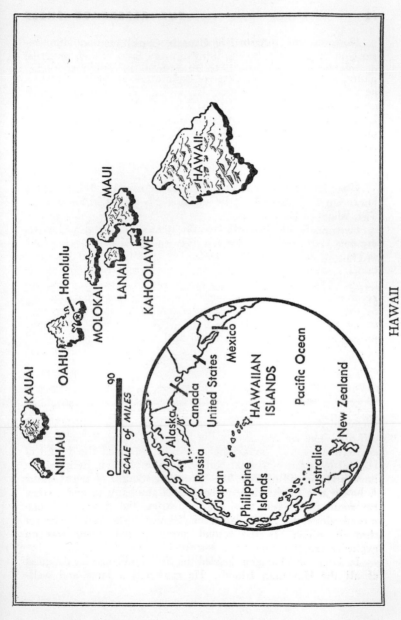

HAWAII

From News Explorer. p 2. Ap. 17, '59. Reprinted by permission from News Explorer. © 1959 by Scholastic Magazines, Inc.

Arrival of Captain Cook

Captain James Cook, the great English sea captain and explorer, was on his third voyage of exploration in the Pacific when he first sighted the Hawaiian Islands in 1778. His two armed vessels, the *Resolution* and the *Discovery*, anchored in Waimea Bay, Kauai, on 20 January and Cook, accompanied by twelve marines in three armed boats, went ashore. The natives immediately prostrated themselves before the explorer, believing him to be an incarnation of their god, Lono, returning in fulfillment of an old prophecy.

Cook left the Islands, promising to return. He did so a year later. On 17 January 1779, he anchored his vessels in Kealakekua Bay, Island of Hawaii. . . .

Here again the Englishman was treated as a god and given presents. All went well for ten days and then *pilikia* (trouble) set in. It started with the realization that Cook and his companions were not gods but mortals, as were the natives themselves. Quarrels in trade occurred, and thefts. The natives became angry when a fence around a temple was cut up for fuel by the visitors. Then a large boat belonging to the *Discovery* was stolen by natives who broke it up to obtain iron. Cook determined to take the Island king aboard the *Discovery* and hold him until the stolen craft was restored. A fight resulted, and Captain Cook and seventeen natives were killed.

Kamehameha the Great

Cook, as he explored each of the inhabited islands, found them ruled as independent kingdoms by hereditary chiefs called *alii nui*. The emergence of a Big Island chieftain, Kamehameha, changed all that. Kamehameha first consolidated the Island of Hawaii by a series of great battles. In one of them, he is said to have had the aid of Pele, the Hawaiian goddess of the volcano. A battle was in the making between Kamehameha and Keoua. En route from Hilo to the Kau district, the forces of Keoua moved along the active crater of Kilauea. The first group got through safely. As the second group passed, there was an explosive eruption and every warrior in it was killed.

In 1795 Kamehameha decided the time had come for conquest of all the Hawaiian Islands. He mustered a large and well-equipped army and sailed for Maui. Meeting little resistance there, he destroyed the village of Lahaina and laid waste to the western portion of the island.

His forces then took possession of the island of Molokai and sailed on to Oahu. After a few days of preparation his army marched up Nuuanu valley where Kalanikupule, the king of Oahu, stood with his forces. The Oahu warriors fought bravely but were driven up the valley and hundreds of them perished when they were pushed back over the *pali* (cliff) at the head of the valley. It is an event celebrated in ancient and modern Hawaii songs. The Nuuanu *pali* today is one of the world's greatest scenic masterpieces. . . .

Kamehameha I will always remain a hero to his Hawaiian people. It was he who consolidated the Islands under a rule strong enough to withstand a century of foreign jockeying for favored position in these strategic Islands. He and his descendants were to rule the Islands for one hundred years until just before Hawaii became a territory of the United States.

Vancouver Arrives

About this time foreign vessels began to visit the Islands, principally on trading or exploration missions. In 1791 one of them anchored off Kauai to collect sandalwood, establishing a long and profitable sandalwood trade with China. An important foreign visitor was Captain George Vancouver, British naval explorer, who made three visits beginning in 1792. He brought to Hawaii the first bulls and cows ever seen there, and presents of orange trees, grapevines, and other useful plants. Vaucouver also gave Kamehameha much valuable advice on the management of his monarchy, the training of his troops, and how to deal with foreigners.

In 1820 an event of considerable importance occurred. The first missionaries arrived after a long voyage around the Horn from New England. They found a fertile field for Christianity. The American missionaries gained success when they aligned themselves with the chiefs to combat the distillation of hard liquor, a breakdown in morals, and the spread of infectious diseases.

Russia Tries to Move In

The Islands prospered under the Kamehameha kings. Foreign trade developed steadily, as did internal commerce, agriculture, and industry. Sugar and coffee were becoming established crops.

With Japan closed to foreigners, Hawaii became the center for the whaling industry in the Pacific. Foreign vessels, men-of-war and cargo ships put into Honolulu harbor in increasing numbers.

In 1814 the *Bering*, a Russian trading vessel, was wrecked on the coast of Kauai. Much of the cargo was salvaged by natives. In 1815 the Russians sent an agent to Hawaii presumably to recover the lost cargo but actually to establish a Russian post.

A year later the agent was reinforced by the arrival of two more Russian ships. He landed his men in Honolulu and began building a fort there. Kamehameha ordered them sent away. The Russians went instead to the island of Kauai where, aided by natives, they began building a new fortress. When news of this reached the king on Oahu, he ordered the Kauai governor to expel the Russians at once. This was done after some fighting, and the foreigners were deported to California. Thus ended the dream of Russian conquest in the Hawaiian Islands and the first known attempt at foreign interference with the affairs of the Pacific Kingdom.

The United States and Hawaii

A quarter of a century passed, and in 1842 the United States formally recognized the Kingdom of Hawaii.

Queen Liliuokalani was a handsome and a brilliant woman. She reigned for not quite two years, beginning in January 1891, and was in trouble right from the start. Her reign, although brief, is important. Her dethronement led in succession to the establishment of a provisional government, a Hawaiian republic, and eventually, to annexation by the United States.

Early in her regime the queen clashed with her ministers when she attempted to abolish, by means of a new constitution, some of the restrictions placed upon the monarch. When the ministers refused to sign the document, the queen withdrew it.

In the meantime a Committee of Safety had been appointed by leading citizens who had gathered to discuss the situation.

Members of this Committee took steps almost at once to form a provisional government and to reorganize a voluntary military company previously disbanded.

A mass meeting on 16 January 1893 ratified the action of Committee members. That evening the U.S.S. *Boston* landed a force of armed men for the protection of American interests.

The provisional government was organized on 17 January. That afternoon it took possession of the government building and issued a proclamation declaring the monarchial government to be abolished.

On 19 January five commissioners were named to proceed to Washington with full authority to negotiate a treaty of annexation to the United States. Such a treaty was drafted and sent to the United States Senate for approval only to be withdrawn by President Cleveland, who wanted time to investigate the Hawaiian situation.

When their hopes of early annexation to the United States faded, the Hawaiians took another step. A constitutional convention was summoned to draft a constitution for the Republic of Hawaii. The work was completed on 4 July 1894, and the next day the Republic of Hawaii was proclaimed with Sanford B. Dole as president.

Negotiations for the annexation of the new Republic to the United States were resumed soon after the election of President William McKinley. On 6 July 1898, the Senate and the House of Representatives adopted a joint resolution to this effect. It was signed by President McKinley the next day.

United States Flag Flies over Hawaii

The news of the signing of the treaty reached Honolulu on 13 July amid great rejoicing. The transfer of sovereignty was formally completed on 12 August when the flag of the United States was raised over the executive building.

In April 1900 Congress passed the Hawaii Organic Act, establishing the territorial form of government and providing that the Constitution and laws of the United States have the same force in Hawaii as in the continental states. Sanford Dole, president of the Republic, was appointed the first governor of the Territory of Hawaii, taking office on 19 June 1900. Thus Hawaii came into the Union proudly and voluntarily, preferring the American democratic way of life to the many other forms of government she experienced and was offered.

HAWAII'S STRUGGLE FOR STATEHOOD [6]

Marine helicopters buzzed overhead, church bells rang, and little children raced barefoot along country roads, shouting, "Statehood! Statehood—it's come!" Approved by Congress in 1959, statehood arrived 106 years after pro-American King Kamehameha III first began discussions with the United States Government about the annexation of Hawaii to the Union as a new state. After the King died, negotiations lapsed, although the idea of statehood was never entirely abandoned. In his inaugural address as the first governor of the Territory of Hawaii, Sanford B. Dole prophesied eventual statehood, and in 1903, the territorial legislature petitioned Congress for an enabling act which would lead to statehood. The first bill calling for statehood was submitted in Congress sixteen years later by Jonah Kuhio. Dozens of congressional investigations, reports, and recommendations were produced in the years that followed, but Hawaiian statehood, a symbol of the right and ability of the peoples of the Islands to govern themselves, was always blocked.

Hawaii remained under the constitutional control of Congress, which could, at any time, abolish the territorial legislature and local government and place the Islands under a resident commissioner, as was done in the Philippines, or under a Navy commission, as had been done in Guam and Samoa. Hawaii had been threatened with the loss of self-government before. The President and Congress flirted with the idea of commission government . . . in the early 1930's. During World War II, Hawaii became the first sizable territory in American history to be governed by the military. Throughout its history, the citizens of Hawaii had been unable to vote for President or for their own governor. With only one nonvoting delegate to represent them in Congress, the territory did not get its share of Federal money for roads, conservation, improvement of rivers and harbors, or

[6] From *Hawaii Pono: A Social History*, by Lawrence H. Fuchs, professor of politics and dean of faculty at Brandeis University. Harcourt, Brace & World, Inc. New York. '61. p 406-17. © 1961, by Lawrence H. Fuchs. Reprinted by permission of Harcourt, Brace & World, Inc.

land-grant colleges and vocational education. Hawaii, Congress said in repeated sessions following 1935, was not ready for statehood.

Delegates Jonah Kuhio and Victor Houston, after serving in Congress, believed that Hawaii could not achieve optimum economic and social benefits from participation in the American Union unless the territory was transformed into a state. Houston had warned the Hawaiian Sugar Planters' Association as early as May 1929 that the only sure way to prevent discrimination against the Islands' sugar industry was to obtain statehood. Unless Hawaii carried more weight in Congress, the two major props of the industry—the high protective American tariff and the steady supply of cheap labor from the Philippines—might be destroyed. Congress could lump Hawaii with the Philippines as an offshore area and place the Islands outside the American tariff, or, responding to Hawaii's insistence on equal treatment short of statehood, might exclude Filipino labor from the Islands as they had from the mainland.

Opposition to Statehood

But not all of the citizens of Hawaii wanted statehood. Until 1935, the overwhelming majority of the *kamaaina* [born in Hawaii or long resident there] oligarchy of the Islands were steadfastly opposed. The trustees of the Hawaiian Sugar Planters' Association answered Houston by arguing that immediate statehood would be "premature and unwise," and were delighted when congressional sponsors of Filipino exclusion bills included an exemption for Hawaii. The plantations, over 60 per cent of whose laborers were Filipinos, could continue to draw their field workers from the giant archipelago in the western Pacific, and the tariff walls seemed as sturdy as ever. When Houston complained to Henry A. Baldwin [a sugar plantation owner and political leader] that as delegate he had to beg for benefits for Hawaii and that there was constant discrimination against the territory, Baldwin replied that he understood Houston's feeling like a "book agent going around asking for *kokua* [help]." But territorial status was preferable to statehood, he advised, since the voters of the Island were not mature enough to elect a safe-and-sane governor. "The bolsheviks and booze fighters seem to get the big vote, at least on Oahu, and Oahu would come pretty near controlling T. H. elections," predicted the missionary descendant. There was even a risk, suggested Baldwin, that Hawaii would elect a Japanese governor and a strongly Japanese state legislature. Another missionary descendant, Clarence H. Cooke, opposed statehood in a letter to a high-school debating team by asserting that "through appointment of officers by the President of the United States, such as the governor, secretary of the territory and judges, we have always had a better class of men in these positions than states enjoyed through their elective systems." Until 1934, the other owners and managers of Hawaii's sugar agencies and their subsidiaries agreed with Baldwin and Cooke. [For a discussion of the "oligarchy" of Hawaii, see "Hawaii's Economy: Prospects and Problems," in Section IV, below.]

But following the Jones-Costigan Act of 1934, a fundamental reversal occurred in the attitude of many of Hawaii's leading *kamaaina* citizens toward the issue of statehood. The Act classified Hawaii, not as an integral part of the United States, but as a nondomestic producer of sugar, along with the Philippines and Puerto Rico. The practical effect was to increase the amount of sugar that might be marketed by Colorado, Michigan, and other states by as much as 18 per cent, while the Hawaiian quota was cut by 10 per cent. Despite protests from the Hawaiian Sugar Planters' Association, Federal courts supported the right of Congress to discriminate against any territory in setting sugar quotas. Association lobbyists failed to produce a change in congressional will, and suddenly the men who owned and controlled the great agencies saw the wisdom of Houston's argument for statehood.

Sugar Joins Fight

The sugar industry backed Delegate Samuel Wilder King when he introduced a statehood bill to the House of Representatives in May 1935, and supported the Hawaii Equal Rights Commission, created by the territorial legislature in the same year. The Commission was charged with working to assure Hawaiian equality with the states in Federal legislation and to study the advisability of submitting the issue of statehood to a plebiscite. The first act of the Commission was to authorize Governor J. B. Poindexter, its ex officio chairman, to appear before the congressional delegation then in the territory to study the question of statehood.

This was the first of twenty congressional hearings on statehood held between 1935 and 1958, hearings that saw more than 1,000 witnesses and that resulted in the passage of Hawaiian statehood bills by the House of Representatives in 1947, 1950, and 1953, as well as passage of a Senate bill to admit both Hawaii and Alaska in 1951. By 1940, the prostatehood forces in the territory had persuaded the territorial legislature to authorize a plebiscite on the question. The sugar interests, recognizing that Hawaii's position in the domestic market was in constant jeopardy, strongly supported statehood. Joseph Farrington's Honolulu *Star Bulletin*, the *Nippu Jiji*, and the *Hawaii Hochi* endorsed the plebiscite in editorials and news columns. The Honolulu *Advertiser* opposed immediate statehood, mainly on the ground that Americans of Japanese ancestry who held dual citizenship were not yet trustworthy as Americans.

The magazine *Fortune* helped prostatehood forces when it published an Elmo Roper poll in January 1940 which showed that only 55 per cent of the mainlanders questioned believed the United States should go to the rescue of Hawaii if the Islands were attacked, while 74 per cent favored the defense of Canada. The *Advertiser* considered the poll irrelevant, insisting that Hawaii should not become a state until its citizens were Americanized. It pointed to the 37,000 alien-born Japanese in Hawaii who could not become citizens, the 174 Japanese-language schools attended by more than 40,000 young nisei, and the potential dangers of Japanese-language broadcasts. Disturbed by the *Advertiser's* hard-hitting attacks, the *Star Bulletin* published an article by University of Hawaii sociologist Romanzo Adams entitled "Getting the Facts Straight About Statehood—A Myth About Japanese Dominance." Although no group was more interested in the outcome of the plebiscite than the Japanese, most of their leaders refrained from taking a stand to avoid lending credence to the *Advertiser's* allegations. In the plebiscite, two of every three voters affirmed their support of statehood, with the largest pluralities coming from the outer islands. On Oahu, especially in the haole [white] districts, statehood was more controversial, since it was in such areas that fear of the "Japanese menace" had had the greatest influence.

Post-War Efforts

After the war, statehood efforts were vigorously renewed. In 1944, the Hawaiian Equal Rights Commission recommended that its name be changed to the Hawaii Statehood Commission, a proposal adopted by the territorial legislature in January 1947. Later that year, the United States House of Representatives for the first time passed a bill providing for Hawaiian statehood, but the Senate defeated a move to remove the statehood bill from its Interior and Insular Affairs Committee in the following session. The citizens of Hawaii watched as statehood bills were buried in one house or the other, and during the 1950's, they increasingly doubted that statehood would ever be approved by Congress. Statehood commissioners for Hawaii collaborated with Delegate Jack Burns in organizing testimony for congressional investigators. Proponents of statehood repeatedly argued that Hawaii should not pay Federal taxes without voting privileges, that Hawaii paid more Federal taxes than nine other states, that the Islands had a larger population than any other territory at the time of admission to the Union except Oklahoma, and that the per-capita income of its citizens was higher than that of thirty-five states. The peoples of Hawaii, they pleaded, were literate and patriotic, ready to assume the obligations of first-class citizenship.

Suddenly, in 1958, the statehood strategy of Delegate Burns diverged from that of certain statehood commissioners and Governor William Quinn in Honolulu. Following passage of the Alaskan statehood bill by the House of Representatives, Burns agreed with proponents of Alaskan statehood and Democratic leaders in the Senate that it would probably destroy the chances of statehood for either territory if Hawaii and Alaska were joined in the same bill. Burns agreed that it would be wise for Hawaii to wait its turn, even if it meant postponement of consideration of the Hawaiian bill until a new Congress met in 1959. Lorrin P. Thurston, chairman of the Hawaii Statehood Commission and publisher of the now ardently prostatehood *Advertiser*, did not agree that Hawaii's bill should be held up until the following year. Commissioner O. P. Soares said that it was "naïve" to believe that Hawai would be better prepared in the next session "if Alaska goes through this time." Governor Quinn called for an immediate push and wondered why the Hawaii bill should be held up for Alaska.

Alaska-First Plan

It became increasingly clear that Burns not only acquiesced in, but was one of the chief strategists of the plan to separate the two bills and push Alaska first. The theory was simple. Some congressmen opposed Hawaii, others were antagonistic toward Alaska. Why combine these minority oppositions to defeat an over-all bill? Also, Burns maintained, the momentum to accept Hawaii would be irreversible once Alaska achieved statehood. Not only would additional pro-Hawaiian statehood congressmen sit in both chambers, but it would be difficult to discriminate against Hawaii as the only remaining incorporated United States territory. Opponents of the Burns strategy in Hawaii did not agree that the alternatives were a combined bill or Alaksa first and Hawaii second. Thurston pointed out that as long as Delegate Burns was committed to helping Alaska while keeping Hawaii off the House floor, the Hawaiian bill was doomed for 1958. Soares argued that Hawaii's willingness to follow Alaska provided statehood opponents with the argument that "we're going soft on statehood and don't really care any longer." When it was reported that Senate Majority Leader Lyndon B. Johnson and Democratic Speaker of the House Sam Rayburn, both from Texas, were working closely with Burns's two-step strategy, Republicans in Hawaii complained in the *Star Bulletin,* "It is increasingly clear that in a showdown, Hawaii will never get statehood while southern Democrats control key positions of leadership in Congress.

Burns disagreed strongly. The Hawaii statehood bill was dead for 1958, but he had received private assurances from Johnson that it would receive early consideration in the Senate in 1959. Speaker Rayburn was not committed to support statehood, but he agreed not to stand in its way against the majority sentiment in his own chamber. To fortify that sentiment, Burns invited Representative Leo W. O'Brien, Democrat of New York and chairman of a special subcommittee of the House Committee on Interior and Insular Affairs, to visit Hawaii in late November. Strongly sympathetic to Hawaii's statehood request, O'Brien brought two like-minded members of the subcommittee with him to make what the committee called "an intensive inquiry" on the statehood issue.

In January, the three committee members submitted their report, signaling the opening thrust in the last congressional battle for statehood. The report systematically rebutted the major antistatehood arguments of the bill's two principal antagonists in Congress, Senator James Eastland, Democrat of Mississippi, and Representative John Pillion, Republican of New York.

Pillion's main argument was that the influence of the International Longshoremen's and Warehousemen's Union in Island politics and the extent of Communist control in the union were too great to admit Hawaii to statehood. We would be inviting "four Soviet agents to take seats in our Congress," charged the New York representative. Eastland agreed. When informed on the Senate floor that the FBI could identify only twenty-five known Communists in the Islands, Eastland maintained that "they control the economic life of the Islands." A second, but less important, argument advanced by opponents of statehood was that Hawaii's Oriental population would never be fully assimilated into American life. South Carolina Democratic Senator Strom Thurmond, while emphasizing that persons of Japanese ancestry were as moral in their way as any other group, added that they could not adapt to American political institutions. Friends of statehood in the Senate and House pointed out privately that Senators Eastland and Thurmond may have been less concerned about Communist influence in Hawaii or the cultural separatism of the Japanese than they were about the addition of two pro-civil-rights senators to the upper chamber. A persuasive friend of statehood from Louisiana, businessman George Lehleitner, stated that southern opposition, as measured in votes, was even stronger against Alaska than Hawaii. . . . Congressmen were genuinely concerned, insisted Lehleitner, when men of such stature and influence as former Governor Lawrence Judd and industrialist Walter Dillingham lent their support to the charge that Hawaii was dominated by the Communist leadership of the ILWU.

Another former governor, Ingram M. Stainback, also opposed statehood, insisting that a commonwealth arrangement comparable to that existing for Puerto Rico would be more advantageous for Hawaii than admission as a state. The main advantage of commonwealth status, Stainback pointed out, would be exemption from Federal taxation. A handful of citizens who agreed with Stainback formed the Commonwealth party, but all of its candidates were beaten badly in the 1958 election. Commonwealth did not ring a bell with the peoples of Hawaii, and economic and fiscal experts, while agreeing that Island taxes were high, pointed to a 1954-55 study which showed that, after taxation, the average citizen of Hawaii had $4 to every $1 left for the Puerto Rican citizen, indicating the ability of the Islands to support statehood economically.

Opinion of Islanders

A comprehensive private public-opinion survey on all the Islands in 1958 revealed that 23 per cent of the haoles [whites] and 27 per cent of the Hawaiians polled strongly opposed statehood. Congressional opponents of statehood would have rejoiced had they known of these results. Only 43 per cent of the sample favored immediate statehood; 24 per cent showed some degree of opposition, and the remainder were apathetic. Of the largest ethnic groups in the Islands, only the Japanese revealed a clear majority backing immediate statehood. Favoring immediate statehood were 62 per cent of the citizens of Japanese ancestry, 44 per cent of the Chinese, 39 per cent of the Filipinos, 33 per cent of the haoles, and only 30 per cent of the Hawaiians and part-Hawaiians. An intensive 1959 survey of the fourteenth representative district on Oahu showed that respondents who had previously replied that they were "neither for nor against statehood" or that they were "opposed but would go along with it," would probably vote in favor of statehood in a referendum that put the issue squarely, yes or no. Still, 37 per cent of the Portuguese, 34 per cent of the haoles, and 32 per cent of the Hawaiians interviewed in the fourteenth district refused to endorse statehood.

Antistatehood sentiment in the Islands correlated frequently with hostility toward Japanese. . . . When the voters of the fourteenth representative district on Oahu were asked in early 1959 if they felt that any racial group or groups in the Islands had too much power, 60 per cent of the Hawaiians and 56 per

cent of the Portuguese in the sample replied yes. Of those who
answered affirmatively, nearly nine out of ten Hawaiians and
Chinese, eight of ten Filipinos and haoles, and nearly seven of
every ten respondents of Portuguese extraction specified the
Japanese.

The survey revealed that tensions between the Hawaiians and
Portuguese on one hand and the Japanese on the other were
recognized explicitly by members of the first two groups. Latent
hostilities between haoles and Japanese were also uncovered,
although haoles were much less open than the Portuguese [gen-
erally not considered haoles] and Hawaiians about their feelings.
Filipino resentments toward the Japanese persisted, as was shown
by intensive individual interviews.

Overwhelming Endorsement

Despite opposition to Hawaiian statehood, the strategy of
Delegate Jack Burns was validated in the second session of the
Eighty-fifth Congress when both houses voted overwhelmingly to
admit Hawaii to statehood. All that remained was for the voters
of the territory to endorse the statehood bill in the June 1959
primary election. Every major group in the Islands, from the
newspapers to the Hawaiian Sugar Planters' Association to the
ILWU, urged statehood. Not a single important political figure
publicly disagreed. Statehood was no longer an academic question. The Congress of the United States had endorsed it. The
voters on every major island in the territory, despite the complex
ethnic tensions intertwined with the statehood issue, overwhelmingly voted yes. The final count was seventeen to one,
with prostatehood victories in every representative district, and
significant antistatehood sentiment expressed only in small Portuguese and Hawaiian precincts. The only one of the Islands'
240 precincts to reject statehood was tiny Niihau, all of whose
107 registered voters were Hawaiian or part-Hawaiian. On that
little island, invariably overwhelmingly Republican, Hawaiians,
still trying to recapture the past, registered their protest to the
final act in the absorption of Hawaii into the American Union.
There, the seven out of nine voters who said no to statehood
probably would have said yes to a restoration of the monarchy.

But to the majority of Hawaii's citizens, justice in the Islands had finally been done.

Justice—what did it mean? For years, Hawaii's leaders had complained that it was unjust for Islanders to be excluded from first-class citizenship. Now, the peoples of Hawaii would be on an equal legal footing with their fellow citizens on the mainland. But justice within Hawaii was another issue. Statehood symbolized, but did not create, the vast changes that were taking place in the Islands' economic, political, and social systems, making it a "just" society.

There are tests of a just society: Is decision-making widely shared? Are goods and services widely distributed? Is creative talent rewarded without discrimination between sexes or among races and religions? To these questions, Hawaii could answer—with qualifications—in the affirmative, and could confidently prophesy a stronger, less-qualified yes for the future.

Was decision-making widely shared in the year of statehood in Hawaii? Within the past decade, the political system had been transformed from one-party domination to vigorous competition between two well-organized parties; the control of Hawaii's wealth had been widely dispersed; strong labor unions had been established, and competition among labor unions was increasing.

Politics to the Fore

Poststatehood politics in Hawaii featured dozens of able politicians from all races actively seeking to serve the new state government. The proportion of college-educated and professionally trained candidates for state office in 1960 was probably higher than for any other state in the Union. The variety of racial backgrounds of these candidates was incomparable. The Democrats, especially rich in talent, found it difficult to agree on a slate of state candidates before the June primary election. Daniel K. Inouye and others close to Jack Burns persuaded the Delegate to run for governor rather than for one of the seats in the United States Senate, although Burns, assured of a Senate victory, agreed reluctantly. The new governor, under Hawaii's constitution, would be exceedingly powerful and would have hundreds of appointments to make. Against the popular Burns, whose statehood strategy had been vindicated, the Republicans could nominate only one man—the extremely popular appointed Governor, William F. Quinn. For lieutenant governor, Democratic primary voters chose territorial Senator Mitsuyuki Kido over Spark M. Matsunaga; for representative, Inouye defeated Patsy Takemoto Mink; former Governor Oren E. Long and perennial mayoralty candidate Frank F. Fasi were nominated for election to the United States Senate. Republican strategists privately doubted that anyone could beat Inouye, but, hoping to win at least one Senate seat, they pitted Wilfred Tsukiyama against Long and former territorial Representative Hiram Fong, now a successful businessman, against Fasi. The big contest, of course, would be for the governorship. To help Quinn win among voters of Hawaiian extraction, the Big Island's county chairman and popular campaigner, James Kealoha, was matched against Kido.

The Republican Oahu county chairman, Benjamin Dillingham, worked tirelessly to regroup GOP forces against the favored Democratic slate. He repeatedly criticized Burns as a captive of the ILWU and charged that his election would aid the cause of the Soviet Union and the Peiping government of China. But Quinn, rather than Dillingham, sounded the major theme in the Republican campaign. Running on a liberal Republican platform, which he had helped to write, he spoke of eliminating taxes on basic foods, increasing net personal-income-tax exemptions, extending unemployment-compensation benefits, and distributing public lands on a fee-simple basis at rock-bottom prices to citizens of Hawaii. The last idea, introduced in the closing weeks of the campaign, captured the interest of hundreds of voters. Quinn called it the "second mahele" [land reform] after the Great Mahele of the nineteenth century, perhaps without realizing that the mid-nineteenth-century reform was viewed by Hawaiian voters as a fraud against their people. Nevertheless, Quinn and his scheme for land reform represented the desire of a growing number of Republican politicians to identify with the hopes and needs of the voters of various ethnic strains and to avoid positions and symbols that would associate them with the Republican party of the past. Among the new liberals was territorial Representative Frank Judd from Oahu's seventeenth district. Judd, whose famous great-grandfather had arrived in the Islands in 1828, bore a name that, as much as any in the Islands, was identified with the past. But he emphasized the need for the Republicans to establish a liberal record, to become the party of the people. Another missionary descendant, Ballard Atherton, president of the Hawaiian Telephone Company and former chairman of the City Charter Commission, was not a candidate for office, but he encouraged fellow Republicans to adopt a positive approach on the land question and to become sensitive to the special demands of Hawaii's ethnic groups. Hebden Porteus, popular senator from Oahu's fourth district, also decried what he called "110 per cent Republicans who wanted to talk only about the devaluation of the dollar and high taxes." Porteus, an Alexander & Baldwin [one of the "Big Five" sugar factors and business corporations] lawyer, helped write the liberal Republican platform planks on land and taxes, and encouraged large estates to open up more land to home owners. On Maui, plantation executive John E. Milligan joined the liberal Republican faction.

Election Results

When the votes were counted, these Republican liberals, including Quinn, were victorious, proving that the revolution of 1954 had far from destroyed the Republican party in Hawaii. There had never been so close an election in Hawaii's history. Individual Republicans, among them victorious Quinn, Kealoha, and Fong, showed amazing strength in Democratic districts. In addition to the governorship, lieutenant governorship, and one United States Senate seat, the Republicans also recaptured control of the territorial—now the state—Senate. The Democrats won a majority in the new state House of Representatives, Long defeated Tsukiyama, and Inouye won a magnificent landslide victory, to become the first American of Japanese ancestry named to the United States House of Representatives.

Although there is a serious question as to whether the ends of democracy are well served when power is so sharply split between the two political parties that it is difficult for the leaders of either party to be held responsible to the electorate, there could be no doubt that political power in the Islands was now fluid, that opportunities for advancement in politics were open to talent through two keenly competitive political parties.

WHAT STATEHOOD MEANS TO HAWAII [7]

Hawaii comes into the American Union with the experience of more than a century of self-government. Since the adoption of a constitution by King Kamehameha III in 1840, followed in 1848 by a division of the land which removed the physical basis for the earlier feudal system, Hawaii has been ruled under constitutional law—as kingdom, republic, and organized territory. Long before its annexation to the United States in 1898, it had adopted the Anglo-American common law and governmental practices familiar to Americans, which culminated in the deposition of the monarchy in 1893. As a sovereign republic and as a territory of the United States, it has financed and (except during a period of martial law during World War II) has ruled itself with a minimum of assistance and direction from the Federal Government.

The coming of statehood, then, will not basically change the structure or fabric of government in Hawaii. Unlike Alaska, her sister novitiate, Hawaii will not suddenly face the necessity of assuming governmental burdens—for example in public health, highways, education—which had previously been borne in whole or in part by the national Government. On statehood day, no new function will have to be assumed by the government of the new state. The schools, the highway program, the administration of justice, the revenue structure, health and welfare services and, without important exception, all the rest of the governmental program, will continue to operate as on the preceding day, and for the most part under the direction of the same people.

Acting in a community accustomed to self-government, legislatures and governors have kept Hawaii well abreast of governmental practices elsewhere in the nation. It would be easy to compile a long list of statutes—in the fields of public health, education, agriculture, labor, and taxation—in which Hawaii has pioneered or has been in the van of American jurisdictions. It has not looked for leadership to the Interior Department or other agencies in Washington.

[7] From article by Robert M. Kamins, professor of economics, University of Hawaii. *State Government.* 32:156-61. Summer '59. Reprinted by permission.

Impact on Local Government

Changes there will be, of course. The first change is being experienced as this is written, months in advance of statehood. Persons aged 20 are registering for the first state elections, scheduled for June 27 and July 28, as permitted by the state constitution, under the provisions of which the elections will be conducted. (Alaska set the minimum voting age at 19; Georgia and Kentucky have set the minimum at 18; all other states at 21.) . . .

Popular election may be expected to strengthen the office of the governor, particularly since a "short-ballot" constitution gives the governor authority to appoint all department heads as well as members of the state judiciary. Even though Hawaii has a well-developed civil service system, patronage opportunities for the executive will be abundant. A by-product will be the injection of additional zest to political action in Hawaii, already vigorous—with strong Democratic and Republican parties.

If, as appears likely, the office of governor will lie at the center of heightened political activity in this new state, the election of two national senators and one or two congressmen, cannot but add to the enlivenment of partisan competition. Coincidentally, the adoption in 1959 of a charter for the city-county of Honolulu, which enlarges the membership of the municipal council while strengthening the position of the mayor, probably will further invigorate the striving at the polls. . . .

Under rather remarkable constitutional relationships with the Federal Government, one department of the Hawaii government is protected against change by the state legislature. The Hawaiian Homes Commission Act of 1920, a Federal statute, established the Hawaiian Homes Commission, a territorial agency designed to assist Polynesian Hawaiians in maintaining their communities and creating new ones. Relatively large areas of public land have been made available by the commission to persons of Hawaiian ancestry (of at least half blood, in recent years) as residential sites and agricultural homesteads. Hawaiians receiving land grants are given ninety-nine-year leases, for which they pay an annual rent of $1.00. Holders may also receive low-interest loans from the commission.

The state constitution adopts the Hawaiian Homes Commission Act on behalf of the state, agreeing that "the spirit of the Hawaiian Homes Commission Act looking to the continuance of the Hawaiian homes project for the further rehabilitation of the Hawaiian race shall be faithfully carried out." Furthermore, Congress, in the act of admission, permits the amendment (in the constitution or by statute) of administrative provisions of the Hawaiian Homes Commission Act but prohibits the new state from changing the provisions relating to the commission's funds, to change the qualifications to hold land under the act, or to decrease the benefits of Hawaiian landholders, unless permitted by Congress. This last tie to the Federal apron strings Congress would not cut.

Search of the Laws

Attainment of statehood makes it necessary to study the statutes under which Hawaii has been governed. In Washington, the Budget Bureau is examining the Federal statutes applicable to Hawaii, to determine if statehood will change their applicability. (By way of example, in Hawaii as a territory, business transacted has been *ipso facto* considered to be in interstate commerce for the purpose of some Federal laws. In Hawaii as a state, presumably the same legal tests that are used elsewhere in the United States will determine what is interstate commerce and what is not.) Under an executive order, the Budget Bureau is to report its findings to the President.

In Honolulu, meantime the legislature has authorized the Hawaii attorney general to consider the effect of statehood on the laws under which the state is ruled, both those enacted by Congress and those of the Hawaii legislature.

The study is given urgency by a provision in the Admission Act which repeals within two years of the date of statehood all territorial laws enacted by Congress. This refers to laws "the validity of which is dependent solely upon the authority of the Congress to provide for the government of Hawaii" as a territory. . . .

Putting the state constitution into effect changes the administration of the laws as well as their form and content. Hawaii the territory has had a three-member Supreme Court, appointed by the President. Under the constitution this appellate court is expanded to five, appointed by the governor, and it is to be served by an administrative director. The establishment of the latter position, accomplished by the last territorial legislature in anticipation of statehood, was recommended in a 1957 survey of Hawaii's judiciary as being of primary importance to improve the administration of justice. . . .

Effects in Washington

More profound effects of statehood may stem from Hawaii's gaining votes, as well as a voice, in Congress than from changes in the local government of the Islands. The sugar industry, still the largest grouping of private enterprises despite the postwar diversification of Hawaii's economy, has always been concerned about its marketing quota under the sugar acts while Hawaii remained a territory. Now that it is a state with as many Senate votes as any other, Hawaii's quota seems more secure. If production on the shrinking acreage utilized by cane plantations should increase over a million tons—Hawaii's approximate annual allotment on the national market—perhaps the quota can be enlarged for the state of Hawaii. Producers of other local agricultural crops, notably coffee, which has recently suffered from depressed world prices, are now beginning to ask if the new senators and representative cannot obtain coverage for their crops under the farm price support programs.

Statehood also promises to insure the stability of another source of mainland dollars, the largest—defense expenditures. Hawaii's economic development in recent years may be viewed as a race against possible disarmament or movement of military establishments out of Hawaii. If the Islands are to be demilitarized ultimately (and from their position in the Pacific the people of Hawaii are at least as concerned as any other portion of America's population with the dangers of continued international tensions), two senators and a representative may be able to cushion the economic shock by obtaining federally financed public works in larger quantity than Hawaii the territory could have expected.

Hawaii is land-hungry, and statehood may cause the release by military agencies of substantial acreages held since

World War II, currently put by the United States to infrequent or marginal use. Under the Admission Act, each Federal agency having control over any property in Hawaii is required within five years of the date of statehood to report to the President concerning its continued need for each parcel. If the President determines that any land is no longer needed by the United States, the act provides that it shall be returned to Hawaii.

By such transfers, Hawaii would regain at least a portion of the public lands which were ceded to the United States in 1898 at the time of annexation. Hawaii's government hopes that the areas returned will be substantial, particularly on the island of Oahu, where a rapidly increasing population is pressing hard against limited amounts of readily usable land. The land so transferred to the state government will become, under the Admission Act, a public trust for the support of the public schools, for the betterment of native Hawaiians, for development of farm and home ownership, and for similar purposes.

Furthermore, the Admission Act applies to Hawaii the Submerged Lands and Outer Continental Shelf Lands Acts of 1953. Hawaii has no offshore deposits of oil, the resource which supplied much of the motivation for passing these Federal laws. But it does have shallow tidal lands which can be filled in, now that their control is firmly vested in the state, to supply needed space for an expanding population and tourist trade. With some difficulty, Hawaii obtained congressional permission last year to fill and use a limited area extending from the shores of Waikiki. Now the littoral of any of the Islands can be expanded as the need arises and resources permit.

Economic Stimulus

Obtaining the use of more land, particularly on densely populated Oahu, constitutes the most obvious stimulation of economic growth under statehood. Other influences are less tangible but also important.

The greatest of these is the familiarity which Hawaii will gain for investors and merchants, for tourists and American migrants, as a state of the Union. During the past several decades an increasing part of the mainland population acquired some knowledge of Hawaii and its institutions, but a surprisingly large number of mainland Americans still wondered about the language, the money and the tariff system of the territory of Hawaii. It is already apparent that the state of Hawaii is more familiar, and therefore inspires greater confidence as a place for investment or business enterprise. Without much doubt, the current flurry of economic expansion—the construction of Hawaii's first oil refinery, first steel mills, first cement plants, additional small manufactures, new hotels, shopping centers and residential areas, the commercial exploration of bauxite (the state's only known mineral resource), will be accelerated and sustained by business attracted to Hawaii by the spotlight of statehood.

Accelerated movement of persons to Hawaii from other parts of the United States is also to be expected—movement to a "paradise" which statehood has brought closer, in the popular image, to accustomed American ways. Such an influx, when added to the established population growth of the Islands, will place still greater pressure on the intensively utilized land area of Oahu, forcing an expansion of economic growth in the other seven principal islands of the chain. All of the latter are now relatively underdeveloped, with static or declining populations. The expansion will require the establishment of cheap inter-island travel, now limited to plane and barge traffic, the supplying of water to arid lands, a shift of dairy and truck farming from Oahu to its neighboring islands, the growth of villages into towns and towns into cities, the expansion of commercial and governmental services in all areas—in a word, the over-all enlargement of virtually every phase of Hawaiian activity.

Social Aspects

Those who have found pleasure in living here cannot but view with mixed feelings the prospect of a more crowded Hawaii. There is reason to believe that the changes associated with economic expansion will be gradual, but their cumulative effects will be profound.

A minority in Hawaii who have opposed statehood have feared some of these effects. Many persons of Hawaiian ancestry, justifiably proud of their Polynesian antecedents (and sometimes idealizing the golden days before Captain Cook, before the missionaries, before the revolution which toppled the monarchy, or before the tide of migration from the mainland pulled in by World War II) have forebodings that they and their culture will be lost in the new Hawaii, pushed aside by a more aggressive commercialism. Were this to happen, and it does not yet seem imminent, statehood would not be the cause but rather the symbol of a social evolution of almost two hundred years. What may rather result is a Hawaii which moves closer to mainland living patterns, yet retains in its amalgam much of the graciousness and individuality of the Hawaiian people.

Older Caucasian settlers, of families established in Hawaii for a century or more, may also wonder if their predominance in business, politics and society will be further reduced by statehood. Since World War II, and particularly in the past decade, newer settlers from the Orient have begun to assume leadership in the community. However, members of these very families, not unanimously but in strength, have supported the long drive for statehood along with the rest of the population. . . .

Effects on the United States

Incompletely told, these are some of the effects which statehood will have on Hawaii, and some of the local reactions to the changes. There will also be important effects upon the United States as a whole.

Quantitatively, it might be thought that Hawaii is too small, measured against the rest of the country, to have much bearing on the nation's life. The new state comprises only about three tenths of one per cent of the population of the United States, and two tenths of one per cent of its area. Yet there is good reason to believe that this small region will soon play an important part in the rounding out of America and in its international relations.

To date, because it was initially settled by migrants from Europe and Africa, the mainland United States has had little knowledge of Asia and its peoples, little ability to communicate with them or to understand firsthand their problems, fears and desires. The admission of Hawaii to statehood demonstrates to the nations of the Orient that the racial attitudes of the United States are not what its traducers have said. Statehood also creates in Hawaii a pool of first-class Americans of Oriental ancestry, some of whom (though deplorably few) are able to speak one or more of the languages of the East, who can be called upon to represent the United States in discussions with Asian countries.

The preamble to the state constitution manifests some of the attributes of the people of Hawaii which especially qualify them to serve the United States in the conduct of international relations:

We, the people of the State of Hawaii, grateful for Divine Guidance, and mindful of our Hawaiian heritage, reaffirm our belief in a government of the people, by the people and for the people, and with an understanding heart toward all the peoples of the earth, do hereby ordain and establish this constitution for the State of Hawaii.

BACKGROUND ON THE FIFTIETH STATE [8]

America, in accepting Hawaii as the fiftieth state, is much like a man who finds himself married to a picture bride. He does not really know her, but as he starts living with her he discovers that she is beautiful, intelligent and gifted with a dowry.

Physically, Hawaii is exquisite. Palm trees bend into the wind and glistening lagoons tempt the eye. Across one of the Islands (Kauai) runs a deep geological gash as colorful as the Grand Canyon; it tells, in layer after layer of dazzling rock, the story of how the Islands sprang from volcanic origins. On another island, Hawaii, active volcanoes rise to snow-covered peaks nearly fourteen thousand feet high. Waterfalls are so numerous they are not named and cliffs that drop two thousand feet into the sea are common.

It is a land of flowers, so brilliant that they are difficult to visualize. They blossom all year round: orchids, torch ginger, plumiera, hibiscus and bird-of-paradise. There is the beefsteak plant, with leaves the size of platters and startling red. There

[8] From " 'Aloha' for the Fiftieth State," by James A. Michener, author of *Tales of the South Pacific, Hawaii,* and other novels. New York *Times Magazine.* p 14+. Ap. 19, '59. Copyright © 1959 by James A. Michener. Reprinted by permission of the author.

is the lowly croton, a winsome shrub whose iridescent leaves cover a spectrum of more than twenty colors, dominated by gold and purple and rust. This is my favorite.

But most of all, Hawaii is a land of people, an amalgam of many types. Two per cent are full-blooded Hawaiians, brothers of those Polynesians who inhabit Tahiti and Samoa; 16 per cent are part-Hawaiian, and this segment is growing; 25 per cent are ordinary mainland white Americans, and since immigration from Asia is halted while, with statehood, movement from the mainland will increase, this is the fastest-growing group; 2 per cent are Puerto Ricans; and 1 per cent are from European countries. That leaves 54 per cent as having come from Asia: Filipinos, 12 per cent; Chinese, 6 per cent; Koreans, 1 per cent; and Japanese, 35 per cent, which makes them the largest single ethnic group.

The most important fact about Hawaii is that these varied peoples live together in harmony. There is practically no race discrimination. . . . However, many Caucasians and Orientals prefer to live strictly within their own communities, and there is no great flood of intermarriage. A Caucasian boy who wants to marry a Japanese girl may have a very tough time, indeed—mostly from the Japanese family.

Two common rumors about Hawaii must be rejected. First, Hawaii is not going to be submerged in an Oriental tidal wave. An educated guess would suggest that today the economic control of the Islands is vested as follows: white Americans, 70 per cent; Chinese, 20 per cent; Japanese, 10 per cent. Second, Hawaii is not governed dictatorially by the "Big Five," the informal combination of sugar factors who once ruled the Islands in a benevolent feudalism. The Big Five are still strong, capable and conservative, but they are not major landowners and they do not control the legislature nor do they exercise a veto power over much of anything. Commercially they are an asset to the Islands, and in their junior offices one begins to find smart young Chinese and Japanese.

Credit for the amazing manner in which so many diverse people live together so easily must be given to three groups. First, the gentle Polynesians who inhabited the Islands originally were by nature inclined to accept other races, and the dominant spirit of Hawaii has always been *aloha,* gracious welcome.

Second, the missionaries who stamped the Islands with their rigorous concepts were liberal Congregationalists from New England who believed in fellowship, education and the immanent presence of God. Hawaii's heritage derives from New England, not California, and Chinese immigrants were not abused in the Islands because the missionaries would not tolerate such behavior. It has been said, "These missionaries did not love Chinese and Japanese, but they did love justice." On this basic Christian justice, Hawaii was founded.

But the *aloha* of the Polynesians and the rectitude of the missionaries would have accomplished little if the next wave of immigrants had been unequal to the occasion. Chinese and Japanese in large numbers were imported to work the sugar fields and after indentures of ten years were supposed to go back to Asia. Instead, they saved money, kept out of trouble, and soon owned either stores or lands. They were admirable citizens and built themselves securely into Hawaiian society. Their major characteristic was an overwhelming passion for education, and in the early days it was not uncommon for a Japanese field hand making 77 cents a day to send five children through high school and university. The ablest son might even go on to become a lawyer at Michigan or a doctor at Penn. Among the best-educated people in America are the Chinese and Japanese of Hawaii.

Five additional assets help make Hawaii a fine state. The population is young and vigorous. Of a dozen political leaders, eight will be under forty. . . .

Hawaii is a wealthy state. It pays enormous taxes to the Federal Government. People live well. There are no extensive slums or depressed areas. Citizens save money and invest in the future. If one considers only the financial balance sheet, America got a great bargain when she accepted Hawaii.

Contrary to the popular image, men in Hawaii work hard. Hawaii was not originally suited to sugar and pineapple, for there were deficiencies in the soil and never enough water. Clever men corrected the soil and dug for water—deep wells and miles of tunnels through the hearts of mountains. If Hawaii is a paradise—and I think it is—men made it so.

Hawaii is by far the most advanced state culturally that has ever been admitted to the Union. It has a famous preparatory school dating back to the 1840's, a strong university, fine churches, interesting newspapers and television stations. Its historical libraries are immensely rich, and its symphony and theatrical groups strong. But the intellectual glory of Hawaii is its pair of museums: the Bishop is about the world's best in Pacific lore; the Academy of Arts owns one of the finest collections of Oriental art.

Finally, Hawaii is a forward-looking state. Its labor laws are more liberal than those of many other areas. It spends a high percentage of its income on education. Its health services are first rate and the proud citizen is apt to say, "We have the best hospitals and the poorest jails in America." Hawaii prefers it that way.

I could continue for many pages listing the virtues of Hawaii, but . . . I think it might be more instructive to explain some of the problems that face the Islands.

Land. No large area of the United States is more limited by land shortage than Hawaii. On Oahu, the site of Honolulu, population density is 835 per square mile, a figure comparable to Belgium's and exceeding Indonesia's. At every point this lack of land inhibits growth. Men cannot find land for either their businesses or their homes, and one of the principal reasons people leave Hawaii is the complaint: "We couldn't find a place to live."

The problem is exacerbated by the fact that what land exists is held in large parcels by a few. The six principal owners control 26 per cent of all available land. Sixty owners control 80 per cent, and since they have been able to prevent their holdings from being properly taxed, that burden falls upon personal income.

In Honolulu a man doesn't buy land by the acre. He buys it by the square foot, and a reasonable figure for a good lot would be $2.50 a foot, or about $110,000 an acre—provided he could find one. Choice land runs about $1.2 million an acre. What the home-seeker does is to lease a plot for fifty-five years with the understanding that each ten years the terms of his lease may be renegotiated upward.

Many businesses seem reluctant to launch major projects on land they cannot own and on which they face upward renegotiation every ten years.

Taxes. Since land is not adequately taxed, income has to be overtaxed, and Hawaii is one of the most heavily burdened areas in the world. Personal income taxes quickly rise to the 9 per cent level, topped by an across-the-board levy of 3.5 per cent on any business activity. This makes retirement of people with middle incomes to Hawaii rather unlikely. Artists, writers and musicians should also think twice before fleeing to paradise; they, too, must pay 3.5 per cent on their business activity. And because Hawaii has such a youthful population, much of which earns no income, personal taxes will probably rise rather than diminish.

Economy. Fifteen years ago Hawaii was in a rather more precarious position than now. Then Island income depended upon military expenditures, sugar and pineapples, in that order, and a disruption in any one could have plunged the Islands into depression. Today the economy rests on five pillars. The military investment, represented by sixteen major installations, including Pearl Harbor, Hickam Air Force Base and Schofield Barracks, with 50,000 uniformed personnel, 50,000 dependents and 20,000 civilian employees, accounts for 38 per cent of the Islands' income or $327 million yearly; then come construction ($185 million), sugar ($145 million), pineapples ($124 million), and tourism ($100 million).

It seems likely that the last category will ultimately rise to second place, for there are few areas in America more appealing than Hawaii. But this introduces a major problem: as tourists increase, the natural facilities that attract them diminish. The physical appearance of Waikiki has slipped in the past decade and those responsible seem to lack both the vision and the ambition to correct the drift. New resort hotels in less developed areas are needed and such projects are being actively pursued.

Labor-management relations. Hawaii has not yet achieved a mature attitude on the interlocking responsibilities of labor and management. Because the Big Five long refused to permit unionization, labor leaders find it profitable to revive old bitterness in a manner that became unfashionable on the mainland twenty years ago. And because some leaders of the longshoremen's union were at one time communistically inclined, management tends to castigate all labor as extremely radical. However, the smart young executives who are now assuming leadership of the great corporations are finding it possible to work with labor.

Bloc voting. A constant fear in Hawaii is that the various races may begin to vote in blocs, Caucasians voting only for Caucasian politicians, Orientals only for Orientals. But a study of voting records fails to show that this has so far happened. Governor Bill Quinn, an astute politician guesses: "Hawaii will probably become a lot like Boston. If a Japanese voter doesn't know anyone on the ticket, he'll naturally vote for a Japanese, the way the Irish vote Irish in Boston, on the grounds that 'he's one of us.' But I have found that if any of our voters know the men running, they pick and choose with great intelligence."

Imbalance among the Islands. Hawaii's second permanent headache, after land, is the fact that, while the island of Oahu grows richer and gains in population, the neighboring islands, which are in many respects more attractive, grow poorer and lose population. Thus Oahu, with only 9 per cent of the land, produces about 80 per cent of the income and houses 79 per cent of the population. Legislating thus becomes a dogfight between Oahu and the rest of the pack. If tourists could be lured away from conventional Waikiki to the neighboring islands, part of the necessary corrective would have been undertaken; but since this seems difficult to do, the imbalance will probably worsen.

Lack of support for culture. The fine cultural institutions which I have praised have been largely created and supported by the private charity of the great missionary and industrial families, but the time has come when these older families should not be expected to continue this burden. Yet replacements have not been found. Rich Orientals have not discovered that Uncle Sam, through generous provisions in tax laws, makes it prudent to give money to public institutions.

For example, on the mainland a man who graduates from Harvard may express his mature gratitude with the gift of a chair, but this does not happen in Hawaii where the lack of support suffered by the university is a scandal.

The "da kine" plague. An unnecessary handicap faced by Hawaii is its addiction to pidgin English, a barbarous *lingua franca* derived from bad English, Hawaiian, Chinese, Portuguese and Japanese, all delivered in an incredible sing-song. The phrase "da kine," from "that kind," is used in everything. A man who wants to tell his friend that a sandwich costs too much will sing, "Eh, blalah! Da kine sammitch pipty cent takai too much!"

Sensible parents try to combat pidgin, but it remains a damnable burden. Entire schools succumb to it and occasionally even teachers take the easy way, so that one generation after another hampers itself by addiction to this folly. However, some firms are beginning to reject young people who speak pidgin and the university is trying to stamp out the barbarism.

Lack of a name. A minor, but serious, problem is that there is no name for the people who inhabit Hawaii. A man who lives in Texas is a Texan and is proud of it. I used to be a Pennsylvanian and for a while a New Yorker. But what am I now? I can't be called a Hawaiian, because that name is reserved for the Polynesians. Possibly we will all become "Islanders," but in the meantime the fact that we have no common name perpetuates old cleavages.

Discrimination. Since Hawaii is famous for the fact that all its people live together in enviable harmony, it is regrettable that a few major institutions still practice racial segregation. There are clubs where Orientals are not permitted, fine residential streets where they are not welcome to live. (On the other hand, Orientals have other clubs to which Caucasians are not admitted.) With the passage of years such customs seem bound to vanish. In the meantime they do little harm and do not deter me from stating that people live together more harmoniously in Hawaii than in any other area I know.

Striking a balance between strength and weakness, it is obvious that Hawaii is going to be a strong state. It is young, progressive, adventurous. It is able to pay its way and to contribute richly to American life. Its major contributions will probably be along these lines.

Vacation land. In addition to its great natural beauty, Hawaii has an almost perfect climate. It never gets as hot as New York does in summer. It never gets cold. About ten days a year, when the northeast trade winds fail to blow, things can get a bit sticky. For the rest of the time there is probably no place in the world with a better climate. Hawaii is thus an

ideal vacation land and, with jet aircraft, is practically next
door to places like Chicago and St. Louis.

Leadership in internal problems. It is not yet clear what
kind of men the Islands will send back to Washington. . . .
Possibly one or two will be Oriental, for Hawaii has a wealth
of able Chinese and Japanese who would grace any legislative
assembly in the world. But whoever goes to Washington will
embody the Hawaiian spirit of *aloha,* and will be well grounded
in American principles. Such men, or perhaps women, will
lend our national leadership a breadth of experience which will
be good for America.

The United States faces grave internal problems arising from
race relations. In the next decade states like Alabama, Mississippi, Georgia, and South Carolina will undergo trying experiences in which the tensions of Little Rock may be repeated
many times over. America is going to be pleasantly surprised at
what Hawaii will be able to contribute to the relaxation of
such tensions.

Hawaiian senators and representatives are going to be men of
the most conciliatory character. They are not going to shout
and bellow. By their quiet precept they will encourage all who
seek logical and unemotional solutions. They will be proof
that conciliation is possible.

On the other hand, agitators and men of ill will can no
longer cry, "It can't be done!" In Hawaii, quietly and without
anger, we have done it.

Help with foreign problems. One of America's major concerns is its relationship to foreign powers, and we are trying
to assure uncommitted or wavering nations that they ought to
trust in our good intentions. A serious bar to our efforts has
been the bad publicity stemming from Little Rock. The Communist Chinese and Russians have abused us severely on that
issue.

But with the admission of Hawaii, the Communist propaganda line collapses. Congress has demonstrated anew our historic attitude toward other peoples. We have shown that we
can accept men of varying colors. Russia claims "Americans
hate Orientals." We do not, and we have proved that we don't.

Let me put the significance of Hawaiian statehood this way:
Today the job of every State Department official in Asia and

Africa has become a little easier; the words of every United States Information Service man have become a lot more persuasive.

But the greatest boon to America will be in the realm of the spirit. For sixty-one years our nation held in the middle of the Pacific Ocean a group of islands to which statehood had been implicitly promised. Over the years, because we feared distance and skins of different colors—and perhaps because we feared the responsibility of taking a new step—we failed to fulfill that implied promise. Then, one by one, the reasons against statehood vanished until at last the nation was faced with one simple moral problem: Were we willing to redeem an old pledge?

Those of us in Hawaii will appreciate what a bold step America has taken in extending statehood to the Islands. That Congress chose to do so is a supreme joy to most of the Islanders, and we are determined that America shall never regret that daring decision. And for its part, the United States today is a little stronger, a little more secure, a little more courageous. To me it looks like a great bargain all the way round.

II. LIFE AND SOCIETY IN THE NEW STATES

EDITOR'S INTRODUCTION

Alaska and Hawaii are the "youngest" states in more ways than one. Their populations have an average age which is lower than that of any other state in the Union. Beyond that, as well, the new states appear young at heart. There is a zest and a swing to life in these outlying regions of America that give them—certainly in the case of Alaska and even in the case of Hawaii—a frontier spirit and buoyancy. In their own highly individualistic ways, the new states are clearing new frontiers in the realm of social relations for America.

This is particularly the case in Hawaii, a long-fabled melting pot of race and creed. Here men have learned by the pressure of necessity and thickly-settled living to open their doors to others of widely varying background and nationality. In Alaska, perhaps the rugged conditions of frontier living have made the worth of a human being measurable in terms other than skin pigmentation or national origin. Yet because both of these states have dynamic societies in a state of constant flux, they have their problems, too. Hawaii has made enormous strides within the past decades in bringing its nonwhite population to a status of equality, but there remain some influences working toward an older order of affairs. Alaska strives mightily to do justice to its "natives"—the Eskimo, the Indian, and the Aleut—yet these groups remain in danger of suffering from the injustices of a rapidly evolving society.

This section examines life and the social structure, with particular emphasis upon so-called minority problems. In the first article, a writer whose sympathies are obviously strongly attached to the forty-ninth state gives his colorful impressions of day-to-day living in Alaska. Readers may be surprised to note that all is not dogsled and snowdrift. In the second article an anthropologist discusses the problems of the "new Alaskan Eskimo"—the Eskimo who is aware of mechanical refrigeration and, what's more, appreciates it. The next article is a forceful enumeration of the rights of Alaska's native peoples and the wrongs currently being perpetrated against them. It calls for greater attention to problem areas.

In the final two articles, dealing with race relations in Hawaii, a professor of sociology gives first a historical summary of that state's racial heritage and next an over-all view of the status of racial groups in the Hawaii of today.

LIFE IN ALASKA [1]

The combination of being the largest state in the Union and having the smallest population gives Alaska a statistical portrait of extreme isolation, "bush" living. The population density is less than 1 person per square mile, compared with an average U.S. density of more than 50 per square mile. In some areas of Alaska, a "village" may consist of a handful of Indians or Eskimos or a cluster of hunters' shacks in a permanent camp. Nearly half the 287 inhabited areas of Alaska contain less than 100 persons. In some 30 per cent of the remaining inhabited areas, the population is between 100 and 200. From these figures it is possible to "prove"—and many have done just that—the isolated existence of Alaskans.

However, expect to find most Alaskans living a dull, insular life and you may expect to be disappointed. Actually, nearly three quarters of all Alaskans live in and around the four largest cities . . . [Anchorage, Fairbanks, Ketchikan, and Juneau].

The great majority of Alaskans live comfortably in modern urban and suburban communities. There are, to be sure, rugged individualists who prefer to live in comparatively primitive shacks or log cabins, miles from town, but even these dwellings are usually equipped with modern conveniences—electricity, running water, telephones, and sometimes automatic oil or LP [liquefied petroleum] gas heat. A visitor to Spenard or City View, suburbs of Anchorage, might well believe he had never left Hempstead, Long Island, the outskirts of Los Angeles, or the suburbs of Denver. Many parts of Juneau, in fact, resemble the quiet, picturesque, hilly streets of San Francisco.

[1] From the book *This Is Alaska*, by Harry Kursh, who has traveled widely in Alaska and who has written several books that touch upon the state. Prentice-Hall. Englewood Cliffs, N.J. '61. p 30-42. © 1961 by Harry Kursh. Published by Prentice-Hall, Inc. Englewood Cliffs, New Jersey. Reprinted by permission.

The most distinctive feature of life in Alaska is that it represents a melting pot of Americans from every state in the Union. Consequently, *most* Alaskans tend to live, work and build in the American tradition. Progress is apt to be characterized by bigger and better split-level homes and well-kept lawns, a car in every garage, supermarket shopping, PTA meetings, weekly Rotary luncheons, Lion lectures, and a Chamber of Commerce in every town with two or more merchants.

The most rapid period of population growth for Alaska occurred after World War II. In October 1867, when a sixteen-year-old boy raised the first Stars and Stripes over Alaska, there were only about 500 white persons in the territory and approximately 33,000 aborigines (Eskimos, Indians and Aleuts). Since then the native population has remained almost static, but the total population has increased from 128,000 in 1950 to more than 220,000, including about 47,000 military personnel and their dependents, most of whom are stationed at Elmendorf Air Force Base and Fort Richardson, outside Anchorage, and at Ladd and Eielson Air Force Bases near Fairbanks. However, the military and their dependents have been in Alaska in such great numbers and for so many years that Alaskans tend to consider them part of the total resident population.

For the most part, newcomers from other states should have no difficulty in adjusting to life in Alaska. There is little in Alaskan social and cultural life that may seem foreign or unique to Americans.

A Closer Look at Alaskans

When an Alaskan says "native," he generally refers to an Eskimo, Indian, or Aleut, of whom there are approximately 35,000.

Most Eskimos live in the far north, the Indians in the southeastern areas, and the Aleuts, a relatively small number, in the southwestern areas, chiefly the Aleutian Islands and the Alaska Peninsula. Many of the natives have retained their cultural and tribal traditions, but nearly all speak English and in almost every respect are "Americanized."

There are also about 5,000 other nonwhites in Alaska, mostly American Negroes and Filipinos. The latter came long ago to work in the fishing industries.

Among nonnative Alaskans there are basically two categories of Americans: those who came to Alaska for a specific job or under military assignment and chose to remain; and those who came to find a new way of life. According to an Alaskan market study published by Benton and Bowles of New York, the "average Alaskan is a newcomer. He and his family have lived in the forty-ninth state for only eight or ten years."

Youthful and Young at Heart

Essentially, Alaska is a youthful state. There are proportionately more younger people in Alaska than in any other state. The number of children under five years of age is twice the national average; and the number of Alaskans over sixty-five is half the national average. . . .

This youthful composition of Alaska is one of its principal assets and clearly a basis for rapid growth.

But in recent years Alaska has been attracting an increasing number of newcomers who are young more at heart than in age. Many arrive having successfully raised a family elsewhere and then grown restive with a sedate, almost routine way of life:

Typical was the story of Mr. and Mrs. Ed Perkins, formerly of Seattle, both around sixty years of age. He had been a carpenter, she a teacher. To explain why they came to Alaska and why they enjoy their new life in the forty-ninth state, Mr. and Mrs. Perkins like to tell the story of a friend who came to visit them at the cabin they had built themselves, overlooking an exquisite view of sea and mountains near Cook Inlet, not far from Anchorage. Plainly puzzled and constantly looking about the cabin, the friend would remark, "I don't know why you left the comforts of your Seattle home where all you had to do was push a button; here you don't even have electricity. You even have to carry water to flush that 'modern' toilet you brag about!"

"He kept that up all the time he was here," Mrs. Perkins said, "and he couldn't even see the inlet below us, or the mountains across, or the woods behind us. And while he was here we talked about a camping trip we were going to take. He said, 'Camping trip! Great Scot, you're camping all the time!'"

Most people, young and old, have chosen to remain in Alaska because they are lured by the state's great outdoors or the sense of adventure that comes with working and living in a land that still throbs with pioneer spirit. A forty-two-year-old New Yorker I met near Anchorage, where he was building his own home in a heavily wooded area, told how he had abandoned an active partnership in a prospering business in New York and decided to settle in Alaska after having made a vacation trip to the new state. "It's the spirit of the place that gets you," he said. "Everybody's busy building something. It's exciting."

The great spirit of Alaska is infectious. It is the common denominator of Alaskans everywhere and derives from a sense of sharing in the challenge of building something new. It is mass togetherness.

I shall never forget my conversation with a young former Brooklynite, an intelligent, well-informed man who had not completed high school. Of his eight years in Alaska, he said:

"The most wonderful thing about Alaska is that everybody works together and helps each other. You don't feel as if you are alone in the world. When I lived in Brooklyn, I think I was the most selfish man alive. I wouldn't go around the corner or lift a finger to help anyone, unless I knew it would also help me.

"I've changed up here and love it. One night I got a phone call from a new neighbor, moved in only a few months before, and I had hardly known him. His car had broken down, and he wanted to know if I could come out to help him. I put my coat on, hopped in my car and took off. It was an eight-hundred-mile round trip!"

The former Brooklynite's sentiments are echoed by the Reverend Richard T. Lambert, of Fairbanks, who has said: "This is really not a get-rich-quick area, nor is it a place where one could drift easily alone, living to oneself. One must come expecting to depend upon others and helping other people in turn."

A unique example of the "Alaska spirit" was the time the canneries of Cordova were caught short-handed by an unexpected bonanza in the salmon run. It turned out to be the largest catch in nearly a generation, but help was urgently needed to pack the catch. Almost everyone in town—men, housewives, children, shopkeepers, teachers, even the local banker—turned to in force, donning oilskins and aprons to help the canneries.

Just as horsethieving in the old West was an odious sort of crime, stealing property in Alaska is considered an abominable act of antineighborliness. A stroller down a main street in any town is apt to pass auto after auto filled with an assortment of supplies and personal valuables, but not one door locked. A wealthy Alaskan, who leaves his home for an annual business trip to Los Angeles, and has been doing so for eighteen years, has never locked his front door. Many Alaskans have no front-door locks.

The Alaskan Personality

Alaskan youthfulness and spirit are without doubt the most important "natural" resources in Alaska, motivating Alaskans to work hard. The same spirit also generates a friendliness, a warmth, a charm and informality that may be seen anywhere: crossing the street, at the corner drugstore, or at a PTA meeting. It may be seen at almost any swank cocktail lounge where men in slacks and sweaters mingle freely with women in evening clothes. In fact, a type of dress usually consisting of an "Eisen-hower" jacket and slacks or whipcord trousers is called the "Alaska tuxedo" because so many men show up dressed that way at social events.

But it is not an affectation, a calculated attempt to be differ-ent. It is a way of life in Alaska. The message is obvious, Alaska's way of saying, "I am a nonconformist, a rugged individualist at heart. I like being with people but I don't like people telling me what I should or shouldn't like for myself."

I saw a rather vivid demonstration of this couldn't-care-less attitude on several occasions in Anchorage. Involved was a husky young man who sported a thick, red beard, an immense handle-bar mustache, begrimed coveralls, and an old felt hat cut to fit atop his head like a precarious fez. At the end of a day's labor on his homestead, not having a car, nor time to change into something more formal, he would drive into Anchorage aboard his open tractor, roll casually along the modern shopping section (Fourth Avenue) and maneuver into a parking-meter space just as if he were coming to town in a chauffered limousine. He'd jump from his tractor, pause to chat with friends, or go window shopping, or stop in at a cocktail lounge, and at no time did anybody stare at him as though he were an odd-ball.

Where and How Alaskans Live

The great majority of Alaskans live comfortably in conventional homes within city or town limits. As a matter of fact, there has been an increasing demand for apartment dwellings in Alaska's larger cities. In the urbanized centers there are modern supermarkets, ranch homes, split-level homes, and Cape Cods, with and without attached garages. There are movie houses, cocktail lounges, bowling alleys, the usual shortage of parking space, and the ubiquitous pneumatic drill, symbol of a changing society.

In contrast, almost every urban area has its share of Alaskans who live in comparatively crude shacks or log cabins, erected by do-it-yourselfers making use of backyard timber. Some "shacks" are authentic leftovers of the Klondike age, but usually with all the comforts of modern living. Some Alaskans even *prefer* the Klondike look. In one log cabin, the type seen in travelogues on Alaska, I saw a roomful of the most luxurious Hollywood-fashion, white leather furniture money could buy. The owner, an Alaskan businesswoman who preferred the "esthetic appeal" of a log cabin, was also partial to modern furnishings. But she would never trade her log cabin for a mansion.

As a rule, Alaskans are fairly gregarious. But this does not mean they gather in throngs. Most simply enjoy informal get-togethers with friends and just talking around coffee at the kitchen table. (According to the American Telephone and Telegraph files, Alaskans do more talking on the telephone than people in any other state. Alaskans average 630 calls per person annually, compared with 426 for the U.S. average.)

Making conversation in Alaska is easy. When strangers meet, the usual ice-breaker is, "And where are you from?"

Alaskans go to movies, listen to radio, watch television, read a great deal—and drink! They do far more drinking than any other group in the United States, a fact that is immediately obvious to visitors. In most towns, there are cocktail lounges and package liquor stores everywhere. Comedian Joe E. Brown once quipped that Fourth Avenue in Anchorage is the "longest bar in the world," a rather pungent description for nearly half a mile of an almost unbroken line of cafés on both sides of the street. . . . [But] drunkenness on the streets is rare.

All told, there are about a dozen radio stations and five television stations in Alaska, within the range of perhaps 90 per cent of the population. Except for local shows, which feature such popular programs as illustrated talks on hunting and fishing, nearly everything on Alaskan television is on film. Most events of any significance may be at least a week old before appearing on Alaskan TV screens, and sometimes the impact and thrills are gone because the details will have been obtained from radio or newspapers. For example, I once asked a thirty-eight-year-old family man who had accumulated considerable wealth through a successful business (restaurant) after thirteen years in Anchorage, "Since you have made so much money, what is there that you would most like to do now? Return to your home town, live it up?"

"No," he said unhesitatingly, "but I'd sure give a thousand bucks to see a big league ball game."

"Don't you see baseball on TV?"

"Yes. But it's stale. The thrill's gone. I always know the score."

Of six daily newspapers in Alaska, perhaps only the two in Anchorage and the one in Fairbanks resemble modern journalism. But even these do not place great stress on national or international affairs, unless there are Alaska angles to the story. Alaskans who desire to keep up with world affairs usually subscribe to the weekly news magazines or the air editions of the New York *Times*. Quite a few pay thirty cents for same-day Seattle newspapers delivered by air, but an impartial observer would have to say that the thirty cents is wasted, for the Anchorage *Daily News*, and *Times*, and the Fairbanks *News-Miner*, widely and efficiently distributed at ten cents each, are equal if not superior to the Seattle newspapers.

Most Alaskans do not seem to be particularly sports-minded. Except for high school teams and service teams, there is little in the way of organized sport. But Alaskans are certainly fun-minded and will participate actively in community festivities and fairs.

Perhaps the most colorful event in Alaska—if not in the entire North country—is the annual Fur Rendezvous, held in February in Anchorage. The Fur Rendezvous converts Anchorage for several days into a carnival city, and attracts Alaskans from everywhere. It is part of a tradition that goes back to early nineteenth century Alaska, when fur buyers met with Indians to trade, and after trading would celebrate their deals with firewater. During the modern Fur Rendezvous, Eskimos come from the north to display their crafts, perform dramas, dances, and sports; and there are dogsled races in the streets of Anchorage, sometimes for stakes running into thousands of dollars. Men and trucks sometimes work through the night, carting snow from the outskirts to spread about the streets of Anchorage in order to assure good dogsled racing! The event even draws one contestant from as far away as Massachusetts.

There are more culturally advanced forms of entertainment in the major cities, such as concerts and theatrical productions which usually play to standing-room-only audiences. Sometimes the performances are by local talent and are quite ambitious. Anchorage, for instance, has a large symphony orchestra of its own, as well as a choral group numbering 100 to 120 voices, which participate in an annual June music festival. But local community groups have been increasingly sponsoring concerts by well-known musicians and artists invited from the great halls of New York, Chicago and Los Angeles.

Alaskans are avid readers, and support their libraries. A recently constructed library in Anchorage is one of the best-equipped and most modern I have seen anywhere in the world, and there was hardly an afternoon or evening that I did not see the library crowded with school children and adult readers. Typically, the library subscribes to scores of outside publications in order to satisfy the Alaskans' hunger for news and knowledge. Several magazines are published in Alaska. One of these, the *Alaskan Sportsman,* is of exceptional quality in its fiction and nonfiction and tends to reflect the true spirit of Alaskans.

Social Interrelations

Nowhere in Alaska is there any evidence of resentment toward *cheechakos,* newcomers. A possible exception is Juneau, where many of Alaska's oldest families have been established and the few newcomers may feel a certain social "chill" in the air.

But as a rule *cheechako* is a friendly term and newcomers are made to feel welcome. Yet Alaskans can be piqued readily by any sudden intrusion of new ideas—or talent—particularly if such intrusion tends to make some Alaskan enterprise, or institution, or personality, seem mediocre by comparison.

To a great extent this may be due to fear, or insecurity. Many Alaskans have been successful in business, society, or politics as a result of individual tenacity and hard work and sometimes sheer courage, rather than superior talents. As a frontier society, Alaska has attracted many whose abilities are somewhat lukewarm, because it has been relatively easy for them to reach the top and remain there in a frontier setting, as compared with a highly competitive society. Mediocrity is frequently apparent, particularly in business. Accordingly a smart *cheechako*, no matter how skilled, ingenious or experienced, does not impose new ideas drastically or suddenly. He learns to take his time.

Women in Alaska

For the most part, women in Alaska lead a typically American family life, tending to home, children, and garden, and they read about Dan McGrew and the "lady known as Lou" with as much curiosity as women who have never been to Alaska. What is perhaps most characteristic of women in the forty-ninth state is that many work, either part-time or full-time; many join their husbands in outdoor fun; many are quite handy with paint brushes and tools around the house.

Doris Dooley grew so handy with tools soon after her arrival in Fairbanks, about ten years ago, that she was able to start her own business, leasing, installing and maintaining soda dispensing machines and popcorn vendors. It is not unusual to see Doris, a handsome blondish woman in her forties, hop off her truck in Fairbanks, with a kit of plumbing tools on her way to a repair or installation job. In some other state she'd probably be a candidate for town eccentric. But in Fairbanks she's just another Alaskan making a go of things.

Women in Alaska enjoy an unparalleled social and economic equality with men. There are women in trades, politics, business and law enforcement. In Anchorage, a familiar sight is the attractive *motorcycle* policewoman, assigned to traffic enforcement.

Before statehood, there were many laws passed protecting the rights and interests of Alaskan women in such matters as minimum pay ($1.50 per hour), equal pay for equal work, and protection of property rights in marriage and divorce. These laws remain in force.

One aspect of life, however, that affects women in particular, especially housewives with children, is what Alaskans call "cabin fever," supposedly a syndrome of boredom and monotony arising from long periods of darkness and cold during the winter. Cabin fever is said to be epidemic in the interior.

Many ministers and physicians (there are no private psychiatrists in Alaska) told me that "cabin fever" is the principal social "disease" in Alaska and that it accounts for a higher-than-average rate of alcoholism and suicide. Another result of cabin fever, according to many Alaskans, is the standard joke known as "the spring breakup," indicated by a high rate of separations and divorces after the winter.

Statistical data support the view that incidences of alcoholism and suicide in Alaska are above average. But if the rate of divorce in Alaska is any indication of cabin fever, the disease is not nearly as bad as many make it out to be. The latest divorce rate in Alaska was about 2.6 per 1,000 population, but there was almost an identical divorce rate for the entire United States.

However, more significant is the fact that the divorce rate in Alaska in 1945 was much higher—3.9 per 1,000—and has been declining steadily ever since, whereas the divorce rate in the United States has remained practically unchanged.

These statistics, of course, are subject to varying interpretations. It is entirely possible, for example, that when a marriage breaks up in Alaska one of the partners is apt to leave the state and obtain a divorce elsewhere. But the *steadily declining* rate of divorce in Alaska cannot be ignored in view of Alaska's increasing population during the same period. My own feeling is that Alaskan marriages tend to be more firmly cemented because husband and wife share a common goal and affection for their way of life and the new state of Alaska. One minister put it nicely: "If a man and wife stick it out together in Alaska for one full year, not even the Lord can tear them apart."

A rather common misconception about women in Alaska is the oft-heard remark, even among Alaskans, that women go to Alaska to get a man because men outnumber women seven to one.

Single women arrive in Alaska constantly, but not many. Most come to take jobs as teachers or as government workers in Federal Civil Service. There is no basis, however, for accepting the seven-to-one ratio. A liberal estimate would bring it down to more manageable proportions, three to one. Nonetheless, Alaska is no huge mantrap for single women. Most young men in Alaska are already married. There is, however, a definite ratio of three *unmarried* males to one *unmarried* female in Anchorage and Fairbanks—thanks to the unusual preponderance of military personnel in those areas.

But do not conclude that life for unmarried females in Alaska is dull. It is anything but that, particularly in Anchorage and Fairbanks. For one thing, both these cities supply adequate recreational and social resources where young couples can have fun. In both cities, there are many socials at community and religious centers, and there are a great variety of clubs, social, fraternal, professional, and recreational. In Anchorage alone, there are more than 150 active social and professional societies. In addition, the social resources in both cities are substantially augmented by large and well-run functions at the various military bases.

Dating and social life is extremely informal, and there is little chance for monotony because Alaska's young folk represent not the monolithic cultural pattern of a single community, but backgrounds as diverse as America itself. . . .

Religion in Alaska

The density of churches in Alaska is high. One community of 1,500 supports nine churches! There are almost one hundred churches between Anchorage and Fairbanks. Every conceivable denomination is represented. Increasingly, the churches are playing a vital role in the social lives of Alaskans, providing a variety of welfare and counseling services, including a Hospitality House in Fairbanks for job-seeking girls in need. Recently, a $5 million college was started by the Methodist Church in

Anchorage, and plans have been made for an almost year-by-year expansion of the college.

But Alaskans apparently are not fervent about their religion. A well-known religious leader in Alaska said, smilingly, "Alaska is still a missionary country as far as religious life is concerned. People who come here are essentially escapists, nonconformists.

"This is a weekend country. Anyone who has any kind of camping gear and a car takes off with his family on weekends. I don't blame them. I'd join them if I could, and sometimes I do."

Cooperation between religious groups is excellent, although there seems to be an undercurrent of animosity between the major denominations and those of what some call the "fringe" religions, of which there are many in Alaska, operating from store-front churches. But discrimination of any sort, religious, racial, or social, is almost nonexistent. It is definitely antisocial to be a bigot in Alaska.

Travel in Alaska

Many arriving in Alaska for the first time are surprised to find that Alaskans travel about with ease, even in winter. Of the many strange notions held by outsiders regarding travel in Alaska, none was more ludicrous than that revealed by a *cheechako* who thought that during winter, if he had to call for a taxi in Alaska, he'd find himself hopping into a dogsled operated by an Eskimo crying, "Mush!"

In some northern portions of Alaska—and in the isolated bush —the dogsled or snowshoes are still the only means of travel in winter. But even these are rapidly giving way to the airplane.

Alaska is the flyingest place in the world. Everybody, it would seem, has a pilot's license—housewives, ministers, doctors, nurses, lawyers, Indians, Eskimos, Aleuts, salesmen, politicians, hunting and fishing enthusiasts. In fact, many sportsmen who had utilized airplanes avocationally for hunting and fishing have become professional bush pilots.

A few days before my visit to the University of Alaska at Fairbanks, an eighteen-year-old Indian girl landed on the campus in her own airplane to register as a freshman for the coming semester. She had flown, I was told, some six hundred miles over extremely rough country.

According to Alaska Airlines, "78.7 per cent of the population use air transportation regularly. The average Alaskan flies twenty-eight times as much and as frequently as the citizen in the continental United States." Indeed, it is the airplane that is really responsible for the "opening" of Alaska's interior. In this regard the United States Air Force played a significant role shortly after World War II, proving that it was feasible to fly heavy equipment into the heartland of Alaska.

There are about 130 fields and terminals for scheduled air transport in Alaska. Added to these are almost 300 landing strips scattered about the state. An Alaskan, if he does not fly his own airplane, will hop aboard anything from a bush pilot's Piper Cub to a DC-7C or jet as casually as a banker takes a taxi to lunch on Wall Street.

A LOOK AT ALASKA'S NATIVES [2]

The mention of Eskimos may bring to mind a bleak and desolate expanse of snow with a sled trail in view and an Eskimo clinging to the back of a dogsled as he hauls home a freshly killed seal. A visual image of this sort would not be inaccurate even today, but it represents only a part of modern Eskimo life. The old Eskimo way of life is gone forever, and in many respects this is saddening. At the same time, some of the harshness has been taken out of living in the arctic, and even the most conservative Eskimo would not want to return to the days before Europeans and Americans arrived in his country. The whites brought new objects and ideas to the Eskimo, and these have often been accepted. At the same time came new and unprecedented problems.

Eskimos are still the most widely dispersed aboriginal people in the Americas. They are spread from Greenland to Alaska and even overlap into the Soviet arctic; the total Eskimo population is now in the neighborhood of 55,000 individuals. Most Eskimos, wherever they are found, have been drawn into a fur trapping and trading economy, but they usually rely upon wild animals and fish as their main source of food. The seal is still

[2] From "The New Alaskan Eskimo," by Wendell H. Oswalt, Department of Anthropology and Sociology, University of California at Los Angeles. *Américas*. 13:10-13. S. '61. Reprinted from *Américas*, monthly magazine published by the Pan American Union in English, Spanish, and Portuguese.

the most important single food animal for most Eskimos, although in some regions salmon, walrus or whales may be locally significant. Eskimos everywhere are primarily village dwellers living in small isolated settlements of less than three hundred individuals. There is some tendency to form community political organizations, but most daily activities center about a man, his wife and children as the most important economic and social unit. The Eskimo is truly a family man in the broadest sense of the word.

At present more Eskimos occupy the tundras facing the Bering Sea in Alaska than any other region of comparable size in the Far North. The six thousand people living there subsist primarily upon salmon and seal. They know better than anyone else the ways in which to set gill nets in order to catch salmon as these fish migrate up the rivers to spawn. Likewise they know the ways of the seal so very well that to hunt them poses no unusual problems. However, these people have come to want more than just food, clothing, and shelter. They have become accustomed to rifles, ready-made clothing, outboard motors, and foods not available in their territory. Their basic problem is how to obtain these and other desired items offered by the outside world and at the same time not lose their identity as Eskimos, for they are justifiably proud of their cultural heritage.

In order to obtain manufactured goods and U.S. foods these people do many things, the most important of which is trapping. Fortunately for them this is one of the best areas of the world in which to obtain wild mink, and so virtually every man traps for these fine pelts. They also trap muskrats, land otters, and fox in order to exchange the skins for goods at the trading posts. In addition, many of the men work during the summer at the large salmon canneries along the southern sector of the Bering Sea coast so that they may obtain cash. Some men likewise work for wages unloading supply ships. All of these things the Eskimos do well, and they quickly learn to operate new devices such as outboard motors or machinery, but they still have many problems in adjusting to the way of life introduced by the white man. A look at the Eskimos' history will help us understand their present situation.

The first contacts the Alaskan Eskimos had with Europeans were not until early in the nineteenth century. It was during this era that the Russians, who were well-established in southern Alaska, began to explore the coastal regions of the Bering Sea in an effort to find new sources of fur. The Russian explorers and traders were reasonably well entrenched among the Bering Sea Eskimos by the 1850's. They obtained so many of the desired furs that their most northern posts were quite successful. Just prior to the purchase of Alaska by the United States in 1867 the less lucrative trading establishments were abandoned. It is noteworthy that the Russians did not attempt to send settlers into this area, nor did they ever really have a strong hold over the Eskimos. Although the Eskimos traded with the Russians and some Eskimo women married Russian men, most of these outsiders lived in the region only briefly if at all. The most important and enduring Russian introduction was Christianity. Some of the Eskimos were baptized and became members of the Russian Orthodox Church, and there continue to be many practicing Russian Orthodox to this day.

After the purchase of Alaska the people continued to trap, but now they exchanged their pelts for goods at posts maintained by companies trading out of San Francisco. The United States was largely disinterested in these people, and the number of outsiders coming into the country was few until near the turn of the nineteenth century. It was then that two important changes took place. First of all Protestant and Roman Catholic missionaries became active locally, and they have continued their efforts down to the present time. The second change was more transient and came as a result of the discovery of gold in large quantities in northwestern Canada and interior Alaska. The gold strikes brought adventurers from all corners of the world into traditionally Eskimo country. Fortunately or unfortunately the Bering Sea coast of Alaska has no gold-bearing deposits, and so the prospectors soon left the Eskimos to themselves once again.

The Government of the United States did not begin to take an active interest in the people of this area until about the second decade of the twentieth century, and then their concern was still quite casual. The Federal Government opened a small hospital and began to establish schools, but most schools continued to be operated by Protestant and Roman Catholic missionaries. Actually it was not until just before World War II that the United States began to take serious notice of these Eskimos. The Government then established many schools, opened a modern hospital, and built some large airports that greatly facilitated travel into the region. The increased governmental activity has brought many changes, but still the tenor of life has been largely unaffected.

The typical Eskimo village of today is isolated from adjoining settlements and occupied by about 120 persons including a teacher or two, a trader, and perhaps a resident missionary. The villages, located along the coast or adjacent rivers, are a blend of the old Eskimo way of life with the new way of life that has resulted from U.S. influence, but it is the new way that is initially the more apparent. A typical community has a large wooden school building with attached quarters for the teachers. The school is the best-maintained building in the village, and it is here that school children, like their counterparts over much of the world, study for about eight months of each year. In the community there would also be a store with a resident trader, who might be a white or an Eskimo. Most trading establishments are well supplied with an assortment of hardware and foodstuffs, along with some clothing. Another imposing structure is the church, which is most likely Roman Catholic, Russian Orthodox, or Moravian. Villagers take considerable pride in their church, and it is maintained as well as their means permit. The only other large building is likely to be a new armory for the local unit of the National Guard, which maintains Eskimo contingents in some settlements. The armory may be used for community affairs, but more often for military drills and exercises.

In this treeless region many families live in dwellings made from logs that have drifted down the rivers to the sea from the forested areas of interior Alaska. Other families, living where even driftwood is scarce, build their houses primarily of sod. However, there is an increasing tendency for all the people to construct their homes of lumber, which they purchase from the Government or from a local trader. Most homes are single-room dwellings in which there is a wood-burning stove, a table, chairs, beds, and a cupboard, in addition to various storage containers. Throughout the settlement are other structures, such as fish-drying racks, buildings for smoking fish, and food caches. The inevitable crowds of dogs are chained to stakes scattered about the edges of the settlement.

A village of this type certainly gives the impression of tranquillity, except perhaps for the occasional snarls of feuding dogs. The people, when first met, seem reluctant to say very much, not from animosity but because they are genuinely shy and retiring among strangers. Once the awkwardness of initial introductions has been overcome, the visitor finds the Eskimos to be gracious hosts and good friends. Eskimos justifiably have the reputation of being very jovial, but at the same time they are far from idle and carefree. It is essential for them to work hard during most of the year if they are to support themselves. In the summer they are busy fishing, while hunting seals may take place at almost any season. From late fall to late spring they trap. Their year is filled with diverse activities with little time for boredom. Midwinter is the longest period of forced inactivity, but even then the people usually are busy chopping wood for their stoves and repairing equipment that will serve them during the coming spring.

When a visitor has reached a point of real familiarity with the village and its people he soon comes to realize that all is not quite so idyllic as it might appear. There are problems, big and small, that lend uncertainty to arctic life.

For example, hunting migratory waterfowl is no longer as unrestricted as it formerly was. The flat, alluvial tundra region is an important breeding center for ducks, swans, and geese. These birds migrate north in the spring, nest on the tundra, and then return to the south in the fall. For generations the Eskimos have hunted these birds in the spring and, in addition, have killed large numbers of the young throughout the summer. However, for many years treaties between the United States, Canada, and Mexico have restricted all parties, including Alaskans to a fall hunting season for waterfowl. Thus, the Eskimos are legally deprived of a source of fresh food during a season when they need it very much. Occasionally Government enforcement agents fly into the region and arrest Eskimos for hunting the birds out of season.

The Eskimos regard this as totally unfair and point out that they have always hunted these birds in the spring and summer.

The conservationists on the other hand argue that such hunting practices very seriously deplete the breeding stock. It is apparent that neither the Eskimo nor the interested public want to see these birds exterminated, but the vital and perplexing question is how the differences can be reconciled. To begin with, the whites have never learned the Eskimos' beliefs about the birds. If they had they would know that the Eskimos think that waterfowl breed in the north in the summer and again in the south in the winter. For this reason, they feel that the birds will always be abundant. The fact that this idea is not correct can become apparent to the Eskimos only after a widespread program of education has been successfully carried out. At the same time the Government, if it must prohibit the Eskimos from hunting birds out of season, should feel morally obligated to help the Eskimos make up for the loss. This could be accomplished by introducing scientific fur management practices so that the people could realize a greater and richer catch of fur animals. Then, although one source of food would be taken away, another would be substituted through the added income with which to purchase meat.

In order to improve their living standard the Eskimos have become more intensive trappers, and at the same time they are becoming concentrated in larger communities. Not many years ago two or three related families often lived in isolated camps throughout the year, but with the erection of United States Bureau of Indian Affairs schools in the larger settlements more and more families have gravitated toward these villages. The result has been for each man to trap over a smaller area, with a resulting decrease in catch per trapper. Most families cannot move to winter trapping camps now because they have school-age children who must attend school from September through May. The winter trapping pattern now prevalent is for the men to go out in the fall to their trapping camps and return periodically to their village.

This routine is very unsatisfactory for all concerned. The women do not like to be left alone for extended periods of time. The men complain of missing their families and of performing women's work in camp, which takes them away from their trapping. Perhaps more serious is the fact that the boys cannot trap until they are out of school, and this deprives the family of needed income for several years. To solve this problem the Bureau of Indian Affairs might divide the school year into two parts so that the families could go as units to their winter trapping camps. Some of the Bureau of Indian Affairs schools have successfully adjusted the school year to accommodate spring muskrat trapping, but in terms of dollars the muskrat catch is insignificant compared to the mink catch. It would be far better for all concerned to make every effort to improve the mink catch. Considering the general complaint of the whites that the Eskimos are increasingly dependent upon welfare funds, it seems only logical to take a positive step in helping the Eskimos, who want to do more trapping, through a more flexible governmental policy in the schools.

The problems mentioned above are only two among many that confront Eskimos and administrators alike. These are not insurmountable difficulties if both sides are willing to consider seriously the desires and needs of the other. The same would apply to other problems such as village health, village government, and resource utilization in general. The primary barrier seems to be that the Government agents are comparatively inflexible in carrying out their obligations and are guided by policy statements that often show little awareness of village needs. The Eskimos, for their part, tend more and more to distrust administrators and to be prejudiced against new programs before really understanding their aims. The conflicts that do exist are not explosive, but they are quite symptomatic of an unhealthy environment. Unquestionably various programs of education can offer partial solutions, but it is both the Eskimos *and* the administrators who must be reeducated. They must both come to realize that they are viewing different sides of common problems wherein mutual understanding is necessary to arrive at accomplishments fruitful for both.

PROBLEMS FACING ALASKA'S NATIVES [3]

In spite of some good policies, and because of some bad ones, we still have an "Indian problem." And actions of the past century on the old frontier, that we regret, are taking place

[3] From "Indian Rights and Wrongs in Alaska," by Theodore B. Hetzel, associate professor of engineering, Haverford College, and a director of the Indian Rights Association. *Indian Truth.* 38:1-8. O. '61. Reprinted by permission.

now on our last frontier, Alaska, in this time of the New Frontier. We must learn better how to deal with people of cultures that differ from ours for the improvement of our relations both within our own borders and with our world neighbors. . . .

Who Really Owns Alaska?

By the treaty of cession in 1867 Russia sold to the United States not just the sovereignty over Alaska, but the title to the land itself. The legal definition of the Federal Government's title to the land is set forth in the Supreme Court's decision in the Tee Hit Ton case which holds that the natives have no firm title to land except as granted by Congress.

The treaty of cession provided that the members of the civilized native tribes should be protected in the free enjoyment of their property.

The Act of 1884 establishing a civil government in Alaska provided:

That the Indians or other persons in said district shall not be disturbed in the possession of any lands actually in their use or occupation or now claimed by them, but the terms under which such persons may acquire title to such lands is reserved for future legislation by Congress. . . .

Some protection for the land claims of Alaskan natives was written into the Statehood Act but even now, nearly a century after purchasing Alaska, Congress has not acted to establish land titles for natives on the basis of their possessory rights.

To the casual observer and even to most of the natives there appears to be more than enough land for the present population, so that the natives give little thought to the subject.

This apparent abundance of land is far from a true picture of the actual situation. Demands for land by the Atomic Energy Commission, the various branches of the Department of Defense, homesteaders, oil and gas producers, mining interests and the state itself, are already causing the loss to natives of land areas to which they are entitled and which are essential to their economic well-being. This situation grows daily less favorable to the natives. Early action by Congress to reverse this direction is essential.

Because of the provision in the Statehood Act for the new state to select over 100 million acres of land to help meet its expenses of operation, the state automatically becomes an aggressive competitor to deprive the natives of land which they need and which is rightfully theirs. They cannot look to the state to protect their land rights.

Ever since early territorial days the Indian population of Alaska has been persuaded that any landholding as reservations or by a group for a community enterprise would prevent them from enjoying equality, nondiscrimination and full citizenship rights. This has been continued by promoters of the state. Combined with the failure of Congress to provide for the settlement of their land claims this has resulted in most natives becoming economically on a level with the poorest, propertyless *cheechako* (name applied to newcomers).

Native villages are protected against seizure, but in villages that have been surveyed it is possible for a competent native to obtain unrestricted title to his land and to sell it regardless of the effect upon the economy of the native community. A special provision permits a native to obtain title to five acres in one piece. Five acres of tundra is even more pitiful than 160 acres of the Great Plains. It cannot support its owner who has always used extensive areas in different places at different times of year for fishing, trapping and hunting different animals. Many of these traditional hunting areas have been taken from the natives' control by the numerous reservations of the Defense Department, the AEC, Wild Life Refuges, the state, mining, gas and oil producers, etc.

Even those natives of southeastern Alaska, who live principally by fishing, need the security of landownership to protect their bases of operations, and their right to hunt where their ancestors hunted. As a Tlingit Indian in Hoonah told me "We used to get fish in the creeks, but now we have to pay for a permit even to get one fish. We used to go to Glacier Bay for seals—you need seal oil when you eat dried fish—but we are not allowed to go there now."

Those Indians of the interior of Alaska whose livelihood, both subsistence and cash income, has always depended upon hunting and trapping should have set aside for their exclusive use the areas of land that have always been their fields of operation. They have over many years developed practices and methods in taking game that both meet their needs and provide for the conservation of the game. New roads and the airplane make it possible for sportsmen and outside trappers and hunters to move in, take the game and destroy this source of native food.

Shades of the buffalo! As one native said, "Whites have taken over good trapping land where we used to trap. They tell us to keep off." . . .

In the far north large areas of grazing land are needed for the reindeer and caribou, important sources of food and clothing for the Eskimo.

It is equally important that these long-time native residents of Alaska share in the income from the gas, oil and mineral lands that are being developed. As has been the practice in other states, the natives should have the landowner's share of income from these products from areas which traditionally have been in their possession.

At Barrow where natural gas is produced and piped right through the village to supply the Federal installations arrangements should be made so that the natives can secure natural gas for their needs. As it is now they must pay from seventy cents to a dollar a gallon for their fuel.

Schools and Schooling

There is general agreement that education is desirable, and that it is a key to the solution of other problems that beset Alaskan natives. New schools are being built in many places, more teachers employed, teacher qualifications are being raised, and burdens of extraneous duties, such as power plant and radio operator, postmaster, magistrate, hotel-keeper, etc. formerly placed upon teachers are being lightened. All this is good.

Native children, mostly from non-English-speaking homes and isolated communities, do not accomplish as much academically in eight years, in spite of high intelligence, as is expected in the "Lower 48." Their expectations and needs are different too. Yet the academic program is based on typical American standards. In the beginning years the pupils make normal progress, but when class material becomes based on an acquaintance with the greater complexities of modern affairs the children drop behind their nonnative contemporaries. And they drop out.

The Bureau of Indian Affairs conducted a valuable experiment this past summer to prepare above-average eighth grade graduates for successful high school careers. Perhaps even more needed is a similar program for those of only average ability, or a whole year added to the high school program to bring achievement up to regular norms and to prepare students better for college.

School program and policy are determined in Washington and Juneau. The reasons for them are often not understood either by the students or their parents, and some things which are of importance to the natives are not accepted by the education administrators. Many natives depend on boats and outboard motors. But there is no instruction in boatmaking or outboard repair, except for some shop work at Mt. Edgecumbe, which work is being decreased. There is talk of a vocational high school at Nome. A good idea, but the wrong place.

It is not surprising that boys drop out of school when they do not realize the importance of their studies, and their studies do not include some things they think important. And their parents are not consulted about curriculum. The Bureau should establish local advisory school boards and give them increasing responsibility for decisions affecting their children's education. Most natives would not be able to assume all the responsibilities of school boards at once, but they should be brought into school activities through parent-teacher organizations and into administrative problems wherever possible. We do not approve of the former practice of "kidnapping" Indian children to educate them. We should be sure that we do not now have other practices opposed by the parents.

Hunger Knows No Season

An Alaskan problem that received national attention this past summer is that of the taking of migratory birds which are protected by international treaties. The needs and usages of Eskimos in killing ducks and some other birds when they were in Alaska were probably unknown or overlooked by those who wrote the treaties. The treaties should be revised for the benefit of those who depend on these birds for subsistence, for there is no question but that many Eskimos need this food, and also that the number of birds taken by them is no significant threat to the conservation of the species. It would be simpler, however, to solve the problem by a more understanding enforcement of the regulations. The treaty with Mexico protects those ducks which live temporarily in Mexico, therefore as no eider ducks get that far south they need not be included in those listed for protection. The treaty with Canada states "that special protection shall be given . . . the eider duck . . . by such other regulations as may be deemed appropriate." When the eider were threatened with extinction that meant more strict protection of course, but now that that is not the case the propriety of appropriate regulation is established.

Natives Endangered by "Project Chariot"

Another problem for the Eskimos is the Atomic Energy Commission's Project Chariot, a proposal to experiment with the use of atomic energy to blast a huge excavation. Scientists have been studying the geology, flora, fauna and weather of the area. The natives of the vicinity have been told that there will be no ill effects due to radiation and fallout. However, if one could be so sure of the results it would not be necessary to conduct the experiment, and the assurances are suspect because some findings and recommendations have been published in advance of the gathering of scientific data basic to the recommendations. Political rather than scientific factors seem to be in control of Project Chariot.

Many problems illustrate the confusion of information and misinformation in people's minds: the problems accompanying transition from a hunting to a cash economy, how to get better housing, the effect of airplanes on wildlife, the effect of weirs on salmon spawning, legal problems relating to fish traps and fishing and hunting rights, and the social effects of large military bases adjacent to small native villages.

Relatively well-informed people hold conflicting opinions and are sure of contradictory data. This lack of reliable information is a clear indication that Indian-interest organizations should give more attention to Alaska, its people and their problems.

RACE RELATIONS FRONTIERS IN HAWAII [4]

By virtue of its limited size and geographic insularity, Hawaii lends itself peculiarly to a unitary and simplified representation of its social structure. Both the popular and scientific literature abound with references to Hawaii as "the melting pot of the Pacific"—a land where the associations among the numerous ethnic stocks which make up its population are described in terms as idyllic and equable as the climate and the tropical landscape. Indeed, some observers with a scientific tradition have seriously contended that the contentious peoples of more rigorous climes may become transformed into mild-mannered Polynesians simply by living for some years within the beneficent physical environment of the Islands.

Most social scientists, while critical of so simple a theory of social causation, are nevertheless prone to accept the conception of Hawaii as affording a congenial social climate for free and friendly association among peoples of sharply contrasted cultures and racial origins. A prevailing impression of Hawaii, particularly among journalists but also among social scientists, has varied only slightly from the account given by William Allen White, following his experience in the Islands during the initial conference of the Institute of Pacific Relations. Writing under the title "The Last of the Magic Isles," White described Hawaii as the one place in all the world where "the so-called race problem is [not] acute," where the eyes of the dark-skinned men of the "brown, black, and the yellow [races] of the earth and their mulattoes are [not] looking with suspicion and rage and bitterness into the blue eyes of the men of the northern ruling race of today," where "race antipathies have disappeared because . . . race injustices are not in vogue."

Few of the numerous observers of the social scene in Hawaii go much further than the Kansas journalist in interpreting the beneficent race relations as the consequence of the favorable economic situation in which competition is lacking between the "benevolent white oligarchy" and the imported "races from Asia who live upon the lower standard." Thirty years later no less

[4] From article by Andrew W. Lind, senior professor of sociology, University of Hawaii. In Race Relations: Problems and Theory, Essays in Honor of Robert E. Park, edited by Jitsuichi Masuoka and Preston Valien. University of North Carolina Press. Chapel Hill. '61. p 58-71. Reprinted by permission.

a figure than the President of the United States [Dwight D. Eisenhower] utilized much the same idealized conception of the Islands as a major argument in his State of the Union Address for urging statehood for Hawaii:

In the Hawaiian Islands, East meets West. To the Islands, Asia and Europe and the Western Hemisphere, all the continents, have contributed their peoples and their cultures to display a unique example of a community that is a successful laboratory in human brotherhood.

Statehood, supported by the repeatedly expressed desire of the Islands' people and by our traditions, would be a shining example of the American way to the entire earth.

Even the scholarly and intensive studies by Romanzo Adams, pioneer sociologist in the Islands, have been commonly interpreted as supporting a similarly enchanting view of race relations in which there is "the almost complete absence of race prejudice and sustained social tolerance and cultural reciprocity." Actually, Adams' analysis of Hawaiian race relations does not lend itself to such a simplified conception. He did not fail to recognize the existence, particularly among the newly arrived immigrants and in the military circles, of strong traditions adverse to free association and equality of opportunity across racial lines, but he did insist that, owing to a series of historical accidents in Hawaii, there has evolved a prevailing set of practices (rituals) and a corresponding set of doctrines to symbolize racial equality. . . .

According to Adams, it was the deep rooting of racial equality in the everyday practices of the people, reinforced by a long tradition and a corresponding doctrine . . . that such conduct is right and proper which gives to Hawaii its unique and unorthodox quality as a race relations frontier. Individuals or even small splinter groups may be out of sympathy with the racial code and may even privately resist it, but they cannot afford to express these sentiments openly, and eventually even their inner sentiments, according to Adams, come to conform with the social expectations.

Other competent students have focused attention specifically upon the dual or divided character of Island race relations, being less impressed by the dominant code of racial equality than by the equally pronounced tendency to depart from the code. Everett Stonequist, following two years of observation in Hawaii, characterized the Island system of race relations as containing "a pattern of equality and friendliness and a pattern of inequality and prejudice." Evidence of the latter, according to Stonequist, is found particularly in the racial hierarchy on Hawaii's plantations, in the economic and cultural dominance and the social exclusiveness of the white population, and in the ethnocentrism of the various immigrant groups.

This point of view, which has been shared by numerous other observers, suggests a shifting and unstable equilibrium in which the nonwhite groups especially are subject to varying degrees of racial segregation and prejudice. Indeed, it gives to Hawaii's race relations a character not essentially different from that which is commonly attributed to the continental United States. There is a professed code of racial equality on the one hand—a public avowal that the individual shall be afforded opportunity and rewarded on the basis of his native ability and effort rather than on the accident of birth. The actual practice, on the other hand, may fall far short of the ideal. Hawaii's race relations, they contend, are essentially those of the "American dilemma" described by Gunnar Myrdal—the continuing conflict between the values inherent in the "American creed" where the American thinks, talks, and acts under the influence of high national and Christian precepts, and, on the other hand, the valuations of specific planes of individual and group living, where personal and local interests; economic, social, and sexual jealousies; . . . group prejudice . . . dominate his outlook.

A psychologist from South Africa, after several weeks of observation in Hawaii and prodded, no doubt, by the frequent references to "Hawaii's racial harmony," went so far as to state to a group of fellow scientists that "the only real difference between race relations in South Africa and in Hawaii is that in South Africa we practice racial segregation and inequality and readily admit it whereas in Hawaii you also discriminate but your code won't permit you to admit it." There is much the same implication of unconscious hypocrisy among Islanders in the widely quoted comment of Ray Stannard Baker in 1911: "I have rarely visited any place where there was as much charity and as little democracy as in Hawaii." Although he was alluding at the time primarily to the benevolent paternalism which he found so marked in the Islands, he was no less impressed by the barriers existing to "keep the Oriental in his place."

Robert E. Park [whose pioneer work as a sociologist advanced the study of race relations] appears to have been the first to suggest a pluralistic approach to the study of race relations in Hawaii. In his introduction to Romanzo Adams' *Interracial Marriage in Hawaii,* Park restates a conception which had occurred to him at least a decade earlier following some observations in the Caribbean, where he was greatly impressed by the wide variation in the race relations found in the different islands. The possibility of similar differences among various Hawaiian islands with respect to race relations was proposed to Adams as a basic idea for the study and appears in the introduction as follows:

If . . . we may observe civilization [here] as it evolves under something like laboratory conditions, this is due, in part at least, to the advantages of the islands for the purpose of sociological investigation. . . . All kinds of things can and do happen on islands. . . . Every island (of the group) is likely to enclose within the limits of its coastline not merely another community but a different world, each with its own local traditions and way of life, and each more or less self-sufficing and complete in itself. . . . Insularity, in short, encourages individuality and in this sense, it is true that one cannot tell what will happen on an island.

Hawaii's small islands, with their restricted and "neighborly" populations, yield better returns for the students of race relations, according to Park, because there is "little of that mystery and sentiment in regard to race which so readily springs up in more populous communities where local and occupational segregation so easily becomes the basis for the formation of hereditary classes or castes." . . .

Traders and Missionaries

It is against the background of Hawaii's underlying economy that the evolving pattern of Island race relations may be most effectively portrayed. Trade was, in fact, the atmosphere in which contacts between the native Polynesians and the whites were initiated, and the subsequent shifts in the racial complexion of the region have been largely in response to the changing demands of the Island economy. One need not accept the theory of economic determinism to recognize in Hawaii, as elsewhere, the dynamic influence of free land and of open economic opportunity in stimulating immigration and the mingling of diverse peoples. It is within the shadow, so to speak, of two competing economic institutions—the trading center and the plantation—that Hawaii's pattern of race relations has chiefly taken form.

Trade is a . . . relationship in which, theoretically at least, both participants enjoy equal advantage. The very conception of exchange implies that both parties find the relationship to their advantage and that either party may withdraw and thus terminate the relationship if he feels that his best interests are not being served. . . .

Certainly the Yankee trader who soon followed the explorer, drove hard bargains with the natives and gave little thought for their welfare. That the Hawaiian was frequently victimized in these transactions there can be little doubt; but it was a game which required two to play, and its success was dependent upon the satisfaction of both of the parties. Moreover, the purely exploitative aspects of the relationship could not continue if the Westerners expected to conduct business and to live permanently in the Islands. The natives were not likely to continue doing business with a trader who was known to be a scoundrel. . . .

The Christian missionaries have frequently been credited with introducing the tradition of equality into the race relations of Hawaii, and unquestionably they did much to stabilize this trend and to give it doctrinal support. What is perhaps not commonly recognized is that the missionaries came to Hawaii in the wake of and, to some degree, by the consent of the traders. Despite the acrimonious struggle for power between some of the traders and the missionaries, they actually had much in common and each drew support from the other. The missionaries, like the traders, were beholden to the native rulers for their presence and physical well-being in the Islands, and it would have been inconsistent with both their collective interests and their professed doctrine to discriminate actively against the natives. . . .

It is the combined impact of the forces emanating from the trading center on the one hand and the Protestant mission on the other which is largely responsible for Hawaii's much-vaunted equalitarian race relations. The trader, with his dominant concern for profit, and the missionary, with his zeal for winning souls, were by their vocations compelled to treat the native

Hawaiians with deference and respect. They could not afford to give public expression in the Islands to any feelings which they might privately cherish that the Hawaiians were destined by their biological heritage to remain at their stone-age level of culture. And, as Romanzo Adams has insisted, people tend to bring their attitudes into harmony with the behavior that they believe to be expedient. In the field of race relations, people finally come to have the sentiments of respect that their conduct symbolizes. It is therefore a matter of primary importance to the permanent pattern of race relations in Hawaii that the trader and the missionary arrived before (not after) the planter and the soldier. The lapse of some seventy years following Western discovery of Hawaii before the plantation emerged as a dominant factor in the life of the Islands allowed ample time for the earlier equalitarian pattern of race relations to become firmly established, and at least another fifty years elapsed before any considerable military population arrived to offer further competition.

Planters and Soldiers

The combined effect of certain major social changes in Hawaii before 1850—the dramatic decline in native population from an estimated 300,000 in 1778 to 71,000 in 1853, the consequent releasing of extensive native lands for other purposes, the acceptance by the Hawaiian monarchy of the rights of private ownership and the alienation of land, and the passing of Hawaii as a major center for the whaling industry of the Pacific—these all served to create the necessary conditions for the rise of the plantation frontier in the Islands. The critical significance of the plantation as affecting race relations arises out of its political functions and role. In order to assure the necessary supply of responsible and tractable labor, in a region where such workers are distinctly at a premium, the planter is compelled to assume the part of a political overlord, and the plantation acquires many of the characteristics of a semi-independent state.

In Hawaii, as on other plantation frontiers, the natives had little incentive to accept the onerous conditions of labor on the emerging agricultural estates. Their simple economic needs could readily be satisfied without submitting to the long arduous hours of work under a foreign taskmaster. Since slavery, the device so commonly utilized in other plantation regions, could not be employed, the planters were obliged to import the bulk of their workers from overseas and to hold their labor supply as best they could by a highly stratified social system based upon race. Commencing in 1852 and continuing for nearly a hundred years, the European and American promoters of Hawaii's sugar and pineapple plantations recruited some 400,000 workers from such widely separated regions as China, Korea, Japan, the Philippines, Spain, Portugal, Germany, Norway, Puerto Rico, and the islands of the south and central Pacific. Although the total demand for plantation workers in Hawaii could readily have been supplied entirely from a single region relatively close at hand, such as China, better control, particularly during the early history of the plantation, could be obtained by dividing the labor force among sharply contrasted ethnic stocks and by maintaining distinct physical and social barriers between them.

Thus it is that most of the groups known as races in Hawaii have been drawn to these Islands to supply plantation labor, and the very conception of race as a divisive category is largely a function of the plantation system. Before the middle of the last century the only major distinctions were between the natives and the haole, with minor recognition of the national groupings within the larger category of foreigners. Chinese plantation workers, following their arrival in considerable numbers during the 1850's and 1860's, came to stand out as a special group with a status inferior to that of the haole group with whom they had previously been classified, and beginning in 1866 the Chinese were recognized as a separate racial group in the census of Hawaii. Similarly, the Portuguese, Spanish, German, and Norwegian immigrant laborers, although sharing a common European and Christian heritage with the American and British planters of the Islands, have consistently been treated as distinct racial groups and have so been classified in the official census as long as their place within the Island economy was primarily at the level of plantation labor. . . .

With the economic maturation of plantation agriculture, following World War I, there occurred a reversal in the conditions of the Hawaiian labor market such that unskilled workers, far from being in great demand, are now excessively available. The planter no longer needs to conserve or coerce his workers, since the supply is more than ample, and the pressure to use race as a control device is consequently largely removed. The traditions of the past, however, die hard, and the plantation still remains a symbol of racial, as well as class stratification. . . .

The loss of Hawaiian political independence and the acceptance of territorial status under the United States [in 1898], although by no means attributable exclusively to plantation pressures, symbolized to the masses a further intrenchment of the plantation pattern of race relations. To the native Hawaiians, particularly, annexation reflected a serious loss of prestige, and it was generally interpreted as a public confirmation of the dominant position of the haole, a fact which had hitherto been publicly recognized only within the plantation.

Actually the transfer of citizenship from the Hawaiian Republic to the United States had mixed consequences with respect to race relations in the Islands. On the one hand, the earlier property qualifications for certain elective offices and the exclusion of Orientals from citizenship under the constitution of the Republic were eliminated. The American Bill of Rights was extended to all residents of the territory regardless of racial ancestry. All persons born within the Islands were for the first time granted the rights of citizenship. On the other hand, disparities between legal rights and practices also became increasingly apparent as a considerable number of Americans from the mainland, bearing racial attitudes which were alien to Hawaii, flocked into the newly acquired territory. It is significant, however, that most of these *malihinis* (newcomers) either absorbed "the unorthodox race doctrines" of Hawaii, particularly if they lived in the urban centers, or they returned to the States. A sizable number of mainlanders could not become accustomed to the racial practices which they encountered, and it is probable that their decision to return to the States was motivated in part by a feeling of disgust with Hawaii's racial unorthodoxy.

A new dimension in Hawaiian race relations was introduced shortly after annexation with the arrival of increasing numbers of military personnel. The soldier, whose exercise of power figures so prominently in establishing the superior position of the white man on so many other colonial frontiers, did not seriously figure in the Hawaiian situation until well after a century of contact with the Western world. The first permanent garrison of American troops was established on Oahu shortly after the transfer of sovereignty in August 1898, but it was not until after World War I that Hawaii emerged as the major American military outpost in the Pacific. Hawaii's rapid rise as a military frontier is symbolized in the expanding number of persons returned by the census as "soldiers, sailors, and marines," or in "national defense," from 1,608 in 1910 to 29,057 in 1940, of whom the overwhelming majority were mainlanders. The climax was reached after "Pearl Harbor" when the military personnel completely outnumbered the adult civilian population of the Islands.

The significance of the military population, which Romanzo Adams in the early thirties apparently regarded as the most serious threat to "Hawaii's race mores," is derived, however, less from the numbers involved than from their isolation and political influence. Like the plantations, the military posts had very much the character of independent states where "traditions of a racial caste system" could be maintained without interference from the local community. The distinctions of rank, inherent in the military structure, could readily be translated into a racial hierarchy, particularly when those in command had been disproportionately drawn from "sections of the country in which doctrines of racial inequality are definitely professed and practiced." . . .

The conflict in viewpoint with regard to race relations between the military and civilian elements of the Island population might not have constituted any serious problem, if the isolation between them had been less complete. To a very considerable degree, the military population has lived in a world of its own, with a minimum of communication with, or understanding of life among, the civilians. Limitations of recreational opportunities on the posts, however, have forced the large number of womanless enlisted men, particularly, to seek contacts with the civilian community under conditions which have not been favorable to understanding on either side. . . .

Under the pressure of national crises and also in response to the mounting economic expenditures of the military establishments in Hawaii, Islanders have sometimes compromised with their local code of racial equality. This was perhaps most noticeable during World War II with respect to the treatment of the

Negro, the latest and least familiar, and, hence, the least acceptable, of the immigrant arrivals. Even within the urban centers, the Negro has encountered some discrimination during and following the war, although not to the extent of irreparably damaging the existing pattern of race relations. The service personnel, on the other hand, have also adapted themselves to the Island expectations, even to the point of choosing wives from among the non-Caucasian residents and remaining permanently in Hawaii.

Last to develop among the distinctive types of social situations affecting race relations in Hawaii is what may properly be called the tourist frontier. Running back as far as 1784 with the publication of Captain Cook's *Voyages of Discovery,* the Hawaiian Islands have held a particular fascination to Westerners as one of the last remaining outposts of romanticism in a world of increasing mechanization and standardization. Unquestionably the prospect of escape from the burdens and responsibilities of a routinized existence at home and the anticipation of a South Seas idyll led many of the first traders to Hawaii, but the full effect of such an appeal did not express itself until well into the twentieth century. It has required the facilities of modern luxury liners, both by sea and air, and the latest promotion techniques of travel agencies and tourist bureaus to exploit fully the propaganda appeal of Mark Twain's panegyric on Hawaii of the last century:

. . . the loveliest fleet of islands that lies anchored in any ocean. . . . No alien land in all the world has any deep strong charm for me, but that one. No other land could so longingly and beseechingly haunt me, sleeping and waking, through half a lifetime as that one has done.

The influx each year of thousands of visitors in search of adventure and stimulation, as well as temporary release from the moral restrictions of their home communities, is bound to have notable consequences upon the race relations of the Islands. The tourist shares with the military personnel the racial attitudes of another community—frequently opposed to those prevailing in Hawaii, at least those prevailing in the urban centers—and as one investing his surplus in the Islands he is sometimes less inhibited than the military in expressing these attitudes freely. Theoretically, therefore, the tourists afford a sort of pipeline for the introduction of mainland conceptions of race relations, and the Islanders economically dependent upon their patronage, notably taxi drivers and hotel operators, tend to "play up" to these imported ideas.

Practically, however, the tourists come into close contact with at least that portion of the local community serving their needs and hence they are better situated than the military to undergo some change in attitude. To a degree at least, the tourist goes abroad to learn, and many become converted to the official Hawaiian doctrine of racial equality. In search of new experience and release from the prohibitions of his home community, the tourist may also discard his former racial prejudices with considerable ease, at least while he is away from home. The most sweeping and enthusiastic endorsements of Hawaiian race relations and the most glowing accounts of the non-Caucasian population have come from visitors who only shortly before had arrived in the Islands, prepared to find fault with the unorthodox human relationships they encountered.

Race Relations in Flux

Contrary, therefore, to the common impressions, race relations in Hawaii are manifestly involved and fluid in character. However distinct the frontier situations just delineated may once have been, now virtually every part of the Islands is affected to some degree by all of these differing forces. . . . Not only has the equalitarian atmosphere of the commercial centers extended into the military and plantation areas, . . . but the urban centers, in turn, have felt the impact of military and . . . plantation forces. Traders and missionaries have become planters, and planters have become traders or have retired in the cities, with a corresponding transfer of influence from one area to the other. . . .

The phenomenal conversion of the Hawaiian people to Christianity within a single generation has given rise to the mistaken impression that the missionary frontier has long since disappeared and that the Christian impact upon race relations is unitary and unchanged. The subsequent introduction of additional population elements created new fields for converts and attracted to the Islands a host of different religious movements, with varying racial emphases, to engage in the process. During the latter half of the nineteenth century, the Catholic, Episcopal,

Methodist, and Mormon missions tended to carry on much the same tradition of race relations as the Congregational pioneers, stressing the value of all peoples in the sight of God. The Catholics were in general less puritanical than their Mormon and Protestant colleagues in their approach to deviations from Western morals encountered among the native and immigrant groups. In contrast to the Protestant and Mormon . . . [attitudes] the Catholic church has been somewhat more inclusive in its appeal and has encouraged marriage across race lines insofar as both parties are Catholics. The introduction of a wide range of the emotionally expressive Christian sects since 1930 has served to extend the Protestant influence somewhat into the lower classes and to promote fraternization across ethnic lines. At the same time, the older Protestant denominations are gradually breaking away from the earlier practice of "racial churches" made necessary by the separate languages of the immigrant groups.

The most striking transformations with respect to race relations have probably occurred with the maturation of the plantations of the Islands. . . . The disposition to keep the immigrant races in "their place" as laborers has greatly diminished. Promotion in economic and social status within the plantation occurs increasingly on the basis of individual merit and ability rather than of race, and residential segregation according to race, once essential for effective labor control, is also gradually declining. Strong resistance to the advanced education of the children of plantation workers lest they acquire "white-collar" tastes and expectations was evident among Hawaiian plantation interests until well along in the 1930's, but such barriers to educational advancement, insofar as they may still exist in the more remote portions of the Islands, have been largely negated by the spread of public and private high schools and colleges.

A wholly intrusive and unexpected element in the breakdown of racial barriers on the plantations since World War II is the sudden spread of unionization. Sometimes described as Hawaii's major revolution, surpassing in social significance the revolution of 1893 in which Queen Liliuokalani was dethroned, the establishment of the ILWU as the bargaining agent for workers in both the sugar and pineapple plantations brought about a degree of collaboration and fraternization across race lines which had never previously been thought possible. Where previously the efforts of labor to secure recognition had been confined to the limited and sporadic demonstrations by workers of a single ethnic group, the unionized workers were forced into active co-operation without regard for ethnic background. The first Island-wide strike on the sugar plantations in 1946 and the first large-scale strike in the pineapple industry in 1947 were also the initial experience of large numbers of Island workers engaging in a common cause with persons outside their own racial community, and although deeply-rooted prejudices could not be im-mediately eliminated, a new tradition of far-reaching significance had become well established.

The integration of plantation workers across racial lines has, however, probably widened the barrier between the predomi-nantly haole employing group, on the one hand, and the com-bined non-haole workers, on the other. The phenomenal in-crease in unionization in Hawaii, from a region which was formerly among the least organized in the United States to one which is now among the most highly organized, has also borne unsuspected consequences in terms of a greater disposition to give free expression to any irritations on the part of the workers. Insofar as the workers have been chiefly of the immigrant races and their grievances have been directed largely toward the large haole employers, this freer expression has seemed to carry a racial animus. The more outspoken manifestations of resentments and irritations, particularly toward the haoles since World War II, far from reflecting an intensification of racial feelings, actually testifies to the removal of restraints and a more normal inter-change across race lines. Where once the haole, especially on the plantations, lived in a world somewhat apart from the non-haole workers and thereby protected from their privately held resentments, he is now within easier range of normal human intercourse, critical as well as friendly.

RACE AND OPPORTUNITY IN HAWAII [5]

Like most of the other island areas of the Pacific which have experienced the penetration of Western commerce and trading practices, in Hawaii the positions of power and of substantial re-

[5] From "Hawaii in the Race Relations Continuum of the Pacific," by Andrew W. Lind, senior professor of sociology, University of Hawaii. *Social Process.* 25:12-14. '61-'62. Reprinted by permission.

wards tended first to be concentrated wholly in the hands of promoters from Europe and America. Only after some years of apprenticeship under the new regime could persons of ethnic groups previously lacking such a tradition be expected to occupy positions of prestige and influence. There is, however, considerable variation among regions in the readiness with which the less privileged groups are given access to the means of qualifying for the preferred positions. In this latter respect, owing to . . . [special] circumstances . . . Hawaii has been better situated than any of the other island areas to afford an equal opportunity to all of its various ethnic groups. By 1950, for example, the earlier disabilities of the immigrant labor groups had been so far overcome as to place the Chinese, most of whose parents or grandparents arrived in Hawaii a generation or two earlier as lowly plantation laborers, in a higher average position with respect to annual income than any other ethnic group. Moreover, in a substantial number of the preferred occupations, the men and women of Oriental ancestry by 1950 had clearly outstripped their earlier mentors of Caucasian ancestry. At the same time we must recognize that not all of the immigrant groups have availed themselves of the opportunities for economic and social advancement to the same degree and that the more recently arrived immigrant groups necessarily operate at a disadvantage as compared to the earlier arrivals.

One of the further significant developments of the past decade, reflecting the changing commercial and business relationships among the various ethnic groups of Hawaii, has been the acceptance of non-Caucasians as officials and directors of the larger and once sacrosanct corporations of the Big Five, Hawaii's interlocking organization of major economic enterprises. The participation of Island-born men of Oriental ancestry in the direction of the plantations on which their fathers served as unskilled laborers a generation ago still seems incredible to observers of the racial scene in most other areas of the Pacific. Increasingly during the past decade the promoters of new business and industrial enterprises expanding from continental United States have found it advantageous to seek out competent young men of Oriental ancestry for key positions, recognizing that their clientele is drawn from a population which is more than half of Oriental ancestry.

As recently as twenty years ago, in the competition between two men of equal technical training for a preferred business position, one of Oriental ancestry and the other a Caucasian, the latter commonly would enjoy the advantage. Today that situation is frequently, although by no means always, reversed, and if anyone, it is the Caucasian rather than the Oriental who complains of being discriminated against.

Similarly, the political control of Hawaii has progressively lost the racial coloration it possessed a half century ago when a small minority of Hawaiian and Caucasian elite dominated the scene. Notably since World War II, the ethnic composition of both the elected and appointed officials in the government of the Islands has tended more and more to approximate that of the entire population of Hawaii, although here also the groups with the least experience or inclination to engage in politics are still underrepresented but not unrepresented. By way of summary and without going into detail, it can be accurately stated that in no other Pacific islands have any immigrant labor groups advanced in economic and social status so rapidly and so far within a comparable period of time.

The most obvious index of a diminishing concern for race and of an equalitarian relationship across ethnic lines is, of course, that of interracial marriage and here also Hawaii has progressed further along the continuum than any of its Pacific island neighbors, for which accurate records are available. Some appreciation of the degree to which this process has already occurred and of its inevitable impact upon the future quality of Hawaii's population and social structure may be derived from the fact that somewhat more than a third of all marriages occur across ethnic lines and a slightly lower ratio of all children born in Hawaii are of mixed ethnic ancestry. As a consequence, it becomes only a question of time—certainly less than another generation—before Hawaii's population will have become so extensively interbred as to make the retention of the present system of racial categories a useless pretense. In most other island areas of the Pacific this same process is also taking place, but at a much slower pace, judging by such data as are available.

III. THE POLITICAL MEANING OF STATEHOOD

EDITOR'S INTRODUCTION

To examine the government of Alaska and Hawaii is to be impressed, once again, with the similarities between these totally different pieces of earth. It would, of course, be expected that new states, in drafting their constitutions, should choose the best from the experience of the forty-eight that came before. Happily, such is the case. Alaska and Hawaii have modeled themselves after the best—notably the much praised state constitutions of New Jersey and Missouri. The constitutions of the new states are both about 10,000 words in length. They are both "progressive" in their concern for safeguarding human rights and liberties. And they both feature a strong executive, investing their governors with the opportunity for imaginative and dynamic rule.

Yet as states their political tests are just beginning. Can Alaska afford statehood? Can she bear the costs of self-government in her vast expanse of territory? Can Hawaii, with its simplified yet highly centralized tradition of government, effectively and fairly administer the realm of her differing peoples and interests?

There is an old tradition in American government which holds that the government which is closest to the people is the best. Such a consideration played an important role in the campaign for statehood in both Alaska and Hawaii. Whatever the costs and risks might be, the people of the new states, in overwhelming numbers, were determined to assume for themselves the burdens and responsibilities that the American Federal system reserves to the states of the Union. Now that those burdens and responsibilities are theirs, the people of Alaska and Hawaii may be older and wiser, but they do not as yet seem to be any sadder. For balanced against the burdens of statehood have come new opportunities for action, not only at the state level, where capable, energetic men are at the helm, but at the Federal level, too, where Alaska and Hawaii now each have two senators and one representative to press their interests and causes.

The first two articles in this section deal with government in Alaska, the last three with government in Hawaii. In the first, Alaska's constitution, devised in an academic atmosphere before statehood—and its resulting political pressures—was actually won, is outlined and analyzed. In the second article Alaska's Senator Ernest Gruening explains and enumerates some of the political benefits that have come to Alaska after four years as a state.

In the fourth article Hawaii's constitution, with its strong executive and its centralized structure, is analyzed by two leading political scientists. Next a specialist in American government for the Library of Congress examines the centralized nature of Hawaiian rule and the problems it may involve. Finally, in the last article, a journalist describes some of the advantages of Hawaii's political system in relation to that state's economy.

HOW ALASKA IS GOVERNED [1]

Alaska's new state constitution according to House Report No. 624 of June 25, 1957, which accompanied the Act of Admission of July 7, 1958, has been declared by political scientists and public administrators "to be one of the finest ever prepared." This modern constitution was found by Congress "to be republican in form and in conformity with the Constitution of the United States and the principles of the Declaration of Independence, and is hereby accepted, ratified, and confirmed."

Perhaps the outstanding characteristic of Alaska's up-to-date constitution is its provision for an extremely strong executive branch of government.

Deeply sensitive of their lack of home rule and of their self-labeled status as "second class citizens," the sturdy frontier people of the new state made sure that residual and active sovereign power rested with themselves, exercisable through their governor in whom they vested great power. In Alaska's state government

[1] From "The Forty-ninth State Sets an Example," by John S. Hellenthal, a member of the Alaska bar practicing in Anchorage, and a member of Alaska's constitutional convention. *American Bar Association Journal.* 44:1147-50. D. '58. Reprinted by permission.

there will be no buck-passing or shirking of responsibility by the governor. . . .

In November of 1955, fifty-five delegates met for seventy-five days at the University of Alaska at College, near Fairbanks, Alaska, and drafted the constitution. The voters of Alaska approved it on April 24, 1956, by better than a two-to-one majority. . . .

Possibly it was fortuitous that at the time the delegates met, congressional approval of statehood seemed very remote. Had the delegates met after passage of the Act of Congress they would undoubtedly have been motivated by political considerations to a greater degree. As it occurred, however, the delegates were able to deliberate in a relatively pure academic atmosphere. . . .

Why is Alaska's constitution regarded as one of the finest?

The basic structure of the new constitution follows the government of typical American states; there are many important features based upon past experience of the forty-eight states.

Judicial System

The Council of State Governments asserts "the judicial article embodies many of the concepts long advocated for good court administration." Some of these are:

(a) The progressive features of the Missouri, California, New Jersey and American Bar Association plans for selecting judges;

(b) The supreme court will make the rules for all the courts, subject to the authority of the legislature by two-thirds vote to amend the rules of practice and procedure;

(c) The chief justice of the supreme court, with an administrative director serving at his pleasure, will administer the entire unified judicial system;

(d) The governor will appoint the judges from names submitted by a seven-man judicial council consisting of three lay members appointed by him, three lawyer members named by Alaska's integrated bar, and the chief justice;

(e) Judges desiring to remain in office, must, three years after their initial appointment, submit their names to the voters of their jurisdiction for approval or rejection; thereafter, superior court judges must do so every six years and supreme court justices every ten years.

Dr. Sheldon Elliott, of New York University Law School, Director of the Institute of Judicial Administration, New York, and a member of the House of Delegates of the American Bar Association, who had assisted New Jersey in its constitutional revision, helped in the drafting of the provisions relating to the judicial branch. The Alaska integrated bar approved the draft and offered many practical suggestions.

It is noteworthy that Alaska's method of judicial selection, patterned after the Missouri plan, met with little or no objection from the bar or the lay public. Under territorial government, Alaska's district judges were appointed for terms of four years by the President, often being chosen from nonresidents. One would excuse long-suffering Alaskans, crying for full local government, had they vigorously opposed any nonelective plan.

A Strong Executive Branch

Perhaps none of the states possesses a stronger executive branch than the Alaska state constitution provides. There are no other independently elected officers, and the governor of Alaska will be held wholly responsible for the conduct of state administration during his four-year term.

Unhappy territorial experiences, resulting from the fact that the smallest details of government were administered by absentee bureaucrats in Washington, undoubtedly influenced this Hamiltonian swing of the pendulum. A strong executive may be the trend in modern state government, as evidenced by the 1947 New Jersey constitution, which creates an executive department very similar to Alaska's.

Unique features of constitutional provisions relating to the executive portion of the state government are:

(a) The secretary of state succeeds to the governor's office in case of vacancy and is nominated at the primary election like other candidates. At the general election, however, a vote for the governor is considered a vote for the secretary of state of the same party running jointly with him. This insures that both governor and secretary of state will be of the same party. At Alaska's primary of August 26, 1958, there was some criticism of this innovation because of the possibility that successful candidates for governor and secretary, though of the same party, might be of very divergent political philosophies. Some believe the constitution will ultimately be amended to provide that the governor shall appoint the secretary of state.

(b) Executive departments are limited to twenty, in order to avoid waste, duplication, and an executive hedgerow. New Jersey's 1947 constitution contains a similar provision.

(c) The governor, subject to being overruled by the legislature, can reorganize departments and transfer functions among them.

(d) Individuals appointed (and removable) by the governor, but confirmed by the legislature, will head principal departments. Boards or commissions may head departments, if the legislature so provides, but their principal executive officer must be approved by the governor although the board may be authorized by the legislature to appoint him.

A Truly Representative Legislature

Territorial legislatures were not representative of the people and of the diverse areas of Alaska, with the result that relatively uninhabited regions exercised disproportionate power and frequently enabled a determined minority to throttle desirable legislation.

The membership of the legislature consisting of twenty senators and forty representatives was carefully apportioned in both houses according to population and geography, with emphasis upon area in the Senate and upon population in the House. Small House and Senate districts assure that the less populated communities as well as the large cities are represented.

Some modern and progressive features of the article dealing with the legislature are:

(a) Automatic reapportionment every ten years by the governor acting on the advice of an independent board.

(b) Annual legislative meetings of unspecified length.

(c) Annual salaries for legislators.

(d) Veto or reduction of items in appropriation bills is possible. A three-fourths or two-thirds vote of the legislature, meeting in joint session, depending on whether a revenue and appropriation measure or other bill is involved, is required to override a governor's veto.

(e) It is mandatory that a legislative council be established to meet between legislative sessions.

(f) A constitutional provision requires legislative regulation of the practice of lobbying.

Many Modern Constitutional Provisions

Voting age lowered. Nineteen-year-olds are permitted to vote. High school trained students with elementary civics and government fresh in mind should be well suited to enjoy the full rights of their citizenship. Many believe that youthful voting will tend to curb delinquency problems by instilling a sense of responsibility following high school, rather than requiring young men and women to mark time until they are twenty-one years of age.

Up-to-date declaration of rights. Alaska's constitution accents human rights that have been stressed in current times. Thus— "No person is to be denied the enjoyment of any civil or political right because of race, color, creed or national origin," and "the right of all persons to fair and just treatment in the course of legislative and executive investigations shall not be infringed."

Martial law. The martial law provision is unique, namely "martial law shall not continue for longer than twenty days without the approval of a majority of the members of the legislature in joint session."

Finance. Earmarked funds are done away with, rigid tax and debt limits are abolished. No state debt for capital improvements can be contracted without approval by the state electorate. The governor must submit to the legislature a detailed annual budget; the legislature shall appoint an auditor to conduct legislatively prescribed postaudits.

Merit system. The legislature must establish a system under which the merit principle will govern the employment of persons by the state.

New approach to local government. Evils of county governments with unchangeable boundaries, many elected officials, and overlapping tax authority are sought to be avoided by the creation of "borough" governments corresponding to counties, and to exist together with city governments as the only two classes of local government. Organized boroughs will be created as needed. Provision for home rule in cities and boroughs is made. Service areas to provide special and limited services in organized and unorganized boroughs may be established. The constitution is sufficiently elastic to permit retention of traditional forms of local government, should the legislature so desire; cities, however, must be extended maximum home rule by virtue of a self-executing provision of the constitution.

This approach is largely without precedent. The aim is desirable "to provide for maximum local self-government with a minimum of local government units, and to prevent duplication of tax-levying jurisdictions." Enlightened, inspired and unselfish legislation will be needed to accomplish this end within the constitutional framework.

Natural resources. Provisions dealing with the abundant natural resources of the new state are advanced and sound. Maximum use is balanced with continued availability for future generations. Disposals of rights in state lands must be preceded by public notice. Mining laws shall follow the pattern of Federal laws and shall be based upon discovery and appropriation of mineral resources.

Where the forty-eight states struggled to protect their resources after statehood, Alaska made provision for their protection prior to admission.

Amendments. Amendments to the new constitution can be proposed by a two-thirds vote of each house of the legislature to be effective after approval of the proposed amendment by a majority of the votes cast at the next state-wide election.

Constitutional convention. Provision is made for a constitutional convention every ten years. After a period of ten years passes without a constitutional convention having been held, the matter of whether or not such a convention shall be held must be placed before the voters; if the majority votes in the affirmative, a convention is held. The constitution drawn at this convention must be ratified by the people. Legislative inaction cannot hamstring constitutional reform.

Initiative—Referendum. The constitution provides for both initiative and referendum.

Many Proposals Rejected After Debate

Specifically rejected constitutional proposals were those for a unicameral legislature; elective attorney general, treasurer and other state officials; provision for "complete" separation of church and state; elected judges; independent boards and agencies; biennial meetings of the legislature; permitting legislators to be elected from districts other than their district of residence, as in England; overriding veto by vote of each house, rather than at joint session; prohibition against payment of public funds for "indirect" benefit of religious or private schools.

Some proposals were rejected as being legislative in nature, and many others on more general grounds, e.g. right-to-work provisions; prohibitions against gambling, and wiretapping or eavesdropping.

Lessons Learned at Constitutional Convention

Many states presently seek constitutional revision; many need a thoroughgoing revamping of their outdated constitutions. The recent experience of Alaska can benefit both groups.

At their convention Alaska's constitutional delegates discovered:

(a) Fifty or sixty delegates can adequately handle the problem of constitutional revision at a unicameral meeting.

(b) Committees should be established at the outset. Alaska created these: Judiciary, Legislative, Executive, Natural Resources, Local Government, Apportionment and Suffrage, Bill of Rights, Finance, Administrative, and Style and Drafting. The committees should hold hearings and report their conclusions in the form of drafts of constitutional articles to the convention floor.

(c) The meeting should be limited in duration. Ninety days is sufficient time.

(d) A handbook should be prepared well in advance, contrasting and comparing constitutional provisions of the forty-nine states on various subjects.

(e) Full use should be made of professional bodies and of individuals devoted to study of political science.

(f) The session should recess for about thirty days at the half-way point to hold public hearings and to explore popular sentiment.

(g) The question of unicameralism should be buried at the outset of the session.

(h) Certain illustrative committee hearings should be televised, as Alaska did, to generate the spirit of constitutional reform.

(i) A secluded university affords ideal environment and atmosphere for constitutional deliberation.

During the more than two years following the adoption of Alaska's constitution by its people and the approval of the Act of Admission, no serious criticism of the constitution has been made by the many powerful foes of Alaska statehood, either during the violent debates in Alaska prior to the elections of April 1956 and August 1958, or during the congressional debates on statehood in 1957 and 1958. The constitution withstood the test of debate. Whether or not a modern and efficient state will result must be determined in ensuing years by the statesmanship of the legislators and their success in carrying out the intent of the constitution framers.

ALASKA'S ACHIEVEMENTS UNDER STATEHOOD [2]

Nearly four years as a state have brought to Alaska tangible results not possible during the long years the forty-ninth state was a territory.

Alaska entered the Union on a footing politically equal to its sister states but economically neglected through years of territorial rule. Efforts during both the Eighty-sixth and Eighty-seventh Congresses were necessarily directed toward correcting this economic inequality.

Federal Government departments and agencies, informed and prodded for the first time by elected, voting congressional representatives of the state of Alaska, have increased their programing for the state by millions of dollars.

Part of the task of the Alaska congressional delegation during these years has been to make certain that existing and proposed Federal programs were tailored to suit Alaska's special needs.

Another part of the task has been to take decisive action with Federal agencies to protect Alaska's interests against encroachment, such as our protests against Russian and Japanese fishing intrusions.

[2] From "Four Years of Unprecedented Achievement—the Greatest Progress in Alaskan History"; extension of remarks in the United States Senate by Senator Ernest Gruening (Democrat, Alaska), October 13, 1962. *Congressional Record*. 108:A7806-12. O. 19, '62.

Many advances have been made in the economic development of Alaska, some of major significance to the future of our state, others of less import but significant nevertheless in clearing away obstructions which would hinder future growth.

A Highway Program for Alaska

One of the most important bills for Alaska approved by the Eighty-seventh Congress is Senate Joint Resolution 137, now a part of the Federal Aid Highway Act which takes the important long-awaited first step toward positive planning and development of a road system within our state. . . .

During my testimony on behalf of Senate Joint Resolution 137 I compared the cost of visits to three large cities in three states by a family of four, mother, father, and two children, ages 10 and 14. The states compared were Oklahoma, Michigan, and Alaska. The Oklahomans followed roads to and from Beaver City to Oklahoma City, a distance of 450 miles and the gasoline cost was $7.50. The Michiganites made a round trip from Alpena to Detroit, 464 miles, for the same amount. The Alaskans' round trip to Anchorage and back to Bethel cost $462 via air highway—since no road exists.

Two New Hydroelectric Projects for Alaska

The Eighty-seventh Congress has shown its interest in the development of Alaska's great natural resources by its authorization of the construction of two new hydroelectric power projects:

First. The Crater-Long Lakes division of the Snettisham project near Juneau.

Second. The Bradley Lake project on the Kenai Peninsula. . . .

Advancement for Rampart

When the Development & Resources Corporation of New York presented its final report on the proposed Rampart [Dam] project to the Corps of Engineers it said the market for power from the project would create a busy and prosperous Alaska which would "almost certainly become a substantial producer of electric-furnace pig iron and steel, ferroalloys, copper, magnesium, chlorine and caustic soda, calcium carbide, abrasives, nitrogen, phosphorous titanium and other products." The study is part of intensive investigations now under way on the proposed project for a $1⅓ billion dam which will have installed capacity of approximately 5 million kilowatts and will produce energy at a cost of 2 mills at the bus-bar and not to exceed 3 mills per kilowatt-hour at tidewater.

Rampart Dam would be the biggest power producer in the free world. Better than $900,000 will have been used for Rampart project studies by the close of fiscal year 1963 on June 30, 1962. The total estimated Federal cost of the survey is $1.3 million which the Alaska congressional delegation hopes can be completed in fiscal year 1964. . . .

The Development & Resources report makes clear that even the tremendous power to be generated by Rampart will be insufficient for Alaska's needs and that a whole Yukon River development will be required. In pursuance of this conclusion, I requested and obtained authorization for the Corps of Engineers to investigate the Woodchopper site upstream from Rampart. . . .

Area Redevelopment Act

How to relieve the problem of chronic unemployment which affected many areas of the nation was a major item confronting members of the Eighty-seventh Congress. Unemployment stood at more than 5 million workers. In Alaska the percentage of unemployed was high in most parts of the state. . . .

The Area Redevelopment Act became Public Law 87-27 on May 1, 1961. The act is administered through the Area Redevelopment Administration in the United States Department of Commerce. ARA brought together a number of Federal Government departments and agencies with resources which could be focused on the problem of helping create new jobs. It helps areas diversify and rebuild their economic base. It creates new employment opportunities through its positive approach, and astute administration of the program has furthered its development.

As this report was being prepared, nine ARA projects, with a monetary value of $1,580,962, have been approved for Alaska. The four training programs and the one public facilities loan will provide jobs for 595 persons, and will help correct the situation which existed early in January 1961, when the state unemployment rate was 18.7 per cent. . . .

Alaska's interest in the ARA program has drawn commendation by ARA spokesmen. The forty-ninth state is one of two in the Union to present an over-all economic development program. This was done in September of 1962 and the program is now under consideration. . . .

Manpower Development and Training Act of 1962

With rapid technological changes occurring in industry, the needs of labor change and the skills become outmoded. The Manpower Development and Training Act provides a positive approach for meeting this challenge. . . .

The program is suited to Alaska and its training and employment needs. . . . Eighty-five per cent of the Alaska labor needs are in the nonindustrial areas and people must be trained to fill the needs of the labor market. Such needs include the development of the oil industry, the expansion of the highway program and the extension of the agriculture potential.

Telephone and Air Transportation Taxes

Alaskans, dependent on air transportation for much of their travel, will benefit from congressional action which I supported. The transportation tax on air travel drops from 10 to 5 per cent on November 15, 1962. The air transportation tax ends June 30, 1963. . . .

The tax on long distance telephone calls is now on a year-to-year extension basis. The current extension expires June 30, 1963. The tax on local calls was removed July 1, 1960.

HOW HAWAII IS GOVERNED [3]

The admission of a state to the Union is a matter of such rarity that the occasion always arouses real interest as to the nature and provisions of the constitution of the new arrival.

[3] From "The Hawaiian Constitution: A Structure for Good Government," by Paul C. Bartholomew, professor of political science, University of Notre Dame, and Robert M. Kamins, professor of economics, University of Hawaii. American Bar Association Journal. 45:1145-8+. N. '59. Reprinted by permission.

The addition of Hawaii to round out our half hundred states is no exception, even though the constitution has actually been in existence since 1950. . . .

The people of Hawaii had not waited for Congress to pass an enabling act before proceeding to the framing of a constitution for the proposed state. In 1950 a convention of elected delegates met in Honolulu and proceeded to draw up a constitution which was signed at Iolani Palace on July 22. This was submitted to the voters of Hawaii and approved by a three-to-one majority on November 7, 1950. The action of Congress in adopting the Statehood Act of 1959 involved approval of this constitution. . . .

Hawaii's State Constitution

All state constitutions have some statement of the rights of persons under the state's jurisdiction. In the Hawaiian constitution this statement (Article I) is called the "Bill of Rights," and it generally follows the Bill of Rights of the Federal Constitution. Here is set forth a recognition of popular sovereignty, the equality of men and their mutual rights and duties. Specific guarantees include life, liberty, the pursuit of happiness, property, religion, speech, press, assembly, petition, due process, grand jury, trial by jury in both civil and criminal cases, proper accusation of crime, witnesses, counsel, habeas corpus, the subordination of the military to civil power, and the right to bear arms through a militia. There are specific guarantees against unreasonable search and seizure, double jeopardy, self-incrimination, excessive bail or fines, cruel or unusual punishment, quartering of soldiers or militiamen and imprisonment for debt. There is a final statement to take care of the "principle of exclusion" that "the enumeration of rights and privileges shall not be construed to impair or deny others retained by the people."

These are the basic rights that are found in all state constitutions. However, other states have additional basic guarantees covering the right of privacy, the location of the power to suspend laws, the prohibition of *ex post facto* laws and the outlawing of slavery. On the other hand there are a number of specific guarantees in the Hawaiian constitution that are not included in all of the other state constitutions, such as freedom of the press. The influence of the Federal constitutional model is here obvious.

Article II concerns suffrage and elections. Twenty years is set as the minimum age for voting. This contrasts with Alaska's nineteen years and the eighteen-year minimum of Georgia and Kentucky. All other states have a twenty-one-year limit. One year is set as the period of legal residence in Hawaii. In other states, this ranges from six months to two years. United States citizenship, registration, and a literacy test of ability to speak, read and write English or Hawaiian are added voting qualifications. The first of these is found in all states while registration and a literacy test are qualifications in about a third of the states.

The date of general elections follows the pattern of all of the other states except Alaska—the Tuesday after the first Monday in November of even-numbered years. The legislature is specifically empowered to prescribe methods of voting, including absentee voting, with the provision that voting is to be secret. The legislature is also charged with determining the procedure for deciding disputed elections but this determination is to be in a court of competent jurisdiction. As is common in other states, persons of unsound mind or those convicted of a felony are barred from voting unless pardoned and restored to their civil rights.

The Legislature

Article III is the legislative article. The Legislature (the collective name for the two houses) is to consist of a Senate of twenty-five members and a House of Representatives of fifty-one members. Only Delaware and Nevada have a smaller total number of legislators except, of course, Nebraska's single house of forty-three. One might have expected that the example set by the Nebraska unicameral experiment would have been followed, but Nebraska remains the only state with a one-house legislature. Members of the Senate and the House are to be elected from districts. Six senatorial districts are set by the constitution, together with the number of senators to be elected from each. The eighteen representative districts and the number of members to be chosen from each are temporarily set in the constitution. Reapportionment every ten years is to be by the governor by the method of equal proportion—the mathematical formula used in the apportionment of the lower house of Congress—among four basic areas in the Islands. Apportionment is to be based on the number of voters registered at the last preceding general election.

This provision requiring the governor to reapportion is unique among the states. In most states this is an exclusive power of the legislature, but California, Illinois, Michigan, Oregon, South Dakota, Texas and Washington provide alternative procedures in case the legislature neglects to reapportion. Arizona, Arkansas, Missouri and Ohio reapportion by means of boards, of which the governor is a member in Arkansas and Ohio, but only in Hawaii is the governor himself authorized to perform the function exclusively. The Hawaiian supreme court is empowered to require "by mandamus or otherwise" that the governor perform this duty, if he fails to do it, or to correct errors he may have made in the process.

Terms of representatives and senators are two and four years respectively, which is the arrangement in thirty states including Alaska. There is provision for overlapping terms with half of the Senate membership chosen at each succeeding election. The legislature is authorized to provide for the filling of vacancies and to set the compensation of members. Qualifications for membership include an age minimum of twenty-five years for the House and thirty for the Senate, residence in the state for at least three years, and the fulfillment of all requirements for voting in the district from which the candidate seeks to be elected. The usual legislative immunities are extended to members.

Sessions of the legislature are to be held annually, those in the odd-numbered years are to be known as "general sessions" and those in the even-numbered years are to be known as "budget sessions." At the latter the only business eligible for consideration and enactment is to be the following: revenue bills, appropriation bills, emergency measures (requiring a two-thirds vote of all members of each house), bills calling elections, bills proposing constitutional amendments, and measures relating to the impeachment or removal of officers.

General sessions are to be limited to sixty days and budget sessions to thirty days. The governor may call special sessions which are to be limited to thirty days. All of these periods exclude Sundays and holidays. Regular sessions are set for the third Wednesday in February. Only Alabama (May), Florida (April) and Louisiana (May) have later meeting dates. Almost all other state legislatures meet in January. Until changed by law, the constitution provides that legislative salaries are to be $2,500 per each general session, $1,500 per each budget session and $750 per each special session.

Unusual provisions governing legislative procedure include the discharge of a committee from further consideration of a bill twenty days after that bill has been referred to the committee. Such recall of a bill is to be by a two-thirds vote of the entire membership of that house. The vote on the final passage of a bill in all cases is to be by a majority of the total membership of that house and is to be by roll call.

The governor has the item veto as applied to appropriation bills, as is true in most states. He has ten days to consider bills normally, Sundays and holidays excluded. Only Georgia and Alaska permit a longer period of consideration. The Hawaii constitution tries to avoid pocket vetoes. Borrowing an innovation from New Jersey's 1947 constitution, Hawaii's new basic law authorizes each legislature to convene on the forty-fifth day after its adjournment *sine die* for the sole purpose of considering bills vetoed by the governor. Vetoes can be overridden only by vote of two thirds of the full membership of each house. However, if the legislature fails to convene after its ordinary session, bills returned by the governor do not become law.

Impeachment procedure is entirely normal by comparison with other states. Charges are to be brought in the House of Representatives and trial is to be in the Senate with a two-thirds vote of the members of the Senate required for conviction.

The Governor

Article IV is the executive article. The governor is chosen by plurality vote. This is true of all states except Georgia, Maine, Vermont and Mississippi, where a majority vote is required. In these states, if no candidate receives a majority of the votes, either the two houses in joint session (Georgia and Vermont) or the lower house of the legislature (Maine and Mississippi) makes the selection.

The term of office of the governor of Hawaii is set at four years, as in thirty states, including Alaska. There is no limit on the number of consecutive terms he may serve as there is in twenty-three other states, also including Alaska. Qualifications include a minimum age of thirty-five years, United States citizenship for twenty years and qualifying as a voter. The governor is ineligible for any other state or Federal office during his term. The constitution provides that his annual salary shall be at least $18,000. The 1959 territorial legislature increased it to $25,000 per annum.

As in all but eleven states, there is a lieutenant governor. He is chosen at the same time, in the same manner, with the same qualifications, and for the same term as the governor, but may be of the opposite political party. . . .

The powers of the governor are of the usual sort found in the other states—to faithfully execute the laws, to serve as commander-in-chief of "the armed forces of the state," to recommend measures to the legislature, and to grant reprieves, commutations and pardons. One unusual feature is the authorization to the governor to appoint an administrative director "to serve at his pleasure." No duties are specified for this office, although this may develop somewhat along the lines of the chief administrative officer (CAO) being established in more and more cities. No other state appears to have an officer comparable to Hawaii's administrative director. . . .

Administrative departments are to be established by law but are limited to twenty "principal" departments. The head of each department is to be appointed by the governor with the consent of the Senate and subject to removal by the same procedure. . . .

An unusual feature of this constitution (and that of Alaska also) is limiting the number of elective executive offices to those of the governor and lieutenant governor. Most state constitutions "freeze" a large number of offices such as auditor, treasurer, attorney general, and superintendent of public instruction in the constitution, all to be chosen by popular vote. This reduces the power of both the legislature and the governor in those states, particularly the governor, and opens the way for intra-administrative feuding. This has been avoided by the framers of the Hawaiian constitution.

The Judiciary

The last of the "big three" divisions of governmental power, the judiciary, is established by Article V. A supreme court and circuit courts are established by the constitution, but the creation of inferior courts is left for the legislature. (There are now twenty-nine district magistrates' courts). The Supreme Court is to consist of five justices including the chief justice. These are to be named by the governor and Senate for seven-year terms. All judges must have been admitted to the bar of the Hawaiian Supreme Court for at least ten years prior to appointment. Mandatory retirement is set at seventy years of age. Removal of judges is to be by a two-thirds vote of the membership of each house of the legislature sitting in joint session. Provision is made for retirement of a judge for incapacity. This is to be done by the governor upon the recommendation of an investigatory board....

It is regrettable that the framers of the Hawaiian constitution did not adopt some variation of the plan used in California and Missouri for the choice of judges, as did Alaska. [See the first article in this section, above.] However, it is good that the example of the thirty-six states that use popular election for the choice of judges was not followed.

Taxation and Finance

Artice VI deals with taxation and finance. There is to be no discriminatory taxation of property owned by citizens of the United States who reside outside the state. All bonds and other instruments of indebtedness of a political subdivision must be authorized by its governing body. The state debt limit is set at an absolute $60 million. More than half of the fifty states have some fixed sum limitation on outstanding unpaid indebtedness. In Hawaii this debt limit can be exceeded when authorized by a two-thirds vote of the total membership of each house of the legislature. However, even with such authorization, the amount of general obligation bonds outstanding cannot exceed a sum equal to 15 per cent of the total assessed valuation of real property in the state. "Instruments of indebtedness" issued for certain specified purposes, and to meet emergencies caused by disaster or act of God, may be issued without regard to the debt limit. The same is true if these instruments of indebtedness are issued in anticipation of revenue collections or to meet "casual deficits or failures of revenue" and are payable within one year. . . .

The executive type of budget is provided. All but six states use this arrangement which establishes the governor as the budget-making authority. He is further given the duty of submitting bills simultaneously with the budget to provide for any added revenues or borrowing that may be necessary to meet the proposed expenditures. This is a practical attempt to eliminate unbalanced budgets. The legislature is to appoint an auditor by majority vote of the members of the legislature in joint session. The auditor has the duty to post-audit and to report to the governor and the legislature.

Local Government

Article VII is the local government article. The legislature is required to create counties as the major political subdivision of the state and may establish other subdivisions. This is the usual pattern among the various states. Only Louisiana with parishes and Alaska with boroughs depart from this pattern. Each sub-division is granted self-government, but this is potentially nulli-fied by the further provision that the exercise of this self-govern-ment is to be done "within such limits and under such procedures as may be prescribed by law."

Article VIII makes it the obligation of the legislature to provide for: (1) the protection and promotion of the public health, (2) the treatment, rehabilitation and care of mentally and physically handicapped persons, (3) assistance for persons unable to live in a manner compatible with decency and health, (4) slum clearance and low income housing, and (5) the conservation of natural beauty spots as well as those of historic or cultural interest.

Article IX directs the establishment of a public school system free from sectarian control as well as a university (the University of Hawaii), libraries, and other institutions. Segregation on the basis of race, religion or ancestry is specifically forbidden. The wall of separation between church and state in this area is guaranteed by the proviso that public funds shall not be used "for the support or benefit of any sectarian or private educational institution." . . .

Natural Resources

Article X is concerned with the conservation of natural resources. The legislature is ordered to vest the powers of management and disposition of these natural resources—agricultural, fish, mineral, forest, water, land, game, and others—in one or more executive boards or commissions. All fisheries of the sea waters are to be free to the public, subject to vested rights. Any possibility of preferential treatment for private interests with respect to natural resources is guarded against by the requirement that the state power over public lands is to be exercised only by general laws except where public agencies are involved. Further, the public lands are to be used for the development of farm and home ownership on as widespread a basis as possible. This last provision reflects the historic background of landownership in the Islands where leaseholding arrangements have been prevalent and (on Oahu) land available for ownership in fee has been in chronically short supply.

The following Article (XI) continues the consideration of home lands by adopting as a law of the state the Federal Hawaiian Homes Commission Act of 1920. The treatment of the Hawaiian Homes Commission Act (under which residential and homesteading properties are supplied at an annual rental of one dollar to persons of at least half-Polynesian ancestry) comprises a constitutional anomaly. The act admitting Hawaii to the Union provides that those sections of the Hawaiian Homes Commission Act which relate to its administration can be amended in the state constitution or by statute, but that other sections, including those dealing with funds, cannot be amended without the consent of the United States. No parallel restriction upon the self-government of an American state appears to have been imposed by Congress, and in the light of the determination of previous similar, but different, restrictions, the provision may be legally vulnerable.

Miscellaneous Provisions

Article XII guarantees to employees in private enterprise the right to organize and to bargain collectively. Those in public employment are extended the right to organize and to present to the government their grievances and proposals.

The boundaries, the capital (Honolulu), and the state flag (the Hawaiian flag, modeled after the British) are established in Article XIII.

Article XIV contains general and miscellaneous provisions, some of which are unusual. The merit principle is adopted for public employment subject to law. Any public employees' retirement system is to be a contractual relationship not subject to diminution or impairment. Loyalty to Federal and state governments is made a qualification for public employment and a constitutional oath is set forth. The "exclusion principle" is recognized with the provision that "the enumeration in this constitution of specified powers shall not be construed as limitations upon the power of the state to provide for the general welfare of the people."

In Article XV are set forth the details of revision and amendment of the constitution. Two methods are provided, by convention and by the legislature. The periodic submission plan is adopted in the requirement that at least every ten years the question of calling a constitutional convention must be submitted to the electorate. The possibility that the Hawaiian legislature may neglect to do this is guarded against by providing that the lieutenant governor must certify the question of calling a convention if the legislature has failed to do so. The legislature may propose amendments by a two-thirds vote of each house at one session after the governor has received at least a ten-day written notice of the final form of the proposed amendment. Alternatively, amendments can be proposed by a majority vote of each house on the proposal at each of two successive sessions.

Regardless of whether the amendment is proposed by convention or by the legislature, it is then submitted to a vote of the electorate at a general election. The proposition must secure a majority of all of the votes cast on the question and this favorable vote must also constitute at least 35 per cent of the total number of registered voters. . . .

The final article (XVI) is the very necessary but transitory Schedule Article. This contains the details and the step-by-step procedure for putting the constitution into effect. . . .

A "Good Structure"

The Hawaii constitution is brief (11,400 words) and generally incorporates the better constitutional provisions of the other American states. Its drafters, however, did not completely avoid the trap of being overly specific in dealing with quantities. The state debt limit of $60 million, which seemed generous when the constitution was drafted nine years ago, is inadequate to the point of temporarily embarrassing the fiscal operation of the new state. The requirement that the lower house be reapportioned on or before June 1, 1959, proves to be ineffective, because the delay in achieving statehood left Hawaii without a state legislature on that date.

In addition, the Congress placed unusual limitations on Hawaii by requiring, in the act of admission, that basic amendments to the Hawaiian Homes Commission Act be approved by the United States in order to be effective. Despite these difficulties and shortcomings, however, the constitution of the state of Hawaii affords a good structure for the governance of the fiftieth state.

HAWAII'S CENTRALIZED GOVERNMENT [4]

There is abundant evidence that, in the transition from territorial status to statehood, no significant change was made or intended in the design of Hawaiian government. That government was, and still is, characterized by a high degree of centralization, ranking with Delaware, North Carolina, and in some respects, Virginia and West Virginia as among the most highly centralized in the nation. For proof of this, one may turn to a number of sources of information— . . . the state constitution, basic laws on the organizational structure of the state government, and significant comments found in published materials relating to state and local government

The Hawaiian Constitution

. . . In four articles at least, there are provisions bearing upon state-local relations and the problem of centralization. These are

[4] From *Centralization of Government in Hawaii*, Library of Congress Legislative Reference Service study, by W. Brooke Graves, specialist in American government of the Library of Congress. mimeo. Library of Congress. Washington 25, D.C. Mr. 30, '62. p 2-11, 18.

Article VII on local government, and Articles VIII, IX and X which are concerned, respectively, with public health and welfare, education, and conservation and development of resources.

In Article VII, the legislature is directed to create counties and authorized to create other political subdivisions, each of which "shall have and exercise such powers as shall be conferred under general laws." This statement in Section 1 is followed by a section granting home rule powers to political subdivisions "within such limits and under such provisions as may be prescribed by law." The concluding Section 5 provides that "this article shall not limit the power of the legislature to enact laws of statewide concern." There is nothing particularly unusual about these provisions, but there is about Section 3 which reads as follows:

The taxing power shall be reserved to the State except so much thereof as may be delegated by the legislature to the political subdivisions, and the legislature shall have the power to apportion state revenues among the several political subdivisions.

In this, it is obvious that a high degree of state control over what, in many jurisdictions, are regarded as local finances, has been retained by the state.

These provisions on local government take on an added significance when viewed in relation to . . . the historical background. County government was established in Hawaii on January 1, 1906, after an earlier act of 1903 had been declared unconstitutional. . . .

It appears that counties in Hawaii were created in part to satisfy the demands of the Congress at the turn of the century. It is reported that "certain factors in pre-territorial Hawaii prior to the organic act of 1900 indicated a desire for more centralization." Professor [Bruce B.] Mason summarized the situation as follows:

These factors were the physical topography, with the only suitable port being at Honolulu; the plantation system with its private government; the desire to keep control over the multitude of immigrants who came to work on the plantations; the dominance of the haoles (whites of North European origin); and the zeal of missionaries to Christianize the Islands. Added to these factors as the territory developed were Republican control, until challenged by the Democrats in the 1950's, and the disfranchisement of Orientals until 1952.

Therefore, even though counties were created, they remained subservient to the central government to such an extent that Norman Meller characterized the situation in 1958 as follows: "Hawaii . . . presents . . . an extreme of centralized administration probably unequaled in any state in the mainland." [*National Civic Review*. O. '59.]

As Hawaii moved from territorial status to statehood, its constitution and recent history seemed to promise somewhat more county home rule, although the constitution continued the state's control of health, education and welfare. In fact, the constitution is very specific on these matters, such phrases as "The State shall provide for," and "The State shall have power" occurring repeatedly in Articles VIII, IX and X. Article VIII deals with public health and welfare, and specifically covers public health, care of the handicapped, public assistance, slum clearance, rehabilitation and housing, and public sightliness and good order. . . .

At the time of the transition, Professor Meller felt that the counties were at the crossroads. The major functions noted were still territorial functions but the 1957 legislature, controlled by the Democrats, promised more home rule and gave the counties new taxing powers and more freedom from administrative supervision. He regarded it as questionable whether Hawaiians would overturn more than fifty years' experience under centralized administration. Professor Mason thought that he saw in a provision in Article IX, calling for state-wide control over education under a board appointed by the governor from panels submitted by local school advisory councils, a possible clue to the future.

Organizational Structure

The organizational structure of Hawaiian government was largely a result of two influences, territorial experience and the then recent example of success in New Jersey with both constitutional revision and executive reorganization. The territorial experience conditioned the thinking of the constitutional convention, the people, and the legislature in favor of centralization, while the New Jersey experience made clear the methods by which their disposition to establish a strong executive and a highly centralized government could be realized.

Hawaii followed New York and New Jersey, and the Model State Constitution as well, in limiting the number of executive departments to twenty. . . .

While the departmental structure is of interest and pertinent to the present discussion, the guiding principles upon which the nature of the organizational structure was determined are of far greater importance. There are, as the Joint [Legislative Interim] Committee Report [to the Hawaii State Legislature, 1959] observes, "several basic concepts which have been applied and tested over the years among the various national and state governments and which may be profitably used as guides in organizing the Hawaii state government. It is worthy of note that the framers of the Hawaii state constitution have explicitly or implicitly incorporated these concepts in the constitution." The concepts are:

1. That executive authority should be commensurate with responsibility.

2. That all administrative agencies should be consolidated into a small number of departments organized by function.

3. That the lines of authority should be clear.

4. That departments headed by a single executive shall be the general rule.

5. That the responsible line officers shall be given adequate staff to assist them in the performance of their responsibility.

6. That organization is dynamic, and a minimum of obstacles should be placed upon the executive branch in its effort to carry out the public will as expressed in law.

Significant Comment in the Literature on State and Local Government

Because they are illustrative and relate to important governmental functions, comments here will be limited to the schools [and] land use. . . .

Schools. During the past several years, former President James B. Conant of Harvard University has been engaged in a comprehensive study of public elementary and secondary education in the United States. . . . In considering the problem of organization, he discusses the diversity and size of school districts in the American states. Placed ninth in the list of the ten largest school districts, as measured both in terms of total population and public school enrollment, stands the state of Hawaii which Dr. Conant characterizes as "the only truly state system in the nation. In Hawaii [he continues] there are no local districts or local school boards or superintendents; school revenues and expenditures are determined at the state level, as are curriculum matters and the hiring and placement of teachers." . . . One could scarcely wish for any more conclusive evidence of the highly centralized character of public education in Hawaii.

Land use. One of the major problems confronting state governments at the present time involves the relations of the states with their municipalities and metropolitan areas. Among the more serious aspects of this problem is land use—planning and zoning, safeguarding of open spaces, and the control of "urban sprawl." While other states dawdle over this problem, accomplishing little or taking no action at all, while the problem grows steadily worse, Hawaii during the 1961 legislative session took decisive action . . . in this field of activity. The new legislation is designed to prevent urban sprawl, to preserve open spaces and to protect high-value crop lands. No other state has moved . . . so far in the direction of state-wide planning and land use control. And obviously, this represents a high degree of centralization in an area which, in other jurisdictions, appears still to be regarded as very largely a local matter.

The new legislation will be administered by a State Land Use Commission which is authorized to set the boundaries and prescribe the use regulations for three major zoning districts—urban, agricultural and conservation. The districts will include all land in the Islands. Within each district, the counties will continue their normal zoning procedures, limited only by the state-defined zones and their regulations. Subdivisions, apartments, shopping centers, and the like, will be permitted in the urban zone, but will be excluded from the other two districts. The National Municipal League reports that "it is generally believed that state zoning will prove successful in Hawaii, and that the simplified government—only five counties and *a highly centralized* state government—will be an important factor." . . . [Author's italics.]

Hawaiian Government in the Decade of the Sixties

. . . What is the outlook for the next decade? What things can or should be done to maintain a state government that is structurally equipped properly to perform its duties and that, at the same time, will be both responsive to the will of the people and responsible? . . .

In the first place, no drastic or sweeping changes in existing arrangements are required. Both the state constitution and the governmental structure are relatively new. With possibly one exception, the question is, therefore, more one of maintaining what has already been established, and making changes or improvements as need arises, rather than contemplating any far-reaching changes at the present time. . . .

[One] problem to be considered . . . is that of popular control of government. This is always important in a democratic society, but is particularly so in the case of Hawaii because of the highly centralized system of government and the very strong executive branch established there. What Hawaii has done is generally in accord with the ideas that leading students of state government have been advocating for many years.

This system (centralization plus a strong executive) does, however, create problems in the field of popular control, in a state and among a people dedicated to democratic ideals. What steps can or should be taken to insure that this government *does not* get out of hand, that it *does* remain both responsive to the will of the people and responsible to them? . . . Three possible procedures or devices . . . have been or are being used for this purpose in other jurisdictions: (1) state-wide citizen organization, (2) a commissioner of investigations; (3) a joint legislative committee on government operations.

GAINS FROM SIMPLIFIED RULE IN HAWAII [5]

The forty-nine other states have good reason to be envious of the fiftieth state.

Hawaii, in addition to its traditional boasts of unbeatable climate and tourist attractions, also lays claim to the most sim-

[5] From "Hawaii Is Termed Governmental Paradise," by Gene Smith, New York *Times* staff correspondent. New York *Times*. O. 16, '60. p 1+. Copyright by The New York Times. Reprinted by permission.

plified and streamlined governmental and fiscal structure of any of the states.

For example, the state has only two levels of government—the state and . . . [five] counties. And the reorganization of the state government in 1959 reduced to eighteen the number of departments that rule. Prior to that there were 104 departments, boards and commissions.

As Governor William F. Quinn explains it:

The pace of economic change in Hawaii has been so rapid in recent years that any understanding of Hawaii's economy based on knowledge of five or ten years ago is largely outmoded. . . .

Recent developments in Hawaii's state finances should be of real interest to the financial community. . . . I doubt that any state can match Hawaii's record in the last year, which includes a general fund surplus equal to nearly 20 per cent of general fund tax revenues, a modest tax reduction, a significant reduction in the state's general obligation debt of 4½ per cent and a capital improvement program of $16.3 million during the present fiscal year financed on a pay-as-you-go basis.

The transition from territorial status to statehood, according to Governor Quinn, has been accomplished with essentially no disruption of governmental processes. As related to the issuance of bonds, the fiftieth state's financial structure is limited to the state itself and four counties—the city and county of Honolulu, which embraces the island of Oahu; the county of Hawaii, which is limited to that island; Kauai County, and Maui County, which includes that island and Molokai and Lanai. . . . [The fifth county is Kalawao, which comprises the leper settlement on the island of Molokai.—Ed.]

The governor's report noted that "never in Hawaii's history has the state or the counties failed to make full interest and principal payment on their bonded debt when due. Never in history has a payment on an Hawaiian revenue bond been missed."

Commonwealth Services, Inc., engineering and consulting concern, . . . concluded that, while Hawaii ranks fiftieth in seniority among the states, "at no point is it fiftieth by reference to such standard measures of economic growth as total personal income, civilian employment, volume of retail trade, construction put in place, bank deposits or total population."

Fast Growth

In the last five years its rate of growth has been nearly twice that of the forty-eight mainland states as a group. Its growth is about as fast as California's but not quite as fast as Florida's or Arizona's.

Output per farm worker is more than double the United States average and the state ranks seventh in average home consumption of electricity—4,736 kilowatt-hours, or 28 per cent above the national average of 3,707 as of June 30.

The governor's report seeks in the main to dispel the idea that Hawaii is just a land of tourists and pineapples, although tourism brings in more than $100 million a year and pineapples account for an additional $130 million.

The garment industry, best known for aloha shirts and the women's muu muu, add $18 million to the state's economy.

Sugar brings in an additional $130 million and Hawaiians look for great expanson in this field because of the present Cuban situation. The cane sugar yield runs above five tons a year per acre, against two tons in Louisiana and Cuba and four tons in Florida.

Defense Expenditures

Also looming large in the economic picture is the military, whose payrolls and purchases of goods and services top $330 million a year. However, the report warns that "in the Hawaii of 1960 . . . Defense Department expenditures represent less than one quarter of Hawaii's total personal income."

Expansion in the state is concentrated in fields such as steel production, cement plants, oil refining, steel pipe fabrication, plastics, electronics and other modern industries. Big-name mainland companies are stepping into the picture all the time.

The Standard Oil Company of California is opening a new refinery this month. Hawaiian Cement and Permanente Cement started their operations this summer and Hawaiian Western Steel's electric melting and rolling facilities are operating on a regular schedule.

Total private and government construction has risen from $97 million in 1955 to $216 million last year and the estimate for this year is $260 million.

In summary, Governor Quinn's report points out that "no state has so few units of local government . . . with no school districts, no townships, no separate municipalities to levy taxes or incur debt." These are the prime reasons for the state's sound investment and financial progress.

IV. THE ECONOMIC MEANING
OF STATEHOOD

EDITOR'S INTRODUCTION

One immediate result of statehood for Alaska and Hawaii was publicity—front-page headlines across the United States welcoming the new states and congratulating them on their fine qualities. Tourists, and even people with permanent residence in mind, flocked in to see for themselves. The result was an economic boomlet which added to the rosy glow of admission to the United States on equal footing.

Tourism is still a major source of income for the new states, but inevitably it has fallen somewhat from its post-statehood peak. Of the two states, Alaska has the greater economic potential by virtue of its vast size, its untapped resources, and its opportunities for expansion. Hawaii, a crowded if halcyon island paradise, has a vexing land problem which admittedly hampers development goals. Both states are attracting imaginative and ambitious men, however, and as far as both are concerned the future trend should be bracingly upward.

This section contains three articles, two of which examine the economies of Alaska and Hawaii in considerable detail. In the first a financial analyst puts his mind to Alaska's economic outlook and determines that, despite a number of weaknesses, long-range prospects are favorable. The second article, from *U.S. News & World Report,* emphasizes some of the economic difficulties confronting the forty-ninth state three years after admission to the Union. In the last article, a writer for *Fortune* draws a lively and fascinating picture of Hawaii's golden era and of the men and ideas that are shaping its future.

ALASKA'S ECONOMY: A SUMMATION [1]

The future progress of the economy and development of our forty-ninth state is more difficult to chart than that of any other

[1] From "Alaska: The Economic Outlook," by Ivan Bloch, director of a private industrial and economic consulting firm with interests in Alaska. *Financial Analysts Journal.* 16:31-42. Ja.-F. '60. Reprinted by permission.

state of the Union. This vast land area of almost 600,000 square miles, with a present population of 220,000 people (of which 50,000 are military personnel), intrigues the imaginative inquirer but baffles the rational analyst. On the one hand, the lure of the unknown brings visions of vast, untapped resources; on the other, the hard facts of operating life in this last frontier often are discouraging but to the venturesome.

Frontier development, historically, has reflected the same patterns. If the breaching of the West had been left to the arithmetic of its promises, as then visualized by the prudent analyst, one might retrospectively conclude that nothing would have happened: no railroads, no frontier towns, no mineral development, no cutting of timber and plowing of virgin soils. To be sure, the winning of the West—as that yet to be achieved in Alaska—may have been an inefficient process, wasteful of men and capital resources. However, in the balance, the eventual total gains have been immeasurably large.

A realistic, hard-headed appraisal of Alaska's potentials can lead to no assured conclusion of fact. For instance, merely looking at the market potential in terms of less than a quarter of a million population—and that alone—is simple and essentially negative; there are dozens upon dozens of communities in the more developed states which contain that much population within a radius of a very few miles. However, if this population is viewed in terms of its unsatisfied needs for goods and services (relatively isolated from supply by distance and transportation costs), in terms of high standards of living, and in terms of specific and sometimes peculiar needs, the opportunity picture comes into some focus.

As in the fruition of the West, natural resources furnish an important even though not always clearly defined base. Again the pattern for Alaska is repetitive of that historical for the West: early accent on gold and precious metals, leading to exploitation of base metals; opening operations in forests and lands, and drilling of vast areas for oil and gas. However, it is necessary to view Alaska in terms of its peculiarities, and less in terms of example which might be sought elsewhere. For Alaska is unique in spite of rationales to the contrary. If it resembles anything familiar, perhaps the northern tier of the other forty-eight states provides some basis for comparison. Even there, the total picture cannot be assembled from a few similarities.

Alaska's 586,400 square miles (almost 400 million acres, or twice the area of Texas) contain a great variety of climatic and physiographic features which, in some measure, bear upon the nature of development. The Southeastern Panhandle, an archipelago, is mountainous, heavily forested, and has a mild, wet climate. Its tidal sweep, and its fjords have supported fisheries for salmon and other species. The truly enormous forests are feeding pulp and paper plants, with more to come. In this area of scenic beauty—although all of Alaska is breathtaking in its vistas—are located the state's capital city of Juneau, with a population of 10,000, the communities of Ketchikan, Petersburg, Wrangell and Sitka.

The Country's Terrain

The massive land body of Central Alaska itself divides into distinguishable physiographic and climatic units. The Kenai Peninsula and the Cook Inlet areas contain the rugged Kenai and Chugach mountain ranges, with a gently sloping platform of land bordering Cook Inlet itself. Anchorage, Alaska's largest city (100,000) is located in a wide plain area bounded to its south by the Chugach Range. North of Anchorage is the vast Susitna River valley, bounded to the north by the Alaska Range. To the east, is the Matanuska Valley, long known for its agricultural lands and development. These areas have a moderate climate, with reasonably cold winters, and warm summers. North of the Alaska Range in which are located Mt. McKinley, Foraker and other majestic peaks, is a vast plain in which flow the Yukon, Kuskokwim, Tanana and their tributaries. Winters are quite cold, with moderate snowfall, and summers are intensely hot.

Fairbanks, Alaska's second largest city, is located in this plain, which is bounded to the north by the Brooks Range which drains into the Arctic Ocean. The Alaska Peninsula comprises very large mountain ranges and large lakes. The Aleutian peninsula is composed on an archipelago of relatively barren islands. Although there are forests in most of the central area south of the Arctic Circle, these have not yet been exploited for more than local needs. Mineral activity in this entire area had a boom start with the Alaska gold rush. Today, mining is sporadic and spotty, with the emphasis on coal (of which Alaska is bountiful), sand and gravel. Agriculture, oriented toward local consumption, is concentrated in the Matanuska Valley, near Anchorage, and the Tanana Valley near Fairbanks. Fisheries, a major contributor to Alaska's economy, are operated in Southeast Alaska, the Prince William Sound, the areas around Kodiak Island, Bristol Bay, and other open-sea areas. Salmon, crab and shell fish are principal commercial species.

Transportation Stresses Air

Transportation to and within Alaska has always been of importance to the development of the state. The air age has been intimately connected with the daily activity of every part of Alaska. Ten certified airlines place the state's communities within easy reach of most cities "outside." It is only a quick four and a half to five hours between Seattle and Anchorage and Fairbanks. New York is fourteen hours away; Chicago not quite twelve hours; and Los Angeles about ten hours. With coming jet travel, even these short trips will be substantially reduced in time. In addition, a growing number of world airlines now utilize Anchorage as a hub for transpolar air routes to Europe and the Far East, and Fairbanks is likely to share this position also. The Alaskan has been weaned on the airplane. Outside of numerous certified airlines serving all sections of Alaska, and ubiquitous charter operations, the number of privately owned aircraft is greater in Alaska than anywhere else in the world. Air freight moves intra- and inter-Alaska in enormous, growing quantities.

Waterborne commerce is of extreme importance. The pioneer steamship services of Alaska Steamship Company has been supplemented with numerous tug-barge operations on a frequent and scheduled basis from Puget Sound, Columbia River and California coastal points. Good harbors are found in nearly all coastal parts of Alaska. Panhandle communities all have deep-draft harbors. The Prince William Sound area has all-year, deep-draft ports at Cordova, Valdez, Seward and Whittier, the last two also serving the Alaska Railroad. . . .

The Alaska Highway provides the sole overland motor route to and from Alaska. Considerable all-year traffic exists on this highway, including growing truck movements. The portion in

Alaska is excellent, whereas the Canadian graveled section—1,200 miles—remains to be paved. Within the new state are only 5,100 miles of roads, of which about 2,000 are paved. About two thirds of the total mileage is open to all-year traffic.

No rail facilities exist between Alaska, Canada, and the mainland states. . . . Studies are now under way by the United States Alaska International Rail and Highway Commission to reinvestigate the possibilities of rail system which would link Alaska with West Coast points. Whether the Pacific Great Eastern, which intersects the transcontinental Canadian National line, 400 miles eastward of Prince Rupert on the Pacific Coast, will be extended further, or whether the Wenner-Gren project on the upper Peace River in northern British Columbia will include a rail link is not yet clear. However, whatever rail route is extended, its Alaskan terminus is most likely to be Fairbanks, the northernmost community served by the Alaska Railroad. This 500-mile federally operated and fully modern facility, extends southward from Fairbanks to the Matanuska Valley, to Anchorage and thence to the Prince William all-year ports of Whittier and Seward.

It is on the Alaska Railroad "Railbelt" that most of Alaska's population is concentrated. Fairbanks, about 125 miles south of the Arctic Circle, has a population of around 50,000. Anchorage and its immediate environs has grown from a mere tent city in 1915 to a modern metropolis of some 100,000. . . .

Indices of Economic Development

The population of Alaska has been increasing quite rapidly. From around 70,000 in 1940, the present [1960] total is in excess of 220,000, of which around 50,000 are military personnel. During the period 1951-52, a sharp increase of almost 32 per cent in total number of military personnel was accompanied by an increase of close to 15 per cent in civilian population. While the majority of these new civilians are, in theory, only temporary residents brought by the demands for construction workers in military and defense installations (as for the famous DEW line [Distant Early Warning line of arctic radar stations] and White Alice [a communications system that transmits messages over North America] projects), a large portion remains to swell what might be termed "stable" or "normal" population. This stable population has been steadily increasing year after year, in spite of the seasonal swings which coincide with construction and resources-based activity.

Although it is very difficult to forecast the possible growth of population of the new state, it is likely to continue at an annual total rate ranging between 6 . . . [and] 8 per cent (as contrasted to around 1.6 per cent for the United States). Thus, in 1975, it is likely that Alaska may contain around 750,000 persons, depending on the tempo of development of certain primary industries and the anticipated rate of decrease in total military personnel.

Youthful State

A characteristic of Alaska's population is its youth. In 1950, the United States Census data showed a median age for Alaska of 25.8, whereas that in the United States was 30.1 It appears this disparity continues. Alaska's birth rate per 1,000 population has been steadily increasing: from 23.2 in 1945 to 37.0 in 1956, as contrasted to 19.6 and 25.2 respectively for the United States. Similarly, the Alaska death rate has been substantially under that of the United States, and has been dropping even more rapidly each succeeding year.

The youthful character of Alaska's population reflects itself, obviously, in school enrollment in public primary and secondary systems. Excluding students in Alaska Native Service schools, and the few private institutions, in 1940 there were only 6,312 enrollments. This has grown in rapid fashion: 13,909 in 1950, and 35,888 in 1957. . . .

The gross volume of business also has shown consistent upward gains, more than doubling during the past seven years. . . . Similarly, banking activity has shown remarkably continuous growth. Another significant index of development is found in the continuing rise in airline passenger and freight tranportation inter- and intra-Alaska for certified airmail carriers.

A few other examples can be cited to demonstrate growth. During the period 1947-1957, the number of passenger automobile registrations increased more than sevenfold, from slightly over 7,000 to almost 50,000. Truck registries jumped similarly from about 4,000 to over 17,000. Telephone connections (the majority being in the major cities of Anchorage, Fairbanks, Juneau) increased from 11,000 to over 30,000.

Defense Is Key

The Alaska economy of today is heavily oriented to defense activities. The strategic position of the new state has been reflected in enormous construction of military projects: air fields and their bases; radar and communications systems (as indicated before, comprising the DEW line and White Alice projects); naval bases; and more recently, the emergence of ballistic missile detection, interception and launching facilities. Although precise data on defense expenditures and size of personnel are obviously "classified," it is possible to indicate a total defense expenditure of around $800 million for the period 1950-1957. This can be compared to estimates of the production of Alaska's primary industries for the same period of time: fisheries, $676 million; minerals, $190 million; forest products, $116 million; furs, $47 million; agriculture, $25 million; or a total production of $1,054 million.

The predominant position of the defense establishment and its corollary activities is reflected in the pattern of Alaska's employment. Considering military personnel as employed in a primary industry with a total of 64,100, about 47,000 are in military categories and only 17,100 in construction, mining, lumber and pulp, hunting and fishing, food processing and other primary manufacturing. Most of the 5,863 employed in construction are directly related to military activity. (These data represent reported monthly average employment for 1957.) . . .

The dependence of Alaska's economy on defense considerations has always been a matter of considerable discussion in attempts to visualize the state's future development. The pessimistic view such an economy as tenuous and pose the question "What would happen if the military were to pull out of Alaska?" Those contrary-minded scoff that Alaska's position in world strategy is too important to admit that such a possibility is remotely in sight. The fact remains that each shift in defense technology has caused heavy activity in Alaska, with consequently high rates of expenditures for construction and the establishment of ancillary facilities. Even though there are shifts in the types of defense establishment (such as entailing lesser dollar-value expenditures for the construction of facilities but greater values in the types of equipment established), it can be argued that the net effect on the total economy will remain on a sort of plateau, i.e., that if there are reductions in the value of direct military construction, the shift to highly expert and trained technologists to man the new installations will result in the construction of better housing and related facilities and the employment of higher-income personnel.

One is impressed, however, with the general observation that the pattern of Alaska's development is somewhat similar to that which historically took place in the early days of the western frontier. The establishment of military outposts and garrisons in the 1800's was soon followed by the development of rudimentary service economies, and the rapid exploitation of neighboring natural resources. So in Alaska, the defense economy base has stimulated and enhanced the growth of ancillary primary and service industries. . . .

Even though much of Alaska's economy might be characterized as "taking each other's washing," consolidation and diversification is becoming increasingly evident. A nondefense-oriented economic base is taking shape, principally (and again following traditional patterns of western expansion) in the field of natural resources development, supplemented by the exploitation of Alaska's global transportation position and the expansion of its service establishments.

Resources Development

It is easy to talk of Alaska's "vast untapped resources" but it is not so simple to be precise as to their elements for potential development. This is particularly true with regard to most of its minerals which, although very varied as to their kinds, are widely scattered throughout the immense area of the state, and more usually than not, isolated from consumptive markets by rugged terrain and long distances. If one could generalize as to the controlling elements of resources exploitation in Alaska, one might summarize the situation somewhat as follows:

1. Present local markets (i.e., oriented to Alaska's population and its demands) can support small units of production in agriculture, some construction materials, and in fuels and electric power.

2. Markets along the U.S. West Coast and elsewhere in the other states are and will be shaped by the uniqueness of the

specific Alaskan resource, and the economics of its location (i.e., with regard to lowest cost transportation).

3. The natural resources requirements of Japan and perhaps other Far Eastern nations present an unusual opportunity for Alaskan resources development.

4. The strategic world location of Alaska with regard to transpolar air and sea—and even possibly overland—routes may have profound eventual implications on its development of fuel resources.

Outside of fisheries (which are plagued with vexing problems of resources management), the forests of Alaska are the present source of major-scale resources development. . . .

In contrast to the development of the Alaskan forest industry which is oriented to consumer demands of the United States and Japan, the rendition of value from Alaska's agricultural lands rests upon the needs of local population for certain food products which these lands are capable of producing. . . . Of a total of around 3 million acres believed to be suitable in all of Alaska for agriculture by virtue of soil characteristics and climatic conditions, only about 20,000 acres are now under cultivation. The intensity of the short growing season (long hours of warm sunshine) make possible very high yields of such root crops as potatoes, carrots, turnips and beets; leafy vegetables as cabbage and broccoli in the Matanuska Valley; various cereal crops as wheat, barley, rye in the Tanana Valley. Dairying activity is particularly well established in the Matanuska Valley. Kodiak and some portions of the Aleutians are noted for the initial production of some beef and sheep. The products of this agricultural activity are consumed locally and in 1957 were valued at slightly under $5 million. . . . The winning of land is expensive: the clearing of forest and brush cover from lands otherwise suited for agriculture has been accomplished on a piecemeal basis at very high per-acre costs. . . . Transportation costs on agricultural products provide both a curse and a blessing: on the one hand, the price of certain feeds, of fertilizer and weedicides is high; on the other, freight rates on food commodities from the rest of the United States offer an "umbrella" for the local Alaskan producer. . . .

Tapping Mineral Resources

Although certain mineral resources are known to exist in substantial quantities, the vastness of the new state as yet obscures their extent. It is probable that with the extension of roads and highways, and a greater degree of continuous exploration—utilizing modern geophysical methods—important new discoveries may be made of commercial minerals. One must remark, however, that Alaska has been extensively examined geologically, and that the known variety of mineral occurrences does not necessarily connote commercial quantities.

The gold mining industry of Alaska, in past years, was a major activity. However, of total 1957 mineral production of close to $30 million, sand and gravel, and coal mining now account for equally important values of production, and mercury ranks among major contributors to total value. . . .

Best known of Alaska's mineral resources, and which sustain substantial production year after year, are its coal reserves. . . . The processing of Alaska's major coal resources (estimated substantially in excess of 100 billion tons) offers some interesting, but as yet speculative avenues of approach. For example, the scale of coal mining in the Nenana coal fields about one hundred miles south of Fairbanks on the Alaska Railroad is likely to range between 500,000 to 750,000 tons in the foreseeable future. . . . The vast arctic coal reserves may become important to world markets if the proposed harbor on the Arctic Ocean to be constructed through the use of nuclear explosives (Operations Plowshare) becomes reality. . . .

Search for Oil

Of greatest interest in very recent years has been the discovery of what appears to be commercial quantities of oil and possibly natural gas in certain areas of Alaska. Geological authorities deem a large portion of Alaska as "including rocks that theoretically could contain oil deposits." Exploration and land leasing have been at fever-pitch during the past five years, in such as the Kenai Peninsula, the Alaskan Peninsula and Bristol Bay areas, along portions of Prince William Sound, in the enormous interior areas of the Yukon and Kuskokwim basins, and north of the Brooks Range along the arctic drainages beyond the Arctic Circle. In common with oil and gas exploration, speculation has moved through cycles of extreme optimism, rank discouragement, and again back to considerable hopes that producing areas can be found. . . .

The Alaskan oil situation has brought forth activity in exploration and drilling by virtually every major company and many others. California Standard, Richfield, Phillips, Humble, Union of California, Ohio, Sunray Mid-Continent, General Petroleum, Shell, and many others have established exploratory operations in many sections of the state. Similarly, geophysical exploration companies, drilling, and various other types of supporting firms have established quarters in major communities of central, western and northern Alaska. It is estimated that in Anchorage alone, these activities have brought forth a payroll of at least $3.5 million a year. The possibilities of expansion are highlighted by the recent announcement by California Standard that it will drill additional wells in the Kenai Peninsula and continue exploration at a total cost for 1960 of $3 million. Similarly, late in the fall of 1959, Richfield received approval by the Federal Government for a major exploration program for oil and gas over approximately 1 million acres in the Katalla-Yakataga area on the Gulf of Alaska. . . .

Natural gas reserves are also the scene of considerable exploration and drilling activity. Definitive statements as to possible reserves and commercial quantities have not yet been made by responsible oil companies. However, Union has entered into a contract with the Anchorage Natural Gas Company which obtained a distribution franchise in Anchorage in the fall of 1959. This would necessitate a pipeline from the Kenai fields to Anchorage, a distance of one hundred miles. Other potential fields extend along the Cook Inlet and the upper Matanuska and lower Susitna valleys near Anchorage, and in the far reaches of the Arctic Slopes several hundreds of miles north of Fairbanks.

There has been considerable speculation with regard to the establishment of petrochemical industries in Alaska based on prospective natural gas and oil production. If such chemical units become feasible, it is most likely that these will be oriented with regard to Japanese markets principally, with local and West Coast outlets depending on competitive factors which as yet cannot be stated with certainty.

Vast Hydroelectric Power

The resources briefly outlined in the foregoing are exhaustible in nature. By comparison, Alaska's hydroelectric potential from its lakes and streams is inexhaustible. Various estimates have been made regarding this potential. Most informed sources indicate a possible development of at least 20 million kilowatts of installed capacity. Development to date has been meager and in relatively small sites such as Eklutna (30,000 kilowatts) of the United States Bureau of Reclamation near Anchorage, Cooper Lake (15,000 kilowatts under final stages of construction) by the Chugach Electric Association of Anchorage, and numerous smaller plants in southeastern Alaska. . . .

Some truly giant projects have been under various stages of preliminary investigation throughout Alaska. One of the most impressive in terms of potential capacity at very low cost per kilowatt-hour is the Taiya project near Haines. This would involve the diversion of headwaters of the Yukon River in Canada to a power plant with a capacity of around 2 million kilowatts in coastal Alaska. Another enormous project entails two dams on the Copper River. The Wood Canyon and Peninsula Projects would also have a possible capacity of 2 million kilowatts. However, the largest of all entails a tremendous dam and a reservoir having an area surpassing that of Lake Erie on the Yukon River, some 120 miles northwest of Fairbanks. The Rampart Project, on which initial studies are to begin, would have a generating capacity well in excess of 4 million kilowatts. These very large projects, ranking among the world's biggest, will require many years for investigation, engineering and eventual construction. . . .

In the cursory sketch of natural resources development discussed in the foregoing, it becomes apparent that this will entail extremely large sums of money. Both public and private funds will have to be utilized. In power development, to date, with one or two very minor exceptions, financing has been accomplished either through the issuance of municipal revenue bonds or through loans to local rural electric cooperative associations by the United States Rural Electrification Administration. The very large hydroelectric projects will require very long-term financing at lowest interest rates. Presumably these can be financed only by the Federal Government on traditional repayment bases. Private power development has made no progress in Alaska to this time. Oil and gas exploitation, as well as that for coal and other mineral resources, has been largely by private means save for some basic exploration by Federal and formerly territorial, now state, agencies.

The place of the Japanese market and of Japanese-based investment has been alluded to in prior discussion. The interest of Japan in Alaska is extremely active, and the Alaskans view Japan as a major market opportunity. As a consequence, planning for industrial production or for industrial sales must give weight to this situation. Japan's interest in tapping Alaska's resources is already evidenced by the establishment of the Sitka cellulose pulp operation. Similarly, Japanese geologists and engineers are steadfastly exploring other resources, notably coal and oil. . . .

In contrast to resources development which appears potentially important for national and world markets, except as specifically indicated in the foregoing as for agriculture, the development of manufacturing in Alaska can be viewed in terms of meeting local needs. As pointed out, the total present Alaskan consuming market is measured in terms of its present population of 220,000, and its estimated growth to 750,000 by 1975. Of this total market, about two thirds is in the Railroad Belt including the cities of Anchorage and Fairbanks and their environs. Even if one modifies the estimate in terms of high personal income, the total purchasing power is still quite small as compared with even moderately sized communities in the rest of the United States. However, and this is the difference which bears consideration, the Alaska market is a "captive" of distance and high transportation costs and is isolated from competitive producing centers of manufactured products. . . .

Tourism

One vast area of growing importance entails the outstanding recreational assets of Alaska. The superlative grandeur of Alaska's scenic vistas, its almost unlimited opportunities for all types of outdoor recreation have been well publicized. However, and candor must prevail, the size and characteristics of accommodations and facilities do not begin to be adequate for the tourist potential at hand. This does not imply there are no good facilities in Alaska; on the contrary, some of the hotels and motels (including some now under construction) are comparable to better ones "outside." The fact remains that the number and locations are inadequate, and until more attention is given to the problem, the full recreational potential of Alaska will remain dormant. It has been said, by apologists for the situation, that the seasonal character of Alaska's recreational potential presents an insurmountable obstacle to full development. Actually, no serious attempts have yet been made to develop the year-round opportunities, ranging . . . [the] gamut of winter sports (including cross-country skiing, dogsledding with well-organized hut and lodge facilities), of hiking, mountain climbing and camping, of fishing and hunting and wildlife observation. . . .

With increasing ease of rapid transportation by jet, Alaska's innumerable recreational assets will become accessible to thousands of distant visitors from all parts of the United States, and, by means of the transpolar route, of the world. What is needed is a series of planned and integrated rental or charter transportation services from major airports to lakes, streams and mountain areas in which should be established adequate lodging and eating facilities. A breakthrough by a well organized and financed group in this field is a matter of time, and would be the precursor of substantial similar developments as are taking place elsewhere in the world, as in the Andes, Australia and New Zealand, not to mention European areas.

Business Operating Conditions

Doing business in Alaska is not greatly more difficult or complicated than elsewhere in the United States. To be certain, there are some differences which essentially relate to the establishment rather than operation of enterprises. The climatic hazards are no greater than those obtaining in the northern tier of states. Transportation by air between Alaskan communities is frequent and reliable, as it is with the "outside." Telephone service, especially to other parts of the United States, is excellent although expensive. The shipping of freight by water is time-consuming and, by and large, expensive due to present lack of back-haul. However, it is not an insurmountable obstacle to most business operations.

High Cost of Living

The cost of living in Alaska is high, and artificially so. . . . As might be expected, wage rates are also high although in some categories they are comparable to those which prevail in New York City. Skilled office help is reasonably available; more often than not, permanent commercial establishments draw upon Federal employees wishing to change occupational status. Rentals of office and commercial space are high but, with the increasing number of good, modern office buildings, the situation should become ameliorated. With increasing diversification of enterprise, both quantity and quality of personnel and physical facilities are improving year after year. . . .

The new state's government, in common with its citizens, is even more industry and business-development conscious than most older states. The inquiring industrialist, or businessman, will find the atmosphere conducive to negotiation and discussion. As evidence of this desire to provide all possible incentives to development, on March 29, 1957, the territorial legislature passed comprehensive legislation to facilitate such development. The act . . . enunciates policies and mechanisms for temporary industrial tax incentives which are extremely liberal even though subject to administration and review by a Board and Director of Industrial Tax Exemption. Designated industrial and commercial operations are exempt from income tax upon industrial development income derived during ten years following commencement of operations. Similarly, such exempted businesses are not subject to any license fees, excise or other taxes for a period of ten years except contributions to the Alaska Unemployment Compensation Fund. The property of such businesses . . . [is] also exempted from all taxes (save Federal of course) for periods of years adjusted to the size of the investments. For example, the period of exemption is five years for investment in real or personal property under $1 million, but ten years when such investment exceeds $10 million. . .

Under the United States Congress "Alaska Omnibus Bill" of 1959, Alaska is made eligible to participate in a number of Federal grants-in-aid programs on a comparable basis with other states. It also terminates certain special Federal programs in the new state, and authorizes measures for the orderly transition from territorial to state organization and operations. It clarifies the applicability or inapplicability of certain laws to Alaska. Certain transitional aids are provided to the new state amounting to $28.5 million during the next five years. . . .

ALASKA'S ECONOMIC PROBLEMS [2]

A lot of Alaskans are having second thoughts about statehood now that the bills are coming in.

The jubilation that greeted the birth of this forty-ninth state a little more than three years ago has turned, in many instances, to disillusionment. After nearly one hundred years as a ward of the Federal Government, Alaska has not found the transition from territory to state to be easy.

"Alaska," says its governor, William A. Egan, "is beset by problems as awesome as its geography."

Some of these problems are just coming to the surface. Others have been evident for years. They include:

Deep cutbacks in military spending in Alaska, with a resultant drop in incomes in some areas of the state.

Unexpectedly high costs of state government, coupled with widespread complaints of a growing bureaucracy.

Steadily rising taxes, including cigarette, gasoline and liquor taxes that arc among the highest in any state.

Depressed condition of some of Alaska's traditional industries, such as gold mining, agriculture, fishing and coal mining.

Lack of investment capital to develop new industries which Alaskans believe are the hope of the future.

These major problems, and other lesser ones, are hampering the efforts of Alaskans to give this country's largest state—a land bursting with natural resources—a self-supporting economy.

Despite these handicaps, some residents of this infant state point to developments on the less gloomy side. Among these are:

[2] From "The 49th State—Three Years Later." *U.S. News & World Report.* 52:65-8. Mr. 19, '62. Reprinted from *U.S. News & World Report,* published at Washington. Copyright 1962 U.S. News & World Report, Inc.

New discoveries of oil that have spurred major oil companies to intensified exploration and drilling.

Beginnings of trade with Japan that could provide Alaska with an overseas market easily accessible by water.

Improvement of sea and air transportation that could bring an influx of tourists loaded with dollars to spend.

Prospect of cheap electric power if proposed hydroelectric facilities for central Alaska are built by the United States Government, providing a lure for industries.

Vast riches in natural resources in the interior areas that have scarcely been touched.

Alaskans who look at this bright side of the coin say: "Don't sell us short."

A major source of Alaska's troubles has been the sharp drop in Federal defense spending here. Military construction in the year to end June 30 [1962] will be down to about $38 million —40 per cent of last year's volume when the big radar station at Clear, a $250 million project, was being built.

Government spending normally provides about 50 per cent of Alaska's income. Of this, 40 per cent comes from the Federal Government. So the cutbacks are widening the gap between the state's income and its spending. . . .

Other factors are involved, too. The number of insured workers employed on heavy construction projects, most of them military, dropped from a peak of 10,500 in 1951 to 5,500 in mid-1961.

Big military spending and a short building season have combined to give Alaska a high wage structure. Plumbers get $5.40 an hour, electricians $5.75. Often they work sixty or seventy hours a week.

But high seasonal wages and lack of year-round jobs hurt the economy and lead to high prices. Last year, unemployment in Alaska averaged 12 per cent—about twice the national rate. At winter's peak, in February, unemployment climbs to 50 per cent in some areas.

Prices in Anchorage, a Government survey disclosed, are 27 per cent higher than in Seattle, and prices in Fairbanks are 36 per cent higher. In Anchorage, a haircut costs $2.50, half soles for shoes are $4.50, and milk is 45 cents a quart. In Juneau, eggs are $1.06 a dozen.

House-heating costs in central and western Alaska, where winters are long and temperatures range to 75 below zero, are $75 a month or more.

New cars cost $400 to $500 more than in the Pacific Coast states. There are extra expenses, also, for heavy-duty batteries and heaters to keep engines warm overnight.

Alaska grows only 8 per cent of the food it consumes. All the rest must be brought in, along with practically all consumer goods, at high freight rates.

High wages and prices are an obstacle to development when the cost-plus-fixed-fee clause of military contracts does not apply. Many firms compare Alaskan costs and prices with those elsewhere in the United States and decide against investing.

Alaska, in the last three years, has had to set up an entirely new state government. This has generated other problems.

The division of highways had to take over administration of the multimillion-dollar Federal highway program. The department of fish and game now manages Alaska's abundant wildlife resources. The division of lands now administers the 104 million acres which the state eventually will take over from the Federal Government. Prior to statehood, 98 per cent of Alaska's land was still under Federal ownership. Also, a state judicial system had to be established.

All these new state agencies cost money. This has resulted in soaring taxes and much grumbling about the way things are run.

The number of state employees has reached nearly 4,000, compared with the 750 employed when Alaska was a territory.

State budgets have gone up as services have expanded. The last territorial budget was about $18 million. State budgets have been $33.3 million in 1959-60; $46.5 million in 1960-61; $55.7 million in 1961-62, and $70.4 million proposed for 1962-63, plus $7.9 million in supplemental appropriations for the current [1961-62] year.

The Federal Government granted Alaska a "dowry" of $30 million to aid in transition from territory to state. But, after the state gets $2.4 million in each of the next two fiscal years, this fund will be exhausted. . . .

To many Alaskans, the tax bite under statehood comes as a shock. Taxes were increased last year to raise an extra $3.6

million. For individuals, the state income tax went up from 14 per cent to 16 per cent of the Federal income tax paid.

The tax on gasoline is 8 cents a gallon; on cigarettes, 8 cents a pack; on liquor, $4 a gallon. There is no state sales tax, but a $10-a-year school tax applies to all aged nineteen to sixty.

Despite tax increases, Alaska ranks relatively low among the fifty states in the amount of taxes paid by the average resident per dollar of personal income.

Because of high prices, it takes a $10,000 income to buy the same goods and services that a $7,500 income will buy in Seattle. But Alaskan incomes are about one fifth above the United States average.

Layoffs in military construction have added to the unemployment problem created by unhealthy conditions in some of Alaska's traditional industries.

Since the peak of employment in 1955, jobs have leveled off. In some areas, there has been a drop. The construction workers' union once had 3,300 members. Now there are 900.

Gold mining, once very important, is declining steadily. It is increasingly difficult to cover costs and make a profit at the fixed price of $35 an ounce paid by the United States Treasury.

Agriculture has been a disappointment. Only 25,000 acres out of 1 million rated suitable for farming are under cultivation.

Coal mining has not expanded. Most of the coal mined in the state is used for power generation at military bases.

Fishing, however, appears to be making a comeback after years of decline due to mismanagement and overexploitation. The salmon run of 1961 ranked with the best of thirty years ago, when salmon was Alaska's mainstay.

Alaska is one in name only. It has a tremendous diversity of terrain, climate and resources, spread out over 586,400 square miles—nearly one fifth the size of the rest of the continental United States.

The "panhandle" of southeast Alaska has few people, no access by road, cool summers, and winters only slightly colder than those on Puget Sound. Central Alaska, where the bulk of the population is, can go from 75 degrees below zero to 100 above. The "ice block"—nearly 50 per cent of the state that is mostly frozen tundra, as deep as two hundred feet—is of little use commercially.

Clashes of interest accentuate these differences. Says an Anchorage businessman: "Southeast Alaska is 180 degrees different from us. They have the seafood, forest industries and export; we only have the military. They're inaccessible by road. We're tied to the world's three largest cities—New York, London and Tokyo—by nonstop air service."

Despite all these problems, however, many Alaskans believe their state government will be more flexible, more responsive to changing conditions and to the wishes of its residents, than an "absentee landlord" five thousand miles away in Washington, D.C.

One of the most hopeful developments in recent years—if not in Alaska's history—was the discovery of oil on the Kenai Peninsula in July 1957.

Already, a pipeline has been built to nearby Cook Inlet, where terminal facilities have been installed to load the oil on tankers. In its first year of operation, 5.5 million barrels of crude oil moved through the terminal.

A $10 million refinery is now being built to provide petroleum products for the Alaskan market.

More important, the Kenai discovery may be just a beginning. All geological signposts indicate that Alaska could become this country's top oil-producing state. It now ranks nineteenth among thirty-one oil-producing states.

The search for oil has been speeded by a more liberal leasing policy. Previously, Congress permitted only 300,000 acres of federally owned land to be leased to any one company or individual. This rule has been changed to permit leasing of 300,000 acres of United States-owned land in the northern part of the state and 300,000 acres in the southern part. The state allows 500,000-acre leases on land it owns.

At present, 16,000 exploration leases are in effect, covering 35 million acres. These leases cover less than half of the 80 million acres considered to be potential petroleum sources.

Even though oil is in its infancy in Alaska, it is already proving a major source of income. Last December, competitive bidding on oil leases brought in $15 millon—about twice as much as had been anticipated. One firm alone paid $7,296,000 for leases—$96,000 more than the United States paid to Russia for the entire state of Alaska.

A second industry that Alaskans believe has a big potential is the tourist trade. Alaska has some of the most spectacular scenery in the world, and is a paradise for fishermen and hunters.

One big obstacle to a tourist boom is the difficulty of getting to Alaska. The only way to get there by road is over the Alaska Highway. This road is still unpaved on the Canadian side; it is dusty in summer and muddy in winter.

Beginning later this year, however, there will be an alternate route to Alaska. Motorists will be able to drive from the United States to Prince Rupert, British Columbia, and there take a ferry north through the scenic island passage to Haines, Alaska. From there, highways lead to Anchorage and Fairbanks, in central Alaska.

The idea is to provide a "loop" trip, going one way by the new automobile ferry and returning by way of the Alaska Highway.

Sea and air transportation to Alaska are improving rapidly. More rail and shipping lines are going into the rail-barge business. New jet-plane service has put Juneau within two hours of Seattle.

Over-the-Pole flights from Europe to and from the Orient stop in Alaska. Airport runways at Anchorage and Fairbanks have been extended to handle jets, and terminals are being improved.

About 16,000 transpolar passengers a month pass through Anchorage. There are as many as 60 international flights weekly. Development of Alaska as a center for international air travel is expected to stimulate the flow of tourists.

While oil and tourism seem to be the best bets now, two other things could prove to be even more significant over the long pull.

One possibility is increased trade with Japan. The other is an ambitious Federal project to provide Alaska with abundant, cheap hydroelectric power, which is now lacking. . . .

Already, Japan has poured $150 million into Alaska's forest industry. Alaska has 137 million acres of timber offering 2 million board feet annually on a sustained-yield basis. Only a small fraction of this is being utilized.

In mid-1960, a new pulp mill began operating near Sitka. It was financed by Japanese interests with the help of American investment bankers. It supplies pulp to Japan's rayon industry.

Japan's investment in timber may be just a beginning. The Japanese have affirmed their interest in oil, liquefied natural gas, coal, iron ore, copper and other minerals. It appears wholly possible that Japanese capital, rather than American, may provide the key that will unlock Alaska's vast mineral storehouse.

To develop these resources, Alaska's interior is going to have to be opened up. So inaccessible are many areas that even today the state does not know the extent of its mineral wealth. Practically all known minerals have been found within the state— silver, gold, lead, zinc, copper, mercury, antimony, platinum, chromium, nickel, iron ore, molybdenum and tungsten.

"We have no regrets about statehood," says a labor leader. "All we need is a little more Federal help." There are many who disagree with this view, who say statehood came too soon and with too little preparation.

Alaskans who view the future more as a challenge than a promise point to Scandinavia, on the opposite side of the world. It has a similar geographical location, yet 20 million people live there and have the highest living standard in the world outside the United States.

These Alaskans add: "Russia would give anything to have us back. Then where would the United States be?"

HAWAII'S ECONOMY: PROSPECTS AND PROBLEMS [3]

The first inkling of what impended was an earthquake. The green sea of sugar cane rolled violently under the repeated shocks, then seemed to surge forward upon the doomed village of Kapoho, engulfing it in leafy billows. By dusk, lava fountains were roaring from the cloven earth and a river of incandescent rock drove toward the Pacific, firing the plots of papaya, coffee, and orchids along the way. By dawn the beginnings of a great gray cone had been thrust above the charred plain. "Fire bombs" arched from it into a sky already aflame with red-hot cinders; the first of thousands of fish would soon be dead in the scalding waters offshore; and from deep within the Hawaiian earth were coming the lavas that would put Kapoho to the torch and bury

[3] From "Hawaii's A-Poppin'," by Richard Austin Smith, a *Fortune* magazine contributor. *Fortune*. 61:124-38+. Je. '60. Reprinted from the June 1960 issue of Fortune Magazine by Special Permission; © 1960 Time Inc.

its ashes under many feet of molten rock. Hawaii, the nation's newest state, had begun the 1960's with terrifying evidence that, geologically at least, it was still very much on the make. One day Pele, the goddess of the volcanoes, may raise a whole new island out of the sea in just the way she raised the cone of Kapoho out of the sugar-cane fields.

Meanwhile, the new state has been undergoing profound social, economic, and political changes, some of them more important and only slightly less intense than the spectacle at Kapoho. These changes beneath the tranquil surface of the Islands may escape the attention of casual visitors and even of careful students of statistics. No dry figure on proportional representation, for instance, could express the pride of Hawaii's citizens of Chinese ancestry, many the descendants of coolie laborers, at Hiram Fong's becoming the first person of Oriental parentage ever to sit in the United States Senate. And Henry Kaiser's coming to Hawaii six years ago is, in mathematical lingo, far down in the order of smalls; yet this increment of one to the Islands' population has stood the cement industry on its head and forced the airlines, the hotel owners, and the real-estate developers to break into a sprint lest they be run down by the cartwheeling septuagenarian. The bare figures of booming land prices (this April one parcel between downtown Honolulu and Waikiki was worth $22.50 per square foot, ten times the 1954 valuation) give only a hint of Hawaii's increasingly explosive land situation. With landownership still concentrated in very few hands (four estates possess a whopping 40.5 per cent of Oahu's total acreage), demand is building up as never before, and with it political pressure in the legislature to force more land onto the market, through either heavier taxation or state purchase and resale. No toting up of Hawaii's bank deposits, which jumped from $563 million in January 1959 to $669 million in January 1960, suggests the virtual revolution the Islands have undergone in money matters. "We've had to teach our Oriental citizens that banks are sound and profitable places for the cash they're used to keeping in tin cans and under mattresses," said Rudolph Peterson of the Bank of Hawaii. "The Chinese expect their money to move fast. The Filipinos don't like the idea of having what they own just coming down to some figures in a passbook: they want their wealth where they can handle it.

There's no way to get to them except by word of mouth, so we have a Filipino officer of the bank go out in the cane fields and hold a sort of medicine show or camp meeting to get them to open accounts." The results, he added, are often startling: "One man came in afterward with an oilskin money belt wrapped three times around him. He dropped his trousers to the knees right out on the banking floor getting the thing off, but in it was $17,000. Forty to 50 per cent of our new deposits come from God knows where—mattresses, tin cans, holes in the ground, under the floor boards."

In the broadest sense, the changes in Hawaii can be epitomized in the single word statehood. That one event, plus the millions of dollars in free advertising that attended it, brought tourists in unprecedented numbers. Some 243,000 came in 1959, 41 per cent above the 1958 total, and the record $101 million they spent in the Islands provided new horizons for the tourist business. First-quarter arrivals indicated that 1960 had the makings of an even bigger year for tourism: it topped the comparable months of 1959 by 30 per cent. The First National Bank of Hawaii (until this April the Bishop National) predicted that the number of visitors would reach a million by 1970, almost two million a year in the eighties. The rival Bank of Hawaii predicted tourism would pass the $131 million sugar industry as a major dollar earner by 1963 or 1964. But tourism aside, some of the changes have been long in the making and were merely precipitated or brought into sharp focus after Hawaii joined the Union. Others are as now as statehood itself.

The ABC's of the Fiftieth State

There are some important facts that a tourist might absorb in a fortnight of footing it around the Islands. Situated 2,400 miles southwest of San Francisco and some 3,800 miles southeast of Tokyo, the fiftieth state is a group of seven major islands— Niihau, Kauai, Oahu, Molokai, Lanai, Maui, and Hawaii—all together bigger than the area of Connecticut plus Rhode Island and with more people (660,000) than either Alaska, Delaware, Nevada, New Hampshire, Vermont, or Wyoming. The population contained only 12,000 pure Hawaiians in 1950, less than 3 per cent, and the current census will probably reduce this to an even smaller percentage. The big unknown is whether the Japanese will continue as the largest ethnic group or lose their predominance to the Caucasians. Precensus estimates suggest that each now has roughly a third of the total. Following these are the part-Hawaiians (15 per cent), the Filipinos (11 per cent), the Chinese (6 per cent), with the remaining 4 per cent compounded mainly of Koreans, Puerto Ricans, Negroes, Samoans.

It was a band of New England missionaries, of course, who started the Islands on their way toward Western civilization. They arrived in 1820, forty-two years after Captain James Cook "discovered" Hawaii; the local saying is that they and successive missionary waves came to do good but stayed to do well. The missionaries Christianized the Polynesian natives, moved in on the brawling town of Honolulu with its drunken whalers, established themselves as advisers to the Hawaiian kings, and engineered the Great Mahele, the land division of 1848. Missionaries and other Yankees started the great sugar-cane plantations, where the need for workers was met by importing Orientals under a contract-labor system described as "only a modification of slavery, founded in deceit and maintained by force." In these circumstances the "Big Five," a group of mercantile companies, grew to wield immense local power, financing the plantations, procuring their labor, purchasing their supplies, providing their transport, and selling their products. After an unsuccessful Hawaiian attempt to break the foreigners' religious, economic, and political power, the Islands became a republic in 1894, a territory in 1900, a state in 1959.

The Oligarchs of the Islands

Hawaii's new era was startlingly characterized this March by the head of one of the Big Five companies. "The old caste system," he said with satisfaction, "is breaking down." What he meant by the old caste system, and indeed what most Hawaiians mean when they use the phrase, is not a rigid society of impermeable layers. He referred rather to a small circle of business Brahmins at the summit who had managed to preserve their aloofness and their control while below them the rest of Hawaiian society remained relatively fluid. The economic, political, and social power of this summit group pivoted on the Big Five.

C. Brewer & Company, oldest of the Big Five, was established by Captain James Hunnewell in 1826 with $2,500 worth of trade goods brought in on Hunnewell's vessel. Another sea captain, Charles Brewer, gave his name to the promising mercantile business in 1842.

Theo. H. Davies & Company (nee Starkey, Janion & Company) has been in business since 1845, when the representative of a Liverpool firm arrived in the Islands with a stock of trade goods. Nearly 50 per cent of its securities are held by the Davies family, one of whose members, a young clerk from South Wales, got the company out of serious difficulties in the . . . [1860's].

American Factors (nee H. Hackfeld & Company) was founded by sea captain Henry Hackfeld of Bremen, Germany, in 1849. Branching out of the mercantile business into sugar, Hackfeld brought so much Bremen capital into the Islands that by 1880 a third of Hawaii's sugar plantations were financed by his company. World War I resulted in its seizure by the Alien Property Custodian and rebirth as American Factors.

Castle & Cooke began as a partnership of Samuel Northrup Castle and Amos Starr Cooke, who came to Hawaii in 1837 as members of a missionary company. In 1851 they got a "dismission" from their mission board and founded Castle & Cooke as a mercantile business, subsequently went into sugar.

Alexander & Baldwin was founded in 1894 by Samuel T. Alexander and Henry P. Baldwin, both of missionary stock. Their fathers had started planting sugar cane a generation before when the board of missions asked its clerics to try and get outside work to cut expenses.

Around these five units grew an oligarchy, building up its power from generation to generation, intermarrying and sharing common business and social interests. Interlocking relationships pervaded the whole commercial fabric, linking the Big Five, the banks, the trust companies, ship lines, insurance firms, wholesale and retail outlets, hotels, public utilities, water and irrigation corporations. In this tight system of economic control, power over land was essential, and much of the land was administered by the trustees of the great estates. Washington appointed territorial judges agreeable to the oligarchy and the judges in turn selected the estate trustees and reviewed their actions. Many of the leading families were philanthropically inclined, but the one possession they did not let go was business power. All the way from land to retail trade, control was exercised in such fashion that the way was smoothed for the insider and made almost impassable for the "interloper," as Sears, Roebuck learned in its fight to break into Oahu retailing.

A Distribution of Power

Today Big Five companies are still linked with the two biggest commercial banks, Hawaiian Electric Company, Matson Navigation Company, Hawaiian Telephone Company, and Honolulu Gas Company. And the Big Five still have interlocking directors: Alexander & Baldwin has a director in common with both American Factors and Castle & Cooke, and another man sits on the boards of both C. Brewer and American Factors.

By mainland standards this may seem like a considerable concentration of economic power, but not in the perspectives of Hawaii. It is a far cry indeed from the time when four of the Big Five executives held offices or directorships in thirty to forty Hawaiian enterprises or when fifteen officers or directors of American Factors served as officers or directors of sixty-nine other Island companies. In the changed state of affairs, an American of Chinese descent, Chinn Ho, sits on the board of a major Hawaiian estate, that of Mark A. Robinson, the old prejudice against Oriental trustees finally going down in the face of a need for Oriental business acumen. And a more dynamic land policy is to be expected even from the Bishop Estate, which controls 15 per cent of all the land on Oahu, after last year's selection of State Senator Richard Lyman, a part-Hawaiian, as a trustee. The pay differential between work done by haoles (Caucasians) and that done by Orientals has broken down, and the great white plantation houses are no longer being built. Remnants of paternalism endure primarily on some of the cattle ranches, where the hands seem quite content with a way of life modeled after the *patrón* system of Spanish America, and on Niihau, "the Forbidden Island." Seventh largest of the Hawaiian Islands, with an area of seventy-three square miles and a population of some 200, Niihau is 99.97 per cent owned by the Robinson family and run much as though King Kamehameha IV, the nineteenth century monarch from whom it was bought, were still on the throne. This April the Coast Guard had to send a carrier pigeon to ask residents to search the beaches for a missing transpacific flyer. (The answer: "No strangers on island and we don't expect any.") Sampans are still the means by which the Islanders and their infrequent visitors make the rough seventeen-mile crossing to Kauai. Today Niihau serves as an extreme example of the Hawaii that used to be.

Natural Resource: Beauty

If a single cause can be assigned to the change in the order of things Hawaiian, it is undoubtedly the stimulating jolt of tourism. When mainland greenbacks began to line Hawaiian pockets as never before, revitalizing the hotel business, touching off a building boom, and pushing land prices to new highs, expectations went right up along with everything else. Even the most confirmed standpatter began to expect a great deal more of an economy he'd been happy to accept only a year earlier. In the light of new hopes there occurred a stocktaking that turned up some sobering as well as some heartening facts.

The positive aspects of the Islands' economy are hard to categorize, being largely intangible. An advanced technology, great natural beauty, wonderful weather, and collective open-heartedness are not found in the usual lists of natural resources; nevertheless, their dollar value is tremendous. Hawaii has immense know-how in pineapple and sugar. In particular the research of the Hawaiian Sugar Planters' Association makes the state the world's most efficient cane producer, besides saving the plantations from pestilences that would have been ruinous. The scenery is magnificent: forests of fern and exotic trees like koa and monkeypod; valleys ablaze with orchids, bougainvillaea, torch ginger; angular emerald mountains jutting up from the surf, beaches of white sand or of glistening black lava, even jewel-strewn green ones of olivine; volcanoes crowned with fire and volcanoes capped with snow; waterfalls that plunge down-hill and one that runs uphill. The climate is an asset of great importance in an age when following the sun has become somewhat of a compulsion. *Kau*, the word for season, has little excuse for being in the Hawaiian language: year-round agriculture is standard practice, the October tourist finds the same euphoric temperature as does the June arrival.

The people are warmhearted, outgiving, hospitable, candid. Few indeed are the travelers who come away doubting the reality of the "aloha spirit," that contagious feeling of proportion, serenity, and comradeship that somehow transcends the discordances in Hawaiian society. "The new Hawaii," as a political scientist, Lawrence Fuchs, recently said, "is tolerant of newcomers as the old Hawaii was not. The new Hawaii is a spirit, not a place."

And finally there is Hawaii's geographical situation in the Pacific and its representation of many of the major east Asian races. This means more than just the westward extension of United States boundaries; the citizens of Hawaii have given the mainland a sense of identity with countries and peoples once completely alien. Firmer commercial and cultural ties with the Orient are likely to follow, the way smoothed by Oriental Hawaiians able to speak the Orient's own tongues. In the talking stage is a grand design to capitalize on Hawaii's potentialities as an East-West trade center by establishment of a free port in Honolulu. An East-West Cultural Center at the University of Hawaii, enthusiastically endorsed by the State Department, moved a step closer to realization this April when the Senate unanimously voted it into the mutual-security bill. [The Center began operations in October 1960.—Ed.]

Statistical Serpents in Eden

The negative aspect of Hawaii's economy is to be found in such words as logistics and natural limitations. The island state is 2,400 miles distant from West Coast markets, 4,900 miles away from those on the Atlantic seaboard; freight rates are correspondingly burdensome. Visitors to the Islands, even those from California, have to fly nearly twice the average distance flown on a mainland vacation. As for natural limitations, the 6,435 square-mile area of the Islands is small enough in itself, but mountains, lava fields, and aridity make it even smaller:

only 7.5 per cent is cropland. Consequently, Hawaii must import nearly two thirds of the food needed to sustain its present population, and that population is growing at a faster rate than Japan's. Land availability is already a major problem on Oahu, which contains about four fifths of the people but has only a tenth of the state's area. Oahu now has a greater population density (864 per square mile) than Puerto Rico. Water availability is becoming more or less a problem throughout Hawaii. On Oahu the success of a current water-resource development program will determine how big a population can be sustained there. On the Neighbor Islands, except Kauai, water scarcity on their leeward sides and the tremendous cost of bringing water from the wet, windward sides severely circumscribe agricultural development. These limitations are intensified by a dearth of raw materials and fuel. The Islands possess neither coal nor oil nor any mineral of consequence save possibly bauxite and titanium.

The dollars that keep Hawaii's $1.6 billion economy blooming are earned primarily in agriculture ($290 million), tourism ($101 million), construction ($167 million), or defense ($338 million). Tourism and defense both have the disadvantage of being vulnerable to circumstances beyond Hawaii's control: a mainland depression, or even a recession, could undermine the tourist industry in a hurry; defense budgets are volatile affairs made in Washington, not in Honolulu. Defense at present has a payroll of 50,000 uniformed personnel, 23,000 civilians, or one out of four workers in the labor force, more than any other single activity. As for the agricultural dollar earners, they have their own special problems. Consider the situations in coffee, cattle, pineapple, and sugar.

Kona coffee, the only coffee produced in the States, is grown on the Big Island (Hawaii), mainly on a strip twenty-five miles long and two miles wide. A mountain species of fine flavor, it flourishes mainly at altitudes of 800 to 2,200 feet, getting essential shade not from trees but from "coffee clouds," a cloud bank formed almost daily during the summer months. Production reached a peak of nearly 15 million pounds ($7.2 million) in 1958, but the farmers, mostly Americans of Japanese descent working small leased plots of six acres or so, have been heading into trouble for some time. "It's hard for the boys to get a perspective of the problem," said Shoji Kawahara, a coffee farmer who plainly had the pitch. "The heart of the Kona farm is the family unit. They do the picking. But families have been getting smaller. My father had eleven children; I have three. Help has to be hired at harvest time and that costs money. Then the farmers have been 'keeping up with the Tanakas,' buying two to three party dresses and $2,500 coffee dryers they could do without. With the drop in the price of 'cherry' [coffee berries]—it was 13 cents in 1955, now brings about 5 cents—some are giving up their acreage. The trees are yellow from lack of fertilizer and the morning glories are taking over."

Lately the quality of Kona coffee has deteriorated under hasty processing. This unfortunately has occurred at a time when quality is on the rise in other producing areas, particularly those that turned to newer high-yield strains a few years back. In sum, the prospects of the industry are likely to worsen unless the farmers cut the costs of production, abandon the individualism that leads them to invest heavily in their personal processing facilities, and perhaps band together into a cooperative marketing-and-processing organization.

Home on the Lava Beds

Hawaii's $10.6 million cattle business began in 1793, when Captain George Vancouver presented King Kamehameha I with a bull and a cow, along with sundry other livestock. The animals were promptly declared *kapu* (taboo to kill) and had proliferated into wild herds of thousands by the mid-nineteenth century, when their immunity was revoked. *Vaqueros* from Mexico were brought in soon afterward to teach the Hawaiians "volcano ranching." Today Hawaiian cowboys call themselves *paniolos*, after the original *españoles*, and herd 160,500 head of cattle on a million acres of range land. Richard Smart's 265,000-acre Parker Ranch, begun by a New England sailor back in the last century, is one of the biggest in the United States. But Hawaii's cattle ranges are often parched lava lands, cleared of brush by bulldozer chain, broken up and flattened by sugar-mill rollers so the cattle can get at the grass. To "grass-finish" beef in the Islands takes thirty to thirty-six months, a long way from the cattlemen's goal of twenty to twenty-two months. Feed-lot finishing, which has been tentatively tried in the past year, is very costly, for most feeds have to be imported. Yet without feed-lot finishing, Hawaii's cattle most go to market at lower weights and lower grades. "There's a $1.5 million Navy contract waiting for us," remarked a Maui rancher this March, "if we could just get our grades up from 'good' to 'choice.'"

Pineapple, Hawaii's No. 2 export, is composed of nine variously sized companies, the biggest, with over a third of the pack, being Dole (Hawaiian Pineapple Company). An all-time high was reached with the $124.3 million worth of exports in 1958, and last year's volume was only $1.8 million lower. But the going is likely to be tougher from now on. The industry must pay a special 2 per cent "processing tax" on its gross income. Its plantations are confronted by rising land costs, and in some areas they face the withdrawal of leased pineapple lands for uses of greater value to the owners. On the mainland, a market that is more than 80 per cent supplied by Hawaii, there has been stiff competition from other fruits and juices, frozen and canned, plus some inroads by foreign pineapple.

In the world market, currently accounting for about a tenth of the Islands' sales, the cheap labor, lower freight rates, and government subsidies of some foreign competitors are taking their toll. Hawaii's share of the world supply of solid-pack pineapple has dropped from 75 per cent in 1946 to 69 per cent in 1949 and 57 per cent in 1958. Malaya, Australia, South Africa, Mexico, and Formosa are gaining. Formosa and Hawaii are now neck and neck in West Germany, the biggest Continental market for canned pineapple. Each has something over 36 per cent of this market, where only three years ago the ratio was Hawaii 60 per cent, Formosa 26 per cent. Last year Formosan pineapple was sold in West Germany for as much as 39 per cent less than the Hawaiian product. As the president of Hawaiian Pineapple, H. C. Cornuelle, told his stockholders at the last annual meeting: "Our quality will not carry us all the way if the cost differential between Hawaiian and foreign pineapple widens."

Sugar: More Lumps?

Sugar, Hawaii's greatest export for well over eighty years, is produced by an industry now distinguished by highly efficient operation, diligent research, the world's highest wages for sugar workers in the fields ($12.80 a day), and small prospects for expansion. Currently it is being pinched by forces beyond its control: the rising cost of land throughout the state, and a land scarcity that in the opinion of at least one industrial planner may squeeze sugar out of Oahu by 1970. (This spring American Factors announced that 13,500 acres of sugar-cane land—leased from the Bishop Estate by Oahu Sugar Company—would be turned into a housing development touted as "the largest ever undertaken in the state of Hawaii.") In addition, Island sugar has yet to recover from the 1958 strike. This melancholy affair began so mildly that it was called the "aloha strike" in its early stages. But it soon turned into the most disastrous stoppage on record, thanks in good part to management's clumsy public relations. The four months' stoppage cut Hawaii's sugar production 29 per cent in 1958, and the interruption to the growing cycle is expected to retard sugar output until the 1961 crop. Several sugar companies, among them Ewa Plantation, Oahu Sugar, Pioneer Mill, Kahuku Plantation, McBryde Sugar, and Kekaha Sugar, were still in the red in 1959. But when Island sugar does get back to normal it cannot hope for much more than a sales increase geared to U.S. population growth. "If we want to grow and expand in the sugar business," declared Boyd MacNaughton, president of C. Brewer & Company, "we have to do it outside Hawaii and the U.S." C. Brewer, significantly, is in the process of setting up a 25,000-acre sugar plantation in Iran. And this year Sugar International was formed by C. Hutton Smith of American Factors (Hawaii's biggest sugar agency) with Hawaiian Dredging & Construction Co. and J. H. Pomeroy & Company to establish a Hawaiian-style sugar industry in rapidly developing countries such as the Sudanese Republic.

Islanders Out, Mainlanders In

The sugar industry's new interest in production outside the Islands calls attention to one of the most important changes taking place in Hawaii: a general breaking of the invisible barriers that had isolated Hawaiian business. Hawaiian Dredging is already doing 50 per cent of its business overseas, singly or jointly working on upwards of $150 million worth of contracts from Japan to Kuwait. Declared founder Walter Dillingham: "We've already done the big jobs in the Islands, and we now think of the dredging business as world-wide. There's better potential for it in the Middle East, where we're already operating." Hawaiian Airlines' imaginative young president, Arthur Lewis, has a plan to make the new state the center of a system fanning out all over the Pacific; if the proposition wins CAB approval, and it should, Hawaii may become even more of a "political and intellectual bridge" between Asia and the United States mainland than it is today. And, increasingly, Hawaii's peripatetic businessmen have been sniffing out business opportunities in Japan, Hong Kong, and the Philippines.

While some Island enterprises have been reaching out of Hawaii for larger opportunities, mainland business has been reaching in. Mainland capital is destined to have a profound influence on Hawaii, and very soon. "By 1965," predicted an astute Island financier this April, "mainland capital will be in control here, with an ownership of over 50 per cent." The stake of U.S. insurance companies in Hawaii is already $200 million, twelve times the $17 million of 1948. Standard Oil of California has invested more than $60 million in a new refinery, part of which will go on stream this fall. Sheraton bought Matson's four once-faltering hotels—the Moana, Surf Rider, Royal Hawaiian, and Princess Kaiulani—last June for $18 million. (One difference between the two managements is indicated by this little fact: Sheraton now sells for $400 a month the hotel garbage Matson paid to have hauled away.) Two mainland corporations, American Cement and Cyprus Mines, are the prime backers of a $12 million cement plant (Hawaiian Cement Corporation) to be in operation this summer. Kaiser's Permanente Cement Company has almost finished its own $13.5 million installation on Oahu, and Kaiser's huge Hawaii Kai development is owned by Kaiser Industries (1959 assets: $322 million). The Big Five appeared enormous when they were the only frogs in the puddle; but now that the Big Five, none of which has assets of more than $56 million, are being compared to mainland business, their size suddenly seems to shrink. Moreover, ownership of even the Big Five is changing; two thirds of the stock of C. Brewer & Company, for instance, is held by mainlanders.

In future changes, mainland manpower will be almost as important as mainland capital. Indeed, it has already had an important impact on Hawaii, replacing some managers who owed their jobs to the old school *lei* with professional management. Rudolph Peterson, fresh from the customer-pleasing tradition of Transamerica Corporation, took hold of the haolefied Bank of Hawaii, shook it into an awareness of its opportunities. In four years he more than doubled net profits, increased deposits by two thirds (1959: $303 million). The Honolulu *Advertiser*, a metropolitan daily with a provincial outlook and a plant so antique that heads were set by hand, was stimulated back to health and usefulness in a little over a year by George Chaplin, who had been editor of the New Orleans *Item*. Oregonian Boyd MacNaughton became the first mainlander to head up C. Brewer & Company—the first mainlander, that is, without family connections in the Islands. His performance over the past four years in Brewer's No. 1 spot speaks well for the change: the company's plantations are now considered the most efficient in Hawaii.

The Movers from Within

The rise of mainland influence in Island affairs, however, should not obscure the fact that a number of bright and dynamic individuals, Hawaiian by birth or adoption, are also effectively reshaping the fiftieth state from within. [State] Senator O. Vincent Esposito and House Majority Leader Thomas Gill have been pressing vigorously to reduce the concentration of landownership, particularly on Oahu. A legislative program to force the big estates to disgorge land by threatening condemnation failed to pass last year, although a watered-down condemnation law is now on the books. But the support land reform did get was enough to cause some speedup by the big estates in putting more leasehold homesites on the market. On the bench, the new state supreme court (its first chief justice: Wilfred C. Tsukiyama) can be expected to exercise closer supervision of the land owned by estates than the old territorial supreme court. Such supervision might even induce Hawaii's biggest single landowner, the Bishop Estate, to hire a professional planner for its acreage, holdings worth $6 million just after the war and $120 million today. In the cultural field,

Dr. Alex Spoehr has made the Bishop Museum both an important entomological research center and the world's best assemblage of Polynesian and Hawaiian artifacts; George Barati has built up the Honolulu Symphony from a tiny orchestra with a 1950 budget of $25,000 to eighty-six members and a budget of $178,500. In the world of business, where the change has been most sweeping, three men typify the internal influences bringing about Hawaii's new look: Chinn Ho, Walter Dillingham, and Henry Kaiser.

Fast Decisions in the Hui

Chinn Ho, fifty-six, is representative of a group of high-powered Oriental entrepreneurs (his grandfather was a Chinese farmer) who started out with nothing and now head syndicates (*huis*) of size and importance. It was partially through *huis* that the Islands' Chinese got their first toehold in real estate: during World War II they were ready with cash to snap up the land that some haole families, alarmed by the possibility of invasion, had put on the market. Chinn Ho first broke tradition by being the first Chinese to trade on the Honolulu Stock Exchange and seems to have been breaking some sort of record ever since. The capital of Chinn's *huis*, like all others, is contributed by hundreds of individuals looking for a faster turnover than they could reasonably get from investment in ordinary securities. With a free hand in the management of his *huis*, Chinn has snapped up many opportunities ignored by Hawaii's older, entrenched wealth. His Capital Investment Company and subsidiaries had assets of $1.2 million in 1947, are now worth an impressive $25 million. A dozen enterprises, mainly in Hawaiian real estate, are doing very well indeed, as is a joint venture with Louis Perini to develop 2,200 acres of land on the outskirts of San Francisco. Chinn prides himself on fast decisions, high-leverage investments, and calculated risks. A few years back he bought 9,150 acres of sugar-cane land from Waianae Company for $1.25 million, soon sold 4,000 acres of it for more than $6 million, has watched the remaining acreage steadily increase in value. This year two West Coast developers got an option on $7 million worth of waterfront property adjacent to Waikiki and announced they were going to build a $15 million cooperative apartment hotel on it. Chinn, impressed by the public response to the proposition, moved in fast and bought up their option. There was not even a plan of the building, but within ten days of the announcement prospective owners had plunked down $100 deposits for over seven hundred of the one thousand apartments in the first unit. Chinn's sharp pencil figures there'll be an appreciation in the value of the land of $2.5 million upon construction of the first unit (which would occupy less than half the acreage). If he exercises his right to take a position on the building as well—the tenants will put $12.5 million of their money into that leaving only $5 million to be borrowed—then the profit on the first-unit land and building should run between $5 million and $7 million. Small wonder that Lowell Dillingham, Walter Dillingham's eldest son and the fast-moving president of Hawaiian Dredging (1959 assets: $18 million) should have remarked in February: "We've all missed the boat in land development. Local moneyed interests could have done the developing that mainlanders and the *huis* are doing. The Big Five have plenty of land but they've been so busy trying to keep the sugar industry in a profitable position they haven't had time or effort or money for much else."

Uncle Walter's Still Going Strong

Walter Dillingham, eighty-five, personifies quite a different sort of business influence, though one much admired by Chinn and other rising businessmen, for Dillingham also abhors inactive wealth. Born in the Islands, the son of a Cape Cod schooner captain, urbane, vigorous, astute, "Uncle Walter" has always been a man to reckon with whether on the polo field (he played with sons Lowell, Ben, and Gaylord until he was sixty) or in business. The key Dillingham company is Hawaiian Dredging, begun with $5,000 of borrowed capital in 1902. Since that time it has literally made much of Honolulu, opening up Pearl Harbor, reclaiming Waikiki from the swamp that isolated it, pumping up the coral to provide Jim Dole with a site for an early pineapple cannery and the International Airport with runways for its planes—in all adding some five thousand acres of new land, the lion's share of the made ground on which roughly a third of Honolulu stands. Land and industrial development followed—Dillingham suburbs like Wailupe, and

Dillingham deepwater docks, towboats, barges, a big trucking company (Oahu Transport, ably run by close associate John Walker), a spreading out into sugar (Dillingham is a director of American Factors) and into banking (he is chairman of the Bank of Hawaii).

With such a diversity of interests, Dillingham has had a pervasive influence on Hawaiian business. He has survived numerous skirmishes with Matson and so successfully fought the Big Five that at one time he was known as the Big Sixth. But by and large, he has been a force driving from *within* the prevailing order of things, rather than one functioning independently of it. Last year, however, a single Dillingham project shifted Honolulu's whole axis of retail trade. The immense new Ala Moana center, a $30 million complex of smart shops and big stores (Sears, Woolworth's, Foodland), in effect established a new downtown for Honolulu, supplanting the old, traffic-choked commercial section. Annual sales are expected to reach $40 million, possibly $50 million, compared to $70 million for the downtown district.

The Courtship of Henry Kaiser

At the opposite pole of the Hawaiian business world from Walter Dillingham, opposite in temperament, method, and outlook, is Henry Kaiser. Kaiser's love affair with Hawaii began in earnest in 1954 when he saw droves of tourists being turned away from the few hotels on Waikiki. No more room for hotels on Waikiki beach, he was told, so no more room for tourists. By the following year Kaiser and his community-building partner Fritz B. Burns had become Waikiki's biggest private landowners and the Kaiser-Burns Development Corporation was hard at work turning twenty acres of slums into a resort center (Hawaiian Village) with a two-thousand-foot man-made beach. The Honolulu *Advertiser* correctly observed at the time that a milestone in Hawaiian history was "marked by the entry into these Islands of Henry Kaiser." Within six years Kaiser has built the Hawaiian Village, a nine-hundred-room $15 million hotel complex, the $4 million Kaiser Foundation Medical Center, the $13.5 million cement plant, and established radio station KHVH and television station KHVH-TV. This

year finds him erecting a $5 million addition to the Hawaiian
Village with one hand and with the other working away at
Hawaii Kai, billed as a $350 million resort "city" some twenty
minutes from Waikiki.

Inevitably Henry Kaiser's zealous and jealous courtship of
Hawaii has stirred up one storm after another. When a top
businessman first heard of Hawaii Kai he exclaimed in anger and
amazement: "My God, he's outflanking us at Waikiki." When
United Air Lines flew in a press party in a new DC-8, to publi-
cize the California-Hawaii jet service it would begin in mid-
March, Kaiser stole the headlines with an announcement he
himself was trying to charter or buy "one or more jet planes to
take care of the emergency needs I see growing worse." When
the *Advertiser* ventured to ask editorially what was going to
happen to the homes and leaseholds of a number of families in
the path of the Hawaii Kai development (which will occupy
six thousand acres of Oahu's precious land), Kaiser reacted like
a Bourbon monarch whose divine right had been questioned,
calling the editors cowards, liars, anti-progress, and participants
in a "stop Kaiser" movement. And, of course, Kaiser very soon
indicated that the Islands were now too small for both himself
and Hawaii's Grand Old Man, Walter Dillingham.

The conflict started with the announcement that a new company, Hawaiian Cement Corporation, was going to set up a
$12 million plant, using Oahu coral as its raw material. Main-
land interests (American Cement and Cyprus Mines) were going
to supply the know-how and most of the money, Dillingham and
Bechtel Corporation would build it as a joint venture. Kaiser
immediately announced that he too was going to build a big
cement plant. Before very long Dillingham was growling that
Kaiser men were out buying up coral outcroppings to deprive
Hawaiian's prospective plant of raw material. Kaiser, for his
part, accused the Dillinghams of underhanded tactics in trying
to keep his plant site zoned against "noxious industry." Dillingham, in face-to-face debate, dismissed Kaiser as "a visitor here,"
only to have the visitor invade the dredging business with a
million dollars' worth of equipment. What makes this affair
interesting, however, is economics, not histrionics. Both cement
plants will be in operation this year [1960]. The two plants
can produce 2.7 million barrels of cement, almost three times

the amount Permanente has been shipping in and more than double the estimated 1.1 million barrels now being absorbed in Hawaii. Something is certain to give, but each group is sure it will be the other. "If we have to cut price," said Kaiser recently, "we'll cut it. That's how I broke into the cement business back in the late thirties."

Too Much, Too Soon?

What all this suggests is that Hawaii's most immediate problem is one of maintaining proper balance. Two big cement plants plunked down at the same time in a pocket market is as much a promise of trouble as of progress. And not surprisingly, the building boom is the source of other storm signals. The Islands' leading economist, James Shoemaker of the Bank of Hawaii, called attention in January to the fact that the pace of construction—1959 more than doubling the annual level of only four years ago—had outdistanced both population and consumer buying power. An executive of a chain of co-op apartment hotels was worried about quality: "Some construction is very careless. We shouldn't take advantage of the boom and start building flimsy construction in the outlying areas—it would deaden the atmosphere for Hawaii." More recently, Honolulu's Bishop Street bankers have been voicing concern over the rash of cooperative apartments. The First National Bank and the Bank of Hawaii will accept construction mortgages on co-ops. But once the building is finished these banks do not want the mortgage, and someone else, often a mainland insurance company, takes over.

Looking at Hawaii from the perspective of almost forty years, Alva E. Steadman, board chairman of the Cooke Trust Company and vice chairman of the Bank of Hawaii, observed this March:

I think we're going too fast and I don't see any effective brakes. The boom has all the elements of dangerous explosiveness. The real-estate men are scared to death to make an appraisal for fear somebody else will say the property's worth twice that. People are even buying a chunk of volcano on the Big Island for $895 a lot. I don't believe anybody can predict where Hawaii's going. Most of the supermarkets are undercapitalized. A baking company of which I'm president has had to let some supermarkets take sixty days to settle their bills. They're using our money as working capital in a total amount of $300,000—$50,000 to one supermarket alone. This shows how much of the boom is on credit. We have four more stores now than eighteen months ago, yet gross sales are no greater than eighteen months ago. Imagine what that does to profits! Some will go broke, but that won't solve anything. What in hell can anyone else do with a *used* supermarket?"

Prudent Prospects of Growth

The long and short of it would seem to be that from now on the change in Hawaii should be selective change. If the Islands let their enthusiasm sweep them into overbuilding, a recession would hit Hawaii hard. Even though tourism is incontrovertibly the best hope of the fiftieth state, better a little scarcity than two rooms for every tourist. At the same time, no delay is tolerable in a prudent expansion of tourism to the Neighbor Islands, particularly Maui, Kauai, and Hawaii, nor in making the most of today's circumstances. The six-hundred-mile-an-hour jet is currently working *for* the Islands, bringing tourists there in half the nine hours required by piston aircraft; the big trick is getting them to stay for longer periods of time and capturing for Hawaii's tourist industry a bigger proportion of the travelers using the Islands merely as a stopover. Now would seem to be the time to maximize Hawaii's attractions, before tomorrow's great-circle routes across the Pacific invite bypassing the Islands.

In the past Hawaii has had a way of making even the most ebullient forecasts look bearish. In booming 1955 the best predictions were that 170,000 tourists would come in 1959 and drop $88 million. Today's projections for the next decade—population up 44 per cent to 950,000, gross state product up about 56 per cent to $2.5 billion, upwards of a million tourists spending $573 million a year—these could look just as conservative when 1970 rolls around. Having come so far, Hawaii cannot afford to falter now. And certainly the rest of the nation cannot afford to have it falter. Where else can mainlanders find so marvelous a combination of Yankee ingenuity and grit, Oriental industry and perseverance, a Christian ethic warmed and enlivened by the good will and good humor of the Pacific? Nowhere else is it possible for them to feel so at ease among the Pacific races, whose members are proud to be "first-class citizens" of the republic. Hawaii has the faculty of making even the most moribund mainlander come alive. Sooner or later such a happy awareness will comprehend that Hawaii has also made us partners in the vast world of the Pacific.

V. THE PROBLEM OF DEFENSE

EDITOR'S INTRODUCTION

If the people of the new states were asked to list their major state problems, they might well rank defense at the top. The defense problem has what might be termed a double-barreled effect. On the one hand, both Alaska and Hawaii are continental outposts in vulnerable and exposed geographic positions. Alaska, particularly, is but a short drive across the arctic ice to Soviet Siberia, and her hundreds of miles of coastline remain open and, for the most part, undefended.

On the other hand, military spending has become a key economic prop for both states. Defense expenditures by the Federal Government are the leading source of income in Alaska and Hawaii, and any talk of a military cutback sends shivers through the congressional delegations from both states in Washington. In two important ways, therefore, the nation's defenses are crucially tied to the fortunes of our most recent states.

In the first article in this final section Hanson W. Baldwin, the noted military affairs analyst, raises some disturbing questions about the defense posture of the forty-ninth state. The questions are pursued by Senator Ernest Gruening and the late Senator Richard L. Neuberger, in the second article, which makes a plea for greater military attention to Alaska. The third article describes Alaska's defense posture as of the end of 1962. The concluding article outlines Hawaii's stake in defense spending.

ARCTIC OUTPOST IN THE COLD WAR [1]

Is Alaska—gigantic promontory of North America, closest United States soil to Soviet Russia and newly created state—a strategic asset or a liability?

In Fairbanks and Anchorage and in the bleak, snow-swept streets of Nome, Alaska's sparse population does not spend much time on this question; instead, the size of the anticipated salmon

[1] From "Communique from our Alaskan Outpost," by Hanson W. Baldwin, New York *Times* military affairs analyst. New York *Times Magazine.* p 12+. Mr. 15, '59. Copyright by The New York Times. Reprinted by permission.

catch and the new state legislature's pay scales are of more immediate interest.

But at Elmendorf Air Force Base near . . . [Anchorage] headquarters of Lieutenant General Frank A. Armstrong, Jr., Commander in Chief, Alaska; at Colorado Springs, headquarters of the North American Air Defense Command; at Strategic Air Command headquarters near Omaha, and in the Pentagon, the strategic importance of Alaska and its strengths and weaknesses are again under debate.

Geographically, Alaska's key position is evident from a glance at any map. The peninsula and its long chain of the Aleutian Islands dominate the great-circle shipping and air routes across the North Pacific. Alaska on one flank and Greenland on the other are sentinels for warning, ramparts for defense and advanced bases for counterattack for the North American continent.

Soviet bases in the Chukchi (Chukotski) Peninsula, which is separated by only fifty-five miles of ice-choked Bering Strait from mainland Alaska, are closer by 1,000 miles to the Chicago-Detroit industrial region than any other Russian base. Alaska is a dominant area in the "polar concept" of strategy—attack and defense through the air across the top of the world.

But the acknowledged geographic importance of Alaska is offset, in the minds of some strategists, by two disadvantages.

First, some point out that it is far away from the center of Soviet industrial-military power, which is in European Russia, not in Siberia. But this objection loses meaning as modern weapons achieve almost limitless ranges. (It is only 4,100 air miles from Fairbanks to Moscow and an intercontinental ballistic missile, emplaced at Fairbanks, could reach any part of Russia or China, as well as Western Europe).

The second adverse entry in Alaska's strategic balance sheet is the nature of the country—frigid cold and shrieking winds, inaccessible and unexplored wilds, high costs, difficult supply problems and primitive communications.

There is no doubt that Alaska—the land, the climate, the environment—presents some major problems in military development. Alaska has about one fifth the area of the . . . forty-eight [mainland] states and it is separated from all of them. It has virtually no industry, very few roads, and its one railroad is hundreds of miles from the Canadian system to the south. The

Alaska Highway, 1,523 miles long, extending from the end of the Canadian highway system at Dawson Creek to Fairbanks, is the only land link with the continental states, and it is a gravel road, with limited capacity. . . .

Eskimos in Alaska's two unique National Guard scout battalions are equipped with M-1 rifles and Army radios and they do their forty-eight drills a year and their "summer" camp in March. But to many of them military terminology in English may be difficult—and to explain it in Eskimo may be even more difficult, for the language contains no exact words for such military terms as "tanks" or "tracks." So the instructor, describing what a tank is, uses Eskimo symbolism: "A tank is a walrus with a tin can around it on wheels only they are not really wheels."

Like Russia, Alaska is a contrast between the most primitive and the most advanced, between extremes of heat and cold, snow and rainfall, wind and sun—a wilderness, the last frontier, . . . a land that once before, in World War II, was a base for more than 100,000 troops and ferry route for planes to Russia.

So the problems of rugged wilderness, inadequate communications, primitive living, high costs and extreme climate have been solved before, are being solved today, can be solved tomorrow. But a psychological barrier, compounded in part of fact but in part of legend, of fear, of ignorance, has hampered the full military exploitation of Alaska's strategic position.

This is a land with but few people—perhaps a quarter of a million all told, including some 34,000 men of the armed services, 6,500 civil service employees working for the military, and 33,000 military dependents. Most of the people are crowded around the panhandle area, or Anchorage, Alaska's largest city, or Fairbanks. For endless mile on mile there is nobody.

This is a land with some 33,000 miles of seacoast, guarded by one of the world's most complete radar lines but actually "protected" along its ground periphery only by one thousand Eskimo, Indian and Aleut scouts.

Alaska, in military terminology, is an "overseas theater," with a single unified commander—General Armstrong—over all the armed services. But General Armstrong, unlike other theater commanders, has few forces he can call his own; it has been said of him that he is the only lieutenant general in the Air

Force who commands only two Army battle groups. The two reinforced battle groups—four thousand men—are the principal ground combat forces of the Army in Alaska and only the Army comes clearly and unequivocally under the command of "CINCAL" (Commander in Chief, Alaska).

The Navy's Alaskan Sea Frontier, with headquarters at Kodiak and an outer base at bleak Adak in the Aleutians, is "responsive" to "CINCAL," but its operating forces (twelve naval patrol planes and a handful of small ships in peacetime) come under operational control of the Commander in Chief, Pacific, in peace and war. The Air Force maintains only two combat squadrons—one reinforced—or some sixty fighter-interceptor planes in all Alaska. But "CINCAL" does not control them; General Armstrong wears another hat as Alaskan regional commander for the North American Air Defense Command and as such he operates them for Colorado Springs.

Nor does "CINCAL" have any offensive power. The only missiles in Alaska are two battalions of Nike-Hercules anti-aircraft defensive missiles, which have just been emplaced around Fairbanks and Anchorage. The only bombers in Alaska—normally about twelve or fourteen B-47's—belong to the Strategic Air Command and are rotated to Elmendorf and Eielson Air Force Bases for about two weeks' alert status from home bases in the West and Southwest. "CINCAL" provides them with support and security.

Alaska's strategic concept today is fundamentally defensive. There are only two important target complexes or basic military objectives in the state: the Fairbanks area with the Ladd-Eielson airfields near by, and the Anchorage area, with Elmendorf field and Fort Richardson. These areas are regarded as "stationary aircraft carriers in a sea of tundra"; the insular concept of defense prevails.

These areas, and these only, will be defended. All the rest of the military apparatus in Alaska exists for two other fundamental purposes: to provide early warning of enemy attack to the United States and to provide one 14,600-foot runway at Eielson and the necessary support for SAC's twelve bombers. . . .

But Alaska's defense, as such, is simply enough to prevent the enemy from "taking a Sunday ride." The Russians could saturate our control system, overwhelm Anchorage and Fairbanks with weight of numbers. No defense, as such, can prevent this. Alaska, like all the rest of the world (but even more so because of its proximity to forward Soviet bases) has—and can have—no real defense in the strict meaning of the term in the age of hydrogen weapons, jet aircraft and missiles. Its only real defense today is offense—and Alaska has no offense of its own, only SAC's twelve bombers, their objectives deep in the heart of Russia, not the forward Soviet bases in the Chukchi Peninsula which frown across the Bering Strait. . . .

Yet Alaska is an ideal site for intermediate-range ballistic missiles, or even for intercontinental ballistic missiles. One or two missiles on the bleak and unpopulated outer Aleutians zeroed in on Petropavlovsk could neutralize that threat forever. A squadron deep in the Alaskan Range, or near Kotzebue—back in a fold of the hills—could provide far more defense, not only for Alaska, but also for the continental United States, than all of Alaska's fighter planes and early-warning radar. The Soviet Chukchi bases would no longer be a "dagger" extended toward our continent.

MILITARY NEGLECT OF ALASKA CHARGED [2]

Mr. Gruening: Mr. President, the New York *Times* yesterday printed a letter signed by the two Senators from Alaska and the Alaska Representative in the House taking issue with statements in an article published by the New York *Times'* military expert, Hanson W. Baldwin. . . . Mr. President, Mr. Baldwin had stated that only the important military areas in Alaska around Fairbanks and Anchorage would be defended in the event of a shooting war. Apparently the rest of Alaska and its people would be left undefended. The Alaska delegation felt that it could not allow so mischievous and unwarranted a statement to go unchallenged, and therefore communicated its views to the Secretary of Defense Neil McElroy, asking him for confirmation or correction of this statement for the record.

Secretary McElroy's reply was gratifyingly categorical, to the effect that "there is no military plan in existence, and none has been considered, which contemplates or accepts the concept that

[2] From "Military Defense of Alaska," remarks on the United States Senate floor by Senator Ernest Gruening (Democrat, Alaska) and the late Senator Richard L. Neuberger (Democrat, Oregon), April 27, 1959. *Congressional Record.* 105:6818-19. Ap. 27, '59.

the United States would fail to defend any and all of our
sovereign territory—and that includes, of course, Alaska as an
integral part." This correspondence was printed in the magazine
section of the New York *Times* . . . yesterday, April 26, 1959,
together with a reply by Mr. Baldwin, to whom the New York
Times quite properly accorded the privilege of replying to
Secretary McElroy.

Unfortunately, Mr. Baldwin compounded his error by a
concluding statement in which he alluded to the "potential
danger" that—

A small-scale enemy attack somewhere on the periphery of Alaska
might well create such a political and psychological uproar that it
would create a costly and wasteful military diversion as did the Japanese
on the Aleutians during World War II.

Mr. President, the fact is that what Mr. Baldwin calls a
"costly and wasteful military diversion"—namely, the expulsion
of the Japanese, after their occupation of Attu and Kiska Islands
—would never have occurred if the Federal Government, including successive Congresses, had sensed the military and strategic
importance of Alaska, and had provided the necessary defenses. . . .

The story of the military neglect of Alaska is long; and, although I am familiar with it, it need not be told here. . . . My
point in bringing up this matter today in connection with the
correspondence which was published in yesterday's New York
Times is that I continue to feel very strongly that the defenses
of Alaska are as yet by no means what they should be. In the
course of the last few years, the United States has built a
tremendous number of bases all over the world. They have
been built at great cost. Many of them are of extremely dubious
value. No doubt they were calculated risks when they were
planned and represented the best thinking of our military authorities at the time when they were established. But there is no
question that today our tenure of a great many of these foreign-
based establishments is highly uncertain. There is uncertainty
about whether we shall be able to maintain them, even during
the cold war, in the face of opposition from the governments of
the countries where the United States bases are located; and
this uncertainty applies even in the case of countries which are
manifestly friendly, and whose people we count as belonging to

the free world. In other cases, in the case of countries less free, there is little question that Uncle Sam is being blackmailed, if that may not be too harsh a word, for the right to keep those bases there. If that is too harsh a word, let me say that Uncle Sam is obliged to pay through the nose. There is the further question of whether, with the changing technology of war, these bases have the value that was ascribed to them when they were established.

With the rapid change in the methods of warfare, the validity of these bases, I think, deserves careful reexamination by the Congresses and by the military authorities.

But I wish to point out that whatever defenses we build in Alaska, we build on the firm rock of United States terrain and within the security of a 100 per cent loyal American people. What is built in Alaska is not liable to sabotage, subversion, or other adverse factors which exist in the case of many oversea bases. Alaska's defense should be fully reconsidered, so as to make the forty-ninth state what is an important part of its destiny—namely, to be a bulwark of defense for the North American continent, and thereby for the whole free world.

I repudiate the notion that defending a square foot of American soil is costly and wasteful. But it is much better to have the defenses—and potential offenses—in such shape that no enemy will be tempted, as were the Japanese, to invade any part of our nation. . . .

MR. NEUBERGER: I have been listening with great interest to the discussion of our defenses generally, and those of Alaska particularly, by the . . . [able Senator] from Alaska. Of course, I was especially interested because during much of World War II I was stationed in the Alaska theater of war, as the eminent junior Senator from Alaska knows, because at that time he was the governor of Alaska. I believe he served as governor of the territory of Alaska longer than anyone in Alaska's territorial history.

But the point which I wish to make and which I think is important is this. Reference was made to the New York *Times*. This morning there commenced, on the front pages of the New York *Times*, a most informative series of articles of what the writer has seen in his travels through Siberia. He describes therein vast developments occurring in Siberia in terms of hydroelectric power, railroad construction, highway construction, industrial plants, and an entire, impressive, vast program, which he discusses.

Siberia is opposite Alaska at Bering Strait. If any conflict ever occurs at the roof of the globe, and we pray it will not, it will occur, so far as geography is concerned, between the state of Alaska and Siberia, because at Bering Strait they nearly touch. On a clear day one can see the low headlands of Siberia looming out of the bay, as the Senators from Alaska so well know.

It seems to me the articles which are starting in the New York *Times* emphasize that what has been done in Siberia by the Soviet Union, through vast expenditures of money and resources, should stimulate us in the Senate and the other body of Congress and the President of the United States to bring about a similar program of development in Alaska. Alaska needs roads, highways, a railway connection with the United States, and great hydro-electric power projects to tap such rivers as the Yukon and other great streams which could provide industrial development.

I think the series of articles on Siberia should encourage the Government of the United States to follow Russia's lead, and proceed to develop Alaska, which has not yet been done.

ALASKA: FIRST LINE OF DEFENSE [3]

Militarily Alaska has been called the "forgotten land." Strategically, Alaska is the first line of defense for North America for any possible Soviet-launched aggression.

This strange paradox has led to a controversial approach to the military problems that face the largest state in the Union.

Hanson Baldwin, military writer for the New York *Times*, early this year noted that "Alaska, the forty-ninth state, and the closest United States 'real estate' to the Soviet Union is something of a military stepchild."

There are nearly 34,000 uniformed men scattered throughout Alaska, representing all services. With their dependents they number about 77,000 out of a total population of 227,000 persons.

Military posts are located in all parts of the state, stretching from the now famed DEW Line in the arctic to a Coast Guard unit at Ketchikan.

[3] From "Strategically, Alaska Is First Defense Line." Fairbanks *Daily News-Miner* (Progress Edition). p 32C. N. 28, '62. Reprinted by permission.

But except for a number of transient nuclear-armed Strategic Air Command bombers, and an occasional Polaris submarine operating off the Alaskan coast, the nearest state to Russia does not have a great deal of offensive potential.

This "defense only" attitude on the part of national military planners has not been without controversy. The first official to promote the need for offensive bases in Alaska was the late General Billy Mitchell, who was subsequently court-martialed for his beliefs in air power, and his attitudes toward higher command thinking.

The last person to speak out for offensive weapons in Alaska was General Frank Armstrong, World War II hero, and former commander of all forces in Alaska. He was rumored to have gotten a premature retirement slightly over a year ago for his views.

The present Alaska Command Commander-in-Chief is Lieutenant General George W. Mundy, like Armstrong an Air Force officer and World War II hero.

Soon after the general took command last year, two very strong rumors regarding offensive power circulated throughout the state.

The first concerned the building of a nuclear submarine base in southeastern Alaska, and the other regarded construction of Atlas Missile launching sites here.

The Air Force admitted that it had inspection teams looking over Alaska to find Atlas sites, but to this date none have officially been programed.

The nuclear submarine base was programed for an island in the mid-Pacific Ocean.

Meantime, Alaska remains the best outpost and warning station the continental United States has ever maintained.

First fixed line of warning is the DEW Line, a multimillion-dollar series of radar stations strung along the Arctic Coast. This is backed up with military aircraft warning sites, operated by the Air Force.

Supplementing the electronic sites are the eyes and ears of several thousand Eskimo scouts, who report all strange happenings along the northern and western periphery of the state.

The communication key to the radar stations is White Alice, a system of sites that can speed messages over most of North America in a matter of seconds.

To warn against missiles there is the giant Ballistic Missile Early Warning Site at Clear, on the Alaska Railroad. The Air Force also operates the Donnelly Dome Satellite Tracking Station, near Big Delta.

There is also extensive and sensitive warning type sites located at Shemya, an island near the far tip of the Aleutian Chain.

To back up the fixed stations, the Air Force and Navy also operate round-the-clock flying radar stations. The famed U-2 plane is also known to operate out of Alaska from time to time.

To put teeth into the extensive warning system, there are two forward fighter plane bases in Alaska. These are located at King Salmon and Galena.

Less than a year ago there were only about forty jet fighter planes stationed in the state, placed at the forward bases and Elmendorf Air Force Base near Anchorage.

The fighters are supplemented by Nike-Hercules anti-aircraft missile sites, ringing both Fairbanks and Anchorage.

The air defenses are bolstered by two Army battle groups, one at Fort Richardson near Anchorage and one at Fort Wainwright near Fairbanks.

Except for a handful of Marines at the Kodiak and Adak Naval bases, these are the only "real fighting personnel" in the forty-ninth state.

Fort Greely, an extensive Army base near Big Delta is a training ground and winter equipment testing center.

HAWAII'S DEFENSE-GEARED ECONOMY [4]

The economic importance of defense in Hawaii is fully recognized. It has become the greatest single factor affecting business, income and employment.

Less obvious perhaps is the military importance of the economy of the Islands in strengthening defense potentials here. It provides (1) skilled and semiskilled personnel (as maintenance and repair men for ships, planes and military installations; as

[4] From Hawaii: Patterns of Island Growth; 1958 mid-year report. Bank of Hawaii. Department of Business Research. Honolulu. '58. p 27-8. Reprinted by permission.

nurses and assistants in hospitals; and as accountants, statisticians and clerks in records and supply offices); (2) manned equipment for dredging operations and for the construction of installations and military housing; (3) food and other locally produced items; (4) reserve supplies of mainland products warehoused by local firms; (5) links between military and local utility systems, thus increasing potential capacity and supplying emergency services when needed; and (6) a wide range of recreational facilities and direct personal services for members of the Armed Forces.

In a crisis such aids can be increased manyfold as they were during World War II. Thus the larger and stronger the economy, the more it can contribute to the manpower, the materials' base and the staying power of defense forces in the event of an emergency.

This interdependence of military and economic strength is recognized in Hawaii by a unique military-civilian organization— the "Kokua Council"—comprised of high ranking military officials and leading businessmen. It meets periodically for frank, off-the-record conferences on local problems and has been a potent factor in creating mutually helpful relations between the military and civilian communities.

From the time Hawaii became a part of the United States in 1900 to 1935 defense expenditures here were a minor factor in Hawaiian business. In 1935 they amounted to only about one tenth of the aggregate value of sugar and pineapple. During 1936-41, they rose sharply, and since then have been of primary importance.

At present military personnel, civilian defense employees and the dependents of both groups constitute approximately one fourth of the population of the territory. The outward evidence of this is the system of highways between Honolulu and the primary defense installations—by far the largest and most heavily traveled in the territory.

Counting military personnel stationed here, one in four of our entire population is thus directly dependent on defense for a living—and substantial numbers are indirectly and partially dependent on it. Practically every wholesale, retail and service enterprise on Oahu enjoys at least some patronage from military or defense workers' families, and a number of large firms provide goods or construction and maintenance services under military contract.

In 1957 military expenditures in the territory totaled $308 million (more than the aggregate dollar volume of sugar, pineapple and minor exports).

[By 1960, according to *Hawaii: Planning for Economic Growth,* the 1961 annual economic report of the Bank of Hawaii Department of Business Research, defense expenditures had risen to $373 million and were still rising. The number of civilians employed in the defense establishments had reached 24,200 in June 1961, and the armed forces personnel totaled 53,000.—Ed.]

BIBLIOGRAPHY

BOOKS, PAMPHLETS, AND DOCUMENTS

An asterisk (*) preceding a reference indicates that the article or a part of it has been reprinted in this book.

Adams, Ben. Alaska: the big land. Hill & Wang. New York. '59.

Alaska. Department of Agriculture and the University of Alaska. Agriculture in Alaska. Supt. of Docs. Washington 25, D.C. '58.

Alaska. Department of Natural Resources. Division of Mines and Minerals. Report for the year 1961. The Division. Juneau. '61.

Alaska. Employment Security Commission. Job facts. The Commission. Juneau. F. '59.

Alaska Legislative Council. Final report on borough government. mimeo. Local Affairs Agency. Box 710. Juneau. Ja. '61.

Alaska Legislative Council. Legislative apportionment in Alaska, 1912-61. The Council. Box 2199. Juneau. '62.

Alaska Legislative Council. Legislative handbook on Alaska state government. The Council. Box 2199. Juneau. '63.

Alaska Legislative Council. Revenue and taxation in Alaska. 2 parts. The Council. Box 2199. Juneau. Ja. '62.

Alaska. Resource Development Board. Alaska fact sheet. The Board. Box 2391. Juneau. '62.

Alaska. State Board of Education. Foundation for Alaska's public schools; report of a survey. mimeo. Juneau. S. '61.

Aller, Curtis. Labor relations in the Hawaiian sugar industry. University of California. Institute of Industrial Relations. Berkeley. '57.

*Bank of Hawaii. Department of Business Research. Annual and mid-year economic reports, 1958-62. The Bank. Honolulu. '58-'62.
    Reprinted in this book: Hawaii: Patterns of island growth; 1958 mid-year report. p 27-8.

Brinsmade, E. M. Books on Alaska for young people. Adler's Book Shop. Box 1599. Fairbanks, Alaska. '61.

Carrighar, Sally. Moonlight at midday. Knopf. New York. '58.

Chegaray, Jacques. Hawaii: isles of dreams. Sterling. New York. '59.

Conservation Foundation. Alaska outdoor recreation potential; report to the Outdoor Recreation Resources Review Commission by the Conservation Foundation. Supt. of Docs. Washington 25, D.C. '62.

Day, A. G. Hawaii and its people. Duell. New York. '55.

Day, A. G. Hawaii: 50th star. Duell. New York. '60.

Durand, Loyal, Jr. Hawaii. (Focus. v 9, no 9) American Geographical Society. New York. '59.

Edelman, Lily. Hawaii, U.S.A. Nelson. New York. '60.

Erskine, W. F. White water; an Alaskan adventure. Abelard-Schuman. London. '60.

First National Bank of Hawaii. Department of Economic Research. Brief review of Hawaii for the businessman. The Bank. P.O. Box 3200. Honolulu. '60.

First National Bank of Seattle. Department of Economic Research. Alaska, frontier for industry. The Bank. Seattle. F. '59.

Fisher, F. R. ed. Man living in the Arctic. National Academy of Sciences-National Research Council. Washington, D.C. '61.

*Fuchs, L. H. Hawaii pono: a social history. Harcourt. New York. '61.

Hawaii. Department of Economic Development. Bring your business imagination to Hawaii. The Department. Honolulu. '61.

Hawaii. Department of Economic Development. Facts in focus. The Department. Honolulu. '61.

Hawaii. Department of Economic Development. Information locator: where to obtain information about Hawaii. The Department. Honolulu. '62.

Hawaii. Department of Planning and Research. Geographic statistics for Hawaii. (Research Report no 15) mimeo. The Department. Honolulu. Ja. 15, '62.

Hawaii. Department of Planning and Research. Hawaiian migration, 1950-61. R. C. Schmitt. (Research Report 21) mimeo. The Department. Honolulu. '62.

Hawaii. Department of Planning and Research. Military Statistics for Hawaii, 1961-62. (Research Report 16) mimeo. The Department. Honolulu. '62.

Hawaii. Department of Planning and Research. Population projections for Hawaii, 1960-80. (Research Report 10) mimeo. The Department. Honolulu. '61.

Hawaii. Department of Planning and Research. Research Division. Statistics on the fine arts in Hawaii. (Research Report 17) mimeo. The Department. Honolulu. '62.

Hawaii. Economic Planning and Coordination Authority. Major landholdings in Hawaii: ownership patterns and leasing policies. (Report no 14) The Authority. Honolulu. F. '57.

Hawaii. Governor's Advisory Committee on Finance. State of Hawaii's finances, '60-'62. Department of Budget and Review. Honolulu. '62.

Hawaii. Governor's Committee on Education Beyond High School. Education beyond the high school in Hawaii, 1958-1968. The Committee. Honolulu. '59.

Hawaii. State Planning Office. Provisional estimates and projections of the civilian population of Hawaii, 1940-1980. (Staff Research Memo 30) The Office. Honolulu. '60.

Hawaii Visitors Bureau. 1962 annual program and research report. The Bureau. Honolulu. '62.

Hawaii book; story of our island paradise. J. G. Ferguson. Chicago. '61.

Hulley, C. C. Alaska: past and present. Binfords. Portland, Ore. '59.

Kamins, R. M. Tax problems and fiscal policy in Hawaii. (Report no 1, 1962) University of Hawaii. Legislative Reference Bureau. Honolulu. '62.

*Kursh, Harry. This is Alaska. Prentice-Hall. Englewood Cliffs, N.J. '61.

Kuykendall, R. S. and Day, A. G. Hawaii: a history; from Polynesian kingdom to American state. Prentice-Hall. Englewood Cliffs, N.J. '61.

Lau, K. K. Structure of the Hawaii state government. University of Hawaii. Legislative Reference Bureau. Honolulu. '60.

*Masuoka, Jitsuichi and Valien, Preston, eds. Race relations: problems and theory, essays in honor of Robert E. Park. University of North Carolina. Chapel Hill. '61.
    Reprinted in this book: Race relations frontiers in Hawaii. p 58-71. A. W. Lind.

Moore, Terris. Alaska (Focus. v 13, no 3) American Geographical Society. New York. '62.

Okakok, Guy. Okakok's Alaska; selections from Pt. Barrow News, submitted to the Fairbanks Daily News-Miner, 1955-1959. P. E. O. Sisterhood. 303 Cowles St. Fairbanks. '59.

Palmer, Artis. There's no place like Nome. Morrow. New York '63.

Riwkin-Brick, Anna and Soderberg, Eugenie. Hawaii, a way of life. Macmillan. New York. '62.

Roberts, H. S. Labor-management relations in Hawaii. University of Hawaii. Industrial Relations Center. Honolulu. Ag. '62.

Rogers, G. W. Alaska in transition; the southeast region. Johns Hopkins Press. Baltimore. '60.

Rogers, G. W. The future of Alaska: economic consequences of statehood. Johns Hopkins Press. Baltimore. '62.

Thomas, Tay. Follow the North star. Doubleday. Garden City, N.Y. '60.

Tuttle, Daniel, Jr. and others, comps. Hawaii Democratic and Republican party platforms, 1952-1962. University of Hawaii. Department of Government. Honolulu. '62.

United States. Congress. House of Representatives. Committee on Foreign Affairs. Subcommittee on State Department Organization and Foreign Operations. Center for cultural and technical interchange between East and West (East-West center); hearings, December 13, 1961-January 8, 1962. 87th Congress, 2d session. The Committee. Washington 25, D.C. '62.

United States. Congress. House of Representatives. Committee on Foreign Affairs. Subcommittee on State Department Organization and Foreign Operations. Center for cultural and technical interchange between East and West (East-West Center); report, July 30, 1962. (H. Report no 2060) 87th Congress, 2d session. The Committee. Washington 25, D.C. '62.

United States. Congress. House of Representatives. Committee on Interior and Insular Affairs. Subcommittee on Public Lands. Alaska military land withdrawals; hearings, March 2 and 21, 1961, on H.R. 2279 [and other bills]. 87th Congress, 1st session. Supt. of Docs. Washington 25, D.C. '61.

United States. Congress. Senate. Committee on Agriculture and Forestry. Subcommittee on Agricultural Production, Marketing and Stabilization of Prices. Agricultural land development in Alaska; hearings, August 10, 1962 on S. 2805, a bill to provide for a program of agricultural land development in the state of Alaska. 87th Congress, 2d session. The Committee. Washington 25, D.C. '62.

United States. Congress. Senate. Committee on Commerce. Alaska and Hawaii through routes and joint rates; report, August 1, 1962 [to accompany H.R. 11643]. (S. Report no 1799). 87th Congress, 2d session. The Committee. Washington 25, D.C. '62.

United States. Congress. Senate. Committee on Interior and Insular Affairs. Alaska omnibus bill; report, May 28, 1959, to accompany S. 1541. (Senate Report no 331) 86th Congress, 1st session. Supt. of Docs. Washington 25, D.C. '59.

United States. Congress. Senate. Committee on Interior and Insular Affairs. Subcommittee on Public Lands. Mineral rights for Alaska homesteaders; hearings, June 19, 1959-May 25, 1960, on S. 1670. 86th Congress, 1st and 2d sessions. Supt. of Docs. Washington 25, D.C. '59-'60.

United States. Congress. Senate. Committee on Public Works. Market for Rampart power, Yukon river, Alaska. 87th Congress, 2d session. Supt. of Docs. Washington 25, D.C. '62.

United States. Congress. Senate. Committee on Public Works. Study of highway program for Alaska; hearing before a subcommittee on S.J. Res. 137, February 27, 1962. 87th Congress, 2d session. Supt. of Docs. Washington 25, D.C. '62.

United States. Department of Commerce. Bureau of the Census. Alaska: general population characteristics. (United States census of population: 1960, final report PC(1)-3B) Supt. of Docs. Washington 25, D.C. '61.

United States. Department of Commerce. Bureau of the Census. Alaska: general social and economic characteristics. (United States census of population: 1960, final report PC(1)-3C) Supt. of Docs. Washington 25, D.C. '61.

United States. Department of Commerce. Business and Defense Services Administration. Alaska: its economy and market potential. Supt. of Docs. Washington 25, D.C. '59.

*United States. Department of Defense. Office of Armed Forces Information and Education. Pocket guide to Alaska. (DOD Pam 2-9) The Department. Washington 25, D.C. '56.

*United States. Department of Defense. Office of Armed Forces Information and Education. Pocket guide to Hawaii. (DOD Pam 2-1) The Department. Washington 25, D.C. '55.

United States. Department of the Interior. Bureau of Land Management. Establishing a farm in Alaska. The Bureau. Washington 25, D.C. '61.

*United States. Library of Congress. Legislative Reference Service. Centralization of government in Hawaii. W. B. Graves. mimeo. The Library. Washington 25, D.C. '62.

University of Hawaii. Legislative Reference Bureau. Digest and index of laws enacted and final status table of bills, urgency measures, and resolutions. The Bureau. Honolulu. Je. '62.

University of Hawaii. Legislative Reference Bureau. Hawaii state government organization, selected memoranda. 2v. The Bureau. Honolulu. '59.

Winslow, Kathryn. Alaska bound. Dodd. New York. '60.

Yukiko, Kimura. Social-historical background of the Okinawans in Hawaii. (Report no 36) University of Hawaii. Romanzo Adams Social Research Laboratory. Honolulu. '62.

PERIODICALS

America. 100:635-6. F. 28, '59. Hawaii, our 50th state. B. J. Hartung.

America. 107:661-2. S. 1, '62. Freeze-out in Alaska.

*American Bar Association Journal. 44:1147-50. D. '58. Alaska's heralded constitution: the forty-ninth state sets an example. J. S. Hellenthal.

*American Bar Association Journal. 45:1145-8+. N. '59. The Hawaiian constitution: a structure for good government. P. C. Bartholomew and R. M. Kamins.

American City. 75:121+. Ja. '60. Hawaii, the state without a city.
W. S. Foster.

American Forests. 65:12-13+. Jl. '59. Exploring Alaska. H. H. Bennett.

American Forests. 66:14-16+. Ja. '60. Alaska. R. G. Lynch.

American Forests. 68:20-2+. Je. '62. Hawaii's newest park. John
Dengel.

American Forests. 69:28-9+. Ja. '63. Hop and jump surveying. E. W.
Shaw.

American Forests. 69:32-4+. Ja. '63. Visit to a volcano. J. T. Harrold.

American Heritage. 11:10-14+. F. '60. Isles shall wait for his law.
Bradford Smith.

American Heritage. 12:44-7+. D. '60. Seward's wise folly. R. L.
Reynolds.

American Heritage. 12:64-79. F. '61. Billy Mitchell in Alaska. William
Mitchell.

American Heritage. 13:60-72+. D. '61. Captain Cook's American.
E. M. Halliday.

American Heritage. 13:74-5. F. '62. Billy Mitchell's prophecy; excerpt
from report of 1924. William Mitchell.

American Home. 61:11-14+. Ja. '59. We live in Alaska and love it!

*Américas. 13:10-13. S. '61. New Alaskan Eskimo. W. H. Oswalt.

Annals of the American Academy of Political and Social Science. 335:
38-41. My. '61. University of Hawaii orientation center. S. F.
McCabe.

Antiques. 77:576-7. Je. '60. Knapp paintings of Alaska. P. W. Inman.

Architectural Forum. 114:110-12. Je. '61. Capitol for the 50th state.

Architectural Record. 129:153-6. Je. '61. New capitol for the newest
state.

Atlantic Monthly. 210:73-8. S. '62. Alaska: last frontier. Paul Brooks.

Aviation Week and Space Technology. 71:43+. N. 16, '59. Hawaiian
bids for new Pacific routes. L. L. Doty.

Aviation Week and Space Technology. 75:115+. Ag. 14, '61. Alaska airlines to use, sell Lockheed 60s. A. Sherman.

Better Homes and Gardens. 40:20+. Ja. '62. What it's like to move to
Hawaii. Bob Krauss.

Business Week. p 140-2+. Mr. 14, '59. Hawaii: set to become an
island state.

Business Week. p 201-2. Je. 20, '59. Challenge to Hawaiian tycoon.

Business Week. p 168-70+. N. 28, '59. Mainlanders take over in
Hawaii.

Business Week. p 196+. Mr. 19, '60. Company store.

Business Week. p 141-2+. S. 17, '60. All-out union drive in Hawaii:
labor leaders are competing among one another to sign up the
160,000 unorganized workers.

Business Week. p 57-8+. O. 29, '60. Hawaii's boom keeps climbing.

Business Week. p 124+. O. 28, '61. Hawaii giant jumps to East coast.

Business Week. p 98. O. 20, '62. In Hawaii's bars, it's ti for two; liquor called okolehao.

Business Week. p 81-2. F. 2, '63. Personal business: winter vacation in Oahu.

Christian Century. 76:349. Mr. 25, '59. Hawaii honors its founders.

Christian Century. 76:565. My. 6, '59; 77:1390. N. 23, '60. News of the Christian world.

Christian Century. 76:916. Ag. 12, '59. Hawaii's electorate makes good start.

Christian Century. 80:54. Ja. 9; 80:374. Mr. 20, '63. News of the Christian world.

Christian Science Monitor. p 11. Jl. 3, '58. Alaska: welcome! Hal Painter.

Commonweal. 69:661-2. Mr. 27, '59. Hawaiian statehood.

Congressional Digest. 38:3-32. Ja. '59. Question of statehood for Hawaii.

*Congressional Record. 105:6818-19. Ap. 27, '59. Military defense of Alaska. Ernest Gruening; R. L. Neuberger.

*Congressional Record. 108:A7806-12. O. 19, '62. Four years of unprecedented achievement—the greatest progress in Alaskan history; extension of remarks in the Senate, October 13, 1962. Ernest Gruening.

Coronet. 48:136+. Je. '60. World's roughest police beat. C. E. Hinkson.

Current History. 36:241-2. Ap. '59. Alaska: the forty-ninth state; Proclamation; Flag of the United States. D. D. Eisenhower.

Current History. 41:108-13. Ag. '61. Hawaii: equalization through centralization. H. V. Everly.

Dance Magazine. 34:44-7. Ag. '60. Renascence in Hawaii. Janet Faure.

Department of State Bulletin. 42:130-1. Ja. 25, '60. Secretary sends report to Congress on East-West Center in Hawaii. C. A. Herter.

Esquire. 56:88-90. Ag. '61. Happiest Hawaiians; beach boys. Charlotte Paul.

*Fairbanks Daily News-Miner (Progress Edition). p 32C. N. 28, '62. Strategically, Alaska is first defense line.

Field & Stream. 64:62-6+. My. '59. Trailer trek to Alaska. Jack Parry.

*Financial Analysts Journal. 16:31-42. Ja.-F. '60. Alaska: the economic outlook. Ivan Bloch.

Flying. 65:30-1+. D. '59. Is Alaska expendable? Dave Lewis.

Fortune. 60:139-43. D. '59. To Alaska through a rugged frontier.

*Fortune. 61:124-33+. Je. '60. Hawaii's a-poppin'. R. A. Smith.

Hobbies. 64:116-18. N. '59. Hawaii, our 50th state. Louise Collins.

Hobbies. 66:112-13+. Jl. '61. Hawaii: some early letters. D. H. Hamilton.

Holiday. 26:26-45+. Ag. '59. Alaska. J. W. Bellah.

Holiday. 28:34-55+. Jl. '60. Hawaii. Robert Carson.

Honolulu Star-Bulletin. Ja. 29, '63. Annual progress edition [Articles on all phases of Hawaii].

Horticulture. 39:272. My. '61. Hawaii, our fiftieth state.

House & Garden. 116:34+. Jl. '59. Going places, finding things. Louise Shattuck.

House Beautiful. 103:78+. S. '61. Hawaii: a great state to be in. Marion Gough.

*Indian Truth. 38:1-8. O. '61. Indian rights and wrongs in Alaska. T. B. Hetzel.

Life. 46:14-21. Ja. 26, '59. Living at 30° below: Alaska thrives amid winter gloom.

Life. 46:37-40. Mr. 16, '59. Happy caravan of modern pioneers; Detroiters bound for Alaska.

Life. 46:58-72. Mr. 23, '59. Hawaii: beauty, wealth, amiable people.

Life. 46:75-6. Mr. 23, '59. Pros and cons of Island statehood. Peter Bunzel.

Life. 46:24-5. Mr. 30, '59. Sorely beset '59ers carry on; band of Detroiters.

Life. 46:141-3. Ap. 20, '59. '59ers find promised land; pioneers from Detroit.

Life. 47:41-2+. Ag. 17, '59. Unique Hawaiian look in politics.

Life. 47:37-40. Ag. 31, '59. Hawaii's sunny summer school.

Life. 47:49-52. N. 30, '59. '59ers, now thirteen dig in for winter.

Life. 48:30-1. Ap. 25, '60. Census trek in newest state.

Life. 48:32-5. Ap. 25, '60. For every enumerator hard-to-avoid perils.

Life. 50:87-95. F. 10, '61. Dillinghams of Hawaii.

Living Wilderness. 77:37. Summer '61. Wilderness first policy advocated.

Look. 23:29-31. My. 12, '59. Hawaii, state-to-be where many bloodlines blend in beauty. G. B. Leonard, Jr.

McCall's. 89:228D. O. '61. McCall's visits Hawaii. Horace Sutton.

Mademoiselle. 50:126-9+. Ap. '60. Hedonists in Hawaii; summer school. R. Dionne.

Mademoiselle. 51:143-5+. My. '60. Unfettered life. M. B. Parkinson.

Mademoiselle. 56:18+. Ja. '63. Let's travel.

Mademoiselle. 56:64+. Ja. '63. Hawaii's neighbor islands. Katharine Davis.

Military Review. 41:44-56. F. '61. Alaska: Gibraltar of the North. Willard Pearson.

Monthly Labor Review. 84:459-62. My. '61. Government and bargaining on the Alaska railroad. E. M. Fitch.
Monthly Labor Review. 85:296-300. Mr. '62. Indexes of living costs for Alaskan cities. J. C. Brackett.
Motor Boating. 107:46-7+. My. '61. Icebergs in your ice box. Jean Niemeier.
Motor Boating. 110:42-4+. D. '62. Cruising the Hawaiian Islands, family style. Marian Rumsey.
Nation. 189:166-9. S. 26, '59. Alaska's '59ers. O'Carroll Colvin.
National Business Woman. 38:10-11+. Jl. '59. Fiftieth state. Pauline King.
National Education Association Journal. 48:32-3. Ap. '59. Alaska.
National Education Association Journal. 48:32-3. My. '59. 50th star.
National Geographic Magazine. 115:792-823. Je. '59. Volcanic fires of the 50th state. P. A. Zahl.
National Geographic Magazine. 116:42-83. Jl. '59. Alaska proudly joins the Union. E. H. Gruening.
National Geographic Magazine. 118:1-45. Jl. '60. Hawaii, U.S.A. Frederick Simpich, Jr.
Natural History. 69:6-23. Ja. '60. Landscapes of far Alaska. T. M. Griffiths.
Natural History. 69:36-47. My. '60. First Hawaiians: Polynesian pioneers. Edward Joesting.
New Republic. 140:8. Mr. 23, '59. Idiocy as a catalyst. G. W. Johnson.
New York Times. p 1+. Ag. 22, '59. Hawaii becomes the 50th state; new flag shown. W. H. Lawrence.
*New York Times. p 1+. O. 16, '60. Hawaii is termed governmental paradise. Gene Smith.
New York Times. p 1+. Mr. 13, '61. Hawaii drafts 703-million plan of development over 20 years.
New York Times. p 38. N. 9, '62. Voters reject proposal to move capital from Juneau.
New York Times. p 125. N. 11, '62. Only 17 of Michigan homesteaders who went to Susitna Valley in '59 still there.
New York Times Magazine. p 82-3. F. 15, '59. Faces of the 49th; photographs. S. Carrighar.
*New York Times Magazine. p 12+. Mr. 15, '59. Communique from our Alaskan outpost. H. W. Baldwin.
    Reply with rejoinder. p 62. Ap. 26, '59. E. L. Bartlett and others.
*New York Times Magazine. p 14+. Ap. 19, '59. 'Aloha' for the fiftieth state. J. A. Michener.
New Yorker. 35:20-2. Ag. 29, '59. Our own Baedeker.
New Yorker. 36:98+. Ap. 2, '60. Reporter at large. E. J. Kahn, Jr.
*News Explorer. p 2. Ap. 17, '59. Hawaii, our fiftieth state.
    Reprinted in this book: Map of Hawaii.

Newsweek. 53:29-32. F. 23, '59. Enchanting state.

Newsweek. 53:28-9. Mr. 23, '59. We all haoles.

Newsweek. 53:24. Je. 22, '59. Old island custom; Hawaiian territorial legislature.

Newsweek. 54:21-2. Jl. 13, '59. No fifty on the stump.

Newsweek. 54:22-3. Ag. 10, '59. Surprise: three to two.

Newsweek. 54:19-20. Ag. 31, '59. Yankee Doodle dandy.

Newsweek. 54:68-70+. S. 7, '59. Hawaii's progress and prospects. R. E. Cubbedge.

Newsweek. 54:60. S. 14, '59. Map-making.

Newsweek. 57:29. Ja. 16, '61. Facing the cold facts.

Newsweek. 58:72-3. Jl. 31, '61. History, hula, hoopla; summer school.

Newsweek. 59:84. Ap. 2, '62. Trouble in Hawaii; East-West center.

Newsweek. 59:39-40. Ap. 9, '62. Eye-catching race.

Newsweek. 59:106. Ap. 16, '62. Ukuleles are not enough.

Newsweek. 59:25. Ap. 30, '62. Paradise lost; crack down on kites.

Newsweek. 59:72+. Ap. 30, '62. Pineapple squeeze.

Newsweek. 60:22. D. 10, '62. Manaua's mercy; Hawaii's second drought in two years.

Parliamentary Affairs. 13:489-508. Autumn '60. Hawaii: the fiftieth state. Norman Meller.

Personnel and Guidance Journal. 39:292-9. D. '60. Survey of student attitudes towards campus activities at the University of Hawaii. R. A. Kalish and O. J. Bartos.

Popular Mechanics. 112:57-61. Jl. '59. Alaska's flying bus line. G. X. Sand.

Popular Mechanics. 112:84-90+. S. '59. Other side of paradise. R. M. Botts.

Popular Mechanics. 112:117-22+. N. '59. Toughest railroad you taxpayers own. G. X. Sand.

Public Health Reports. 76:1063-79. D. '61. Hawaiian health.

Saturday Evening Post. 231:19-21+. My. 2, '59. Prosperity hits paradise. F. J. Taylor.

Saturday Evening Post. 232:10. S. 12, '59. Hawaii can sponsor seminars as well as beauty contests.

Saturday Evening Post. 235:26-9. Ag. 25, '62. Hawaii's hustling shepherd. F. J. Taylor.

Saturday Review. 42:62-5. My. 16, '59. Honshu, Hawaii, home. Horace Sutton.

Saurday Review. 42:35-7. S. 5, '59. Alaska: new gold rush. Horace Sutton.

Saturday Review. 42:32-3. S. 12, '59. Anchorage away. Horace Sutton.

Saturday Review. 42:34-5. O. 3, '59. Paradise in limbo. Horace Sutton.

Saturday Review. 43:44+. N. 12, '60. Where the twain will meet. Horace Sutton.

Saturday Review. 43:50. N. 12, '60. Midnight in Kailua. Daniel Taradash.

Saturday Review. 45:39-41. D. 8, '62. Hawaii is to hear. Andre Kostelanetz.

Science Digest. 53:58-65. My. '63. Henry Kaiser: new project, Hawaii-Kai. Leona Elliott.

Science News Letter. 75:6. Ja. 3, '59. Southeast Alaska rises.

Science News Letter. 76:46. Jl. 18, '59. Citizens of Hawaii outlive mainlanders.

Science News Letter. 79:311. My. 20, '61. Ancient Hawaiians.

*Senior Scholastic. 56:10-11. My. 17, '50. Alaska: next stop statehood?
    Reprinted in this book: Map of Alaska. p 10.

Senior Scholastic. 74:8-9+. Ja. 30, '59. 50th star for Hawaii? pro and con discussion.

Senior Scholastic. 74:16. Ap. 3, '59. Hawaii wins our fiftieth star.

Senior Scholastic. 74:12-15. Ap. 10, '59. Aloha Hawaii!

Senior Scholastic (Teacher Edition). 76:19T. Mr. 2, '60. Lush land of luaus and leis. Naomi Rinehart.

*Social Legislation Information Service Bulletin (Washington Bulletin). 82:540-7. N. 25, '58. 49th state.

*Social Process. 25:12-14. '61-'62. Hawaii in the race relations continuum of the Pacific. A. W. Lind.

Sports Illustrated. 16:58-65. Mr. 12, '62. Risk and challenge of the adventure road. Dolly Connelly.

Sports Illustrated. 17:66-70+. Ag. 20, '62. Outer islands: miracles and prophecies. Gilbert Rogin.

*State Government. 31:202-8. Autumn '58. Alaska's struggle for statehood. R. B. Atwood.

*State Government. 31:215-19. Autumn '58. Meaning of statehood to Alaska. T. B. Stewart.

*State Government. 32:146-61. Summer '59. Hawaii: the aloha state. W. F. Quinn; Statehood and Hawaii's people. J. A. Burns; What statehood means to Hawaii. R. M. Kamins.
    Reprinted in this book: What statehood means to Hawaii. R. M. Kamins. p 156-61.

State Government. 33:210-16. Autumn '60. Aloha, malahini. C. S. James and K. K. Lau.

State Government. 34:226-32. Autumn '61. State planning in Hawaii. Frank Lombardi.

Sunset. 124:41+. Mr. '60. Long drive to Alaska.

Sunset. 126:26+. Mr. '61. Around the bend, wilderness; Wailua River excursion, Hawaii.

Sunset. 128:82+. My. '62. Bike cruising in the islands.

Sunset. 129:16. S. '62. Honolulu's big aloha on boat day.

Time. 74:12-24. Ag. 10, '59. Big change.

Time. 75:25. Ap. 25, '60. First year on the Susitna; Fifty-niners.

Time. 75:42+. My. 2, '60. Upgrading in Alaska.

Time. 78:46+. Jl. 21, '61. Awakening in Hawaii.

Time. 80:21. O. 5, '62. Big Ben & young Danny.

Time. 80:82. O. 19, '62. Flight of the five.

Travel. 112:22-6. D. '59. Hawaii's new state. Peter Espie.

Travel. 115:54-6+. Ap. '61. Editor's report: Hawaii. M. M. Davis.

Travel. 118:40-4. O. '62. By freighter around Hawaii. T. B. Lesure.

Travel. 119:64. Ap. '63. New route to Alaska; marine highway.

U.S. News & World Report. 46:101-3. F. 13, '59. If Hawaii becomes
    the 50th state.

U.S. News & World Report. 46:52-3. Mr. 23, '59. Now that Hawaii
    is to be a state.

U.S. News & World Report. 46:78-81. Mr. 30, '59. Sun, sugar, people,
    pineapples.

U.S. News & World Report. 46:80-1. Mr. 30, '59. Where Hawaii stands
    on taxes, labor, races; interview. W. F. Quinn.

U.S. News & World Report. 47:67-70. Jl. 13, '59. State of Alaska one
    year after.

U.S. News & World Report. 50:76-9. Ja. 9, '61. Big boom in the
    50th state.

U.S. News & World Report. 51:90-1. Jl. 17, '61. Thinking of driving
    to the 49th state?

U.S. News & World Report. 51:50--2. S. 4, '61. Fresh look at the
    49th state and how it's making out.

*U.S. News & World Report. 52:65-8. Mr. 19, '62. 49th state; three
    years later.

Wall Street Journal. 158:1+. Jl. 27, '61. Alaska's economy: it's hard
    hit by shifts in defense emphasis, high cost of statehood. R. J.
    Schrick.

Wall Street Journal. 159:1+. Je. 26, '62. Clouds over Hawaii: tourists
    spend less; sugar, fruit industries slip in world markets; construc-
    tion activity off; key prop: military outlays. N. C. Miller, Jr.

Wall Street Journal. 160:1+. Jl. 12, '62. Well-developed state of
    Hawaii is stirred by land reform issue. N. C. Miller, Jr.

Yale Review. 52:72-89. O. '62. Oil barrels and muk-tuk: an Arctic
    year. Daniel McKinley.